PASHTO
Pashto—English
English—Pashto
Dictionary
&
Phrasebook

by
Nicholas Awde
&
Asmatullah Sarwan

HIPPOCRENE BOOKS INC
New York

Historical and cultural background by Fred J. Hill.
Additional thanks to Ian Carnochan,
Thea Khitarishvili, Nicholas Williams,
and Caroline Gates for their help
in compiling this volume.

Typeset & designed by Desert♥Hearts.

For information, address:
HIPPOCRENE BOOKS, INC.
171 Madison Avenue
New York, NY 10016
www.hippocrenebooks.com

Library of Congress Cataloging-in-Publication Data

Awde, Nicholas.
    Pashto : Pashto-English, English-Pashto dictionary
& phrasebook / by Nicholas Awde & Asmatullah
Sarwan
        p. cm.
    English and Pushto.
    ISBN-13: 978-0-7818-0972-6
    ISBN-10: 0-7818-0972-X
        1. Pushto language--Dictionaries--English.
2. English language--Dictionaries--Pushto. 3. Pushto
language--Conversation and phrase books--English.
I. Sarwan, Asmatullah.

PK6791 .A93 2002
491'.593321--dc21

2002038874

Printed in the United States of America.

CONTENTS

Introduction	**5**
A Very Basic Grammar	**10**
Pronunciation Guide	**20**
The Pashto Alphabet	**24**
PASHTO–ENGLISH DICTIONARY	**27**
ENGLISH–PASHTO DICTIONARY	**71**

PASHTO PHRASEBOOK

Etiquette	**116**	Animals	**183**
Quick Reference	**117**	Countryside	**186**
Introductions	**120**	Weather	**188**
Language	**126**	Camping	**190**
Bureaucracy	**128**	Emergency	**191**
Travel	**130**	Healthcare	**195**
Accommodation	**139**	Relief Aid	**203**
Food and Drink	**145**	Tools	**209**
Directions	**154**	The Car	**210**
Shopping	**157**	Sports	**213**
What'sTo See	**166**	The Body	**214**
Finance	**170**	Politics	**216**
Communications	**172**	War	**219**
The Office	**177**	Time	**222**
The Conference	**178**	Numbers	**226**
Education	**179**	Opposites	**229**
Agriculture	**181**	Maps	**231**

INTRODUCTION

Pashto is the language of the Pashtoons, or Pushtuns, who have lived since recorded times in the south-east of Afghanistan and the adjacent Northwest Frontier Province of Pakistan (where they are called Pathans). Their traditional homeland lies south of the Hindu Kush, but Pashtoon groups are spread over a formidable mountain region with their main centers in Kandahar and Kabul in Afghanistan, and Quetta and Peshawar in Pakistan.

In Pakistan, the Pashtoons maintained a strong degree of autonomy under the British Empire and subsequent Pakistan administrations. To the west, Afghanistan was for long the strategic meeting ground of three great imperial powers — Russia, China and the British Empire — and it was here that the Pashtoons along with their fellow Afghans survived major encroachments by the British (who famously lost three separate wars in Afghanistan) and the Tsarist Russians in the 19th century, the result of which helped create a strong, unified state in Afghanistan by 1919.

Internal divisions however continued, and latterly, the 20th century saw this tragic cycle repeated with the invasion by Soviet Russia in 1979, their tattered retreat a decade later, and the battle for control against the ruling Mojahedin and Taliban regimes, a process interrupted only by the West's military intervention in 2001/2.

Voice of a vast region

Pashto (also known as Pakhto, Pakhtu or Pushto) is spoken across a huge continuous area that stretches across Afghanistan from north-west Pakistan to eastern

Iran, with significant pockets of speakers in the United Arab Emirates, India and Tajikistan.

It is one of the official languages of Afghanistan (Dari is the other) that are used in schools, administration, broadcasting and the press. Since the early 1930s the Afghan government in particular has been exerting considerable effort to standardize and publicize the language.

Pashto has been written since the late 16th century in a variant of the Perso-Arabic script — its modified alphabet, standardized in the 18th and 20th centuries, has more vowel sounds than either Persian or Arabic and represents these more extensively.

The variation in spelling of the language's name stems from the different pronunciations found in different regions — Pashtoons say "Pashto" in the south, and "Pakhto" in the north. Like any language, there are regional variants and, despite often confusing attempts to carve it up into various dialects, in general one speaker of Pashto readily understands another.

Although no clear spoken standard form of the language is presently used, the common spelling system reflects the Pashto of Kandahar, and is the form used in this book.

From Alexander to today

Traces of the complex history of the Pashtoons and their language are present in their vocabulary. While the majority of words can be traced to Pashto's roots as a member of the Eastern Iranian branch, it has also borrowed words from adjacent languages for over two thousand years.

The oldest borrowed words are from Greek, and date from the conquest of Bactria, as the region was known, by Alexander the Great in the third century BC. There are also some traces of later contact with the

Zoroastrians and Buddhists whose own empires held political sway over the region during the first millennium.

Pashto has a strong archaic, Sanskrit influence — unsurprising in view of its close geographic proximity to the Indian sub-continent — and it has also been borrowing words from more modern Indian languages for centuries. With the advent of the Islamic period, it borrowed many words from Arabic and Persian.

In recent times, Urdu and English have added to this rich lexicon which also possesses a remarkable facility for coining its own new words — such as **brishnâlik** "e-mail" (literally "electronic letter") — which are accepted by Pashto speakers everywhere.

In Afghanistan, Pashto is developing together with Dari, a close relative of Persian which spoken as a native tongue in the north and west, and which has its own literary tradition. Although Pashto was earlier less used in official documents and in social and political life, nowadays the sphere of its use is expanding all the time with active efforts being made to normalize the language and to create a single literary norm.

Spirit of poetry

Pashto has an extensive and rich written history stretching back many hundreds of years. The earliest existing records are believed to date from the beginnings of the 16th century and consist of an account of the conquest of Swat by the prince Shaikh Mali.

The 17th century saw a massive rise in development in literature, mostly due to a stream of classic poets such as Khushhal Khan Khatak (1613-94), who is known today as the national poet of Afghanistan.

Khushhal was a clan chief who wrote spontaneous and forceful poetry of great charm. His grandson Azal Khan followed in his tradition and was the author of the

Târikh-e Morassa', a history of the Pashtoon people. Popular mystical poets were Abd ar-Rahman and Abd al-Hamid, writing in the late 17th/early 18th centuries. Ahmad Shah Durrani, the founder of the modern Afghan state in the mid 18th century, was himself a poet of note and under his rule Pashto became especially prominent.

Classical Pashto was the focus of study by the soldiers and administrators of the British Empire in the 19th century, and the classical grammar in use today dates from that period. Its status received a further boost when in 1936 it was made the national language of Afghanistan by royal decree.

Pashtoon folk literature is the most extensively developed in the region. Besides stories set to music, there are thousands of two and four-line folk poems traditionally composed by women that reflect their everyday life and attitudes. Meanwhile, modern Pashto written literature has adapted those western literary forms that match forms found in this traditional oral literature. The short story in particular has become a noteworthy feature as a window into the soul of Pashtoon society at home and abroad. These are eagerly read in newspapers, and when collected in book form invariably become best-sellers.

The end of the 20th century saw a rapid expansion of writing in journalism and other modern genres which has brought an element of innovation of the language. Kabul, Kandahar, Peshawar and Quetta are particularly important hubs for newspaper, journal and book publishing, while the Internet has proved to be another popular medium. Meanwhile, there are a large number of long-established radio services based outside of Afghanistan and Pakistan, most notably the Pashto section of the BBC World Service, broadcasting from London. ■

For further background information, see the Introductions to Hippocrene's 'Dari Dictionary & Phrasebook' and 'Urdu Dictionary & Phrasebook'.

- A Pashto man is a **Pёshtun**.
- A Pashto woman is a **Pashtana**.
- The adjective for Pashto is **Pёshto**.
- Pashtos call themselves **Pёshtânё**
- The Pashto language is **Pёshto**.
- Afghanistan is **Afghânistân**.
- Pakistan is **Pâkistân**.
- The Pashto region is **Pёshtonkhwa**.

A VERY BASIC GRAMMAR

Pashto — also known as Pakhto — belongs to the Iranian branch of the Indo-European family of languages. Other members of this branch include Dari, Persian (Farsi) and Kurdish, while relatives in the family include Urdu/Hindi, and, more distantly, English, German, French, Italian and Spanish. Pashto is spoken throughout Afghanistan and is written in a modified form of the Arabic script (see page 24).

—Structure

Like English, the linguistic structure of Pashto is basically a simple one. In word order, the verb is usually put at the end of the sentence, e.g.

Zë ḏâktar yam.
"I am a doctor." (literally: "I doctor am.")

—Nouns

Pashto has no words for 'the,' 'a' or 'an' in the same way as English does — instead the meaning is generally understood from the context, e.g. **ḏâktar** can mean 'the doctor,' 'a doctor' or just simply 'doctor.'

GENDER — As with many other languages, like Italian, German and Arabic, Pashto divides words according to gender, i.e. whether they are masculine or feminine. This can be predictable, e.g. **shëdza** 'woman' (feminine) and **saṛay** 'man' (masculine); or not, e.g. **râdyo** 'radio' (feminine) and **môtar** 'car' (masculine).

Adjectives and verbs agree according to this gender, e.g.

Masculine: **Dâktar râghalay day.**
"The (male) doctor has arrived."
Halak khushâl day.
"The boy is happy."

Feminine: **Dâktara râghalëy da.**
"The (female) doctor has arrived."
Njëlëy khushâla da.
"The girl is happy."

PLURALS — There are a variety of forms for the plural in Pashto; sometimes these are predictable, sometimes not. Some involve a simple change of ending, e.g. **Pështun** 'Pashto man' → **Pështânë** 'Pashtoons,' **shëdza** 'woman' → **shëdze** 'women,' **wazir** 'minister' → **wazirân** 'ministers,' while others have different forms, e.g. **ghar** 'mountain' → **ghruna** 'mountains,' **topak** 'gun' → **topëk** 'guns'. Some don't change at all, e.g. **dodëy** means both 'loaf' and 'loaves,' **gilâs** means 'cherry' and 'cherries', while the word for 'water', **obë**, is always plural.

CASE — In addition to the plural, nouns (and adjectives) in Pashto also adds an extra ending with grammatical function* that depends on where a word appears in a sentence and whether the past or present tense is referred to. Generally predictable, and generated by rules of grammar only, this is best left for more advanced study, but a quick example is as follows:

Present: **Saray kitâb lwali.**
"The man reads the book."

Past: **Sari kitâb wëlwëst.**
"The man read the book."

This sort of switching** is a common feature in many languages across the world, including Hindi/Urdu, Kurdish and Basque.

* Called the 'oblique' case; the neutral form is the 'absolute' case.
** Linguistically, this is called 'ergativity'.

As in languages like German or Urdu, some prepositions/postpositions trigger a case change, e.g. **Kâbëla tër** "as far as Kabul (**Kâbël**)", **pë psho** "on foot (**psha**)".

'OF' — The genitive is formed using **dë** "of", e.g. **dë sari motar** "the car of the man" or "the man's car" **dë ghâsho bors** "toothbrush" (literally: "brush of tooth"), **zmâ dë kor bâghche** "my house's garden" (literally: "my of-house garden"). Sometimes **dë** is omitted, e.g. **Kâbul shâr** "the city of Kabul."

▬Adjectives

Adjectives in Pashto generally change according to the gender of the nouns they modify, usually adding **-a** for the feminine form. Some have a single form for both genders. They generally come before the noun, e.g.

"new" *masculine* **nawëy** — **nawëy motar** "new car"
    feminine **nawe** — **nawe lârëy** "new truck"
"old" *masculine* **zor** — **zor motar** "old car"
    feminine **zara** — **zara lârëy** "old truck"

Some other basic adjectives are:

open **khlâs/khlâsa**	quick **zhër; chatak/chataka**
shut **puri**	slow **sawka**
cheap **arzân/arzâna**	small *person* **wor/wara**
expensive **grân/grâna**	small *thing* **kuchinay/kuchinëy**
hot **tod/tawda**	old *person* **buda/budëy**
cold **sor/sara**	young **dzwân/dzwâna**
near **nizhde**	good **shë**
far **lëri**	bad **bad/bada**
big **loy/loya**	poor **xwâr/xwâra**
long **uzhd/uzhda**	short **land/landa**
huge **ghat/ghata**	one **yaw/yawa**

Some adjectives have irregular forms, e.g. the feminine of

warakây "small" is **wara**. Others do not change for gender, e.g. **takra** "healthy", **khapa** "sad", **nâjora** and **nârogha** both meaning "sick".

Adding **be-** to an existing noun gives the meaning of "without" or "-less", e.g. **khatar** "danger" → **bekhatara** "safe" (= "without danger"), **ma'nâ** "meaning" → **bema'nâ** "insignificant" (= "without meaning"), etc.

▬Adverbs

Most adverbs have a single form with does not change. Some examples:

here **dalta**	up **pâs**
there **halta**	down **lândi**
well **shë**	now **os**
badly **bad**	tomorrow **sabâ**

▬Prepositions

Pashto uses a mixture of prepositions and postpositions (sometimes involving a change of case), in other words words like "in", "at" and "behind" come before or after the noun (remember that in English you can say "who *with*?" as well as "*with* who?"), or sometimes a combination of both, e.g.

of; from **dë**	under **tër ... lânde**
at; in; on **pë**	on **pë ... bânde**
from **lë**	in **pë ... ke**
until; as far as **tër**	to **... ta**

e.g. **pë mez bânde** "on the table", **pë kor ke** 'in the house', **pë Afghânestân** "in Afghanistan", **lë Inglistân** "from England". **Ta** "to" is placed after the noun, e.g. **Zhë Kâbël ta lârëm.** "I went to Kabul."

The sense of English prepositions is also rendered by "preverbs" (see below in the section on verbs).

—Pronouns

Basic forms are as follows:

SINGULAR	PLURAL
I **zë**	we **munzh; muzh**
you *singular* **të**	you *plural* **tâso***
he/she/it **hagha**	they **haghoy****

Use **tâso** for anyone you don't know well or who is older or more senior.

Possessive pronouns are:***

SINGULAR	PLURAL
my **zmâ**	our **zmunz**
your **stâ**	your **stâsi**
his/its **dadë**	their **dëdoy**
her/its **dëde**	

e.g.   **dë hagha râdyo** "his radio"
     dë haghe râdyo "her radio"
     zmâ akhbâr "my newspaper"
     zmunzh akhbâruna "our newspapers"

There is also a system of 'streamlined' forms that join onto the noun:

SINGULAR	PLURAL
my **-me**	our **-mo**
your **-de**	your **-mo**
his/her/its **-e/-ye**	their **-e/-ye**

e.g.   **râdyo-ye** "his/her/their radio"
     akhbâr-me "my newspaper"

Simple demonstratives in Pashto are:
   this/these **dagha; dâ**
   that/those **hagha**

---

* Another form is **tâse**.

** Another form is **duy/doy**.

*** Some have alternative forms: 'my' **dë mâ**, 'your' *singular* **dë stâ**, 'his/its' **dë hagha**, 'her/its' **dë haghe**, 'our' **dë stâ**, 'your' *plural* **dë stâse**, 'their' **dë haghoy**.

When these are used to modify a noun, you simply use the singular forms whether the noun is singular or plural, e.g. **dagha saray** "this man", **dagha sari** "these men", **hagha shēdza** "that woman", **hagha shadzi** "those women".

—Verbs

Verbs are very easy to form, adding a number of prefixes and suffixes to the basic verb form. In fact the underlying structure of Pashto verbs shares similiar concepts to those of the majority of European languages and so its system of regularities and irregularities may soon appear familiar.

Every Pashto verb has a basic form that carries a basic meaning. To this are added smaller words or single vowels that add further information to tell you who's doing what and how and when, e.g.

khwarēl "to eat"
khwarēm "I eat"
wēmikhor "I ate"
wēbēkhoram "I will eat"
khwaralay me day "I have eaten *something masculine*"
khwaralēy me da "I have eaten *something feminine*"

Some verbs, as in European languages, have different stems for different tenses, e.g. **tlēl** "to go" → **hagha dzi** "he goes", **hagha tlē** "he is going".

We saw the personal pronouns above, but these are only used for emphasis. Like French or Spanish, the verb already gives this information:

SINGULAR	PLURAL
I **-ēm**	we **-u**
you *singular* **-e**	you *plural* **-ēy/-âst**
he/she/it **—/-ē/-a**	they **-ē/-e/-i**

e.g.

zë ghwâr̆ëm I want	**mun<u>zh</u> ghwâru** we want
të ghwâ<u>r</u>e you want	**tâso ghwâ<u>r</u>ëy** you want
hagha ghwâ<u>r</u>a he/she/it wants	**haghoy ghwâ<u>r</u>i** they want

These are the most commonly used endings (they can take different forms according to the tense used).

In the second person plural, use **-ëy** as a general ending to address more than one person. You can also use it when speaking politely to an individual although **-âst** will be the preferred form in such situations.

'Not' is **na/në**, e.g. **Leri na day.** "It is not far." **Ma/më** is used with commands, e.g. **wadare<u>zh</u>a!** 'stop!' — **më dare<u>zh</u>a!** 'don't stop!', **më dâre<u>zh</u>a!** 'don't be afraid!'

PREVERBS — In addition to the prepositions/postpositions listed above, Pashto uses 'preverbs' — simple prepositions that are tagged on to the verbs to add to the meaning. Some of the most common are:

bâ away; out of	**râ** towards me
dar towards you	**war** towards him/her/it/them

These can be broad in the way they modify the verb's primary meaning, e.g.

kawël	to give
râkawël	to give (to me)
darkawël	to give (to you)
warkawël	to give (to a third party)

—Essential verbs
—"To be"

The most useful form of the verb "to be" you will need is the simple series of present endings:

SINGULAR	PLURAL
zë yëm I am	**mun<u>zh</u> yu** we are
të ye you are	**tâse yâst/yëy** you are

hagha day *m* he/it is   **haghoy di** they are
hagha da *f* she/it is

e.g. **Zë dâktar yëm.** "I am a doctor."

Simple past:

zë wëm I was	**munzh wu** we were
të we you were	**tâse wâst/wëy** you were
hagha wu *m*/**wa** *f* he/she/it was	**haghoy wë** *m*/**we** *f* they were

Future:

zë ba wëm I will be	**munzh ba wu** we will be
të ba we you will be	**tâse ba wëy/wây** you will be
hagha ba wi he/she/it will be	**haghoy ba wi** they will be

Shta is another form of "to be". The equivalent of the German "es gibt", it tends to be used when the meaning is general rather than specific, e.g. **Râdyo pë mez bânde da.** "The radio is on the table." versus **Pë kota ke râdyo shta.** "There's a radio in the room." (Note the change in word order.)

—"To have" **larël**

Larël is generally the equivalent of the English verb "to have", e.g.

Tsomra payse lâre?   How much money do you have?
Zë sël afghânëy larëm.   I have 100 afghanis.

But some expressions of physical possession or state can be expressed in other ways, e.g.

Dë haghe halëk pë   "That boy has a bad
sar sakht dard day.   headache."
(literally: "Of that boy in head bad ache there is.")

Kaghâz-de bas day? "Do you have enough paper?"
(literally: "Paper-your enough is?")

Of course both can just as easily be translated using **larëm**: **Hagha halëk sakht sar dard lari.** ("That boy a bad head ache has."), and **Të kâfi kâghaz lare?** ("You enough paper have?")

SINGULAR	PLURAL

Present:

zë larëm I have

të lare you have

hagha lari he/she/it has

mun<u>zh</u> laru we have

tâse larëy you have

haghoy lari they have

Future:

zë ba wëlarum I will have

të ba wëlare you will have

hagha ba wëlari he/she/it will have

mun<u>zh</u> ba wëlaru we will have

tâse ba wëlarëy you will have

haghoy ba wëlari they will have

—"To come" râtlël

SINGULAR	PLURAL

Present:

zë râdzëm I come

të râdzë you come

hagha râdzi he/she/it comes

mun<u>zh</u> râdzu we come

tâse râdzëy you come

haghoy râdzi they come

Simple past:

zë râghlëm I came

të râghle you came

hagha râghla he/she/it came

mun<u>zh</u> râghlu we came

tâse râghlëy you came

haghoy râghlël they came

Future:

zë ba râshëm I will come

të ba râshe you will come

hagha ba râshi he/she/it will come

mun<u>zh</u> ba râshu we will come

tâse ba râshëy you will come

haghoy ba râshi they will come

—"To go" tlël

SINGULAR	PLURAL

Present:

zë dzëm I go

të dze you go

hagha dzi he/she/it goes

mun<u>zh</u> dzu we go

tâse dzëy you go

haghoy dzi they go

Simple past:

zë lâṟë**m** I went	**munzh lâṟu** we went
të lâṟe you went	**tâse lâṟëy** you went
hagha lâṟa he/she/it went	**haghoy lâṟël** they went

Future:

zë ba lâṟshëm I will go	**munzh ba lâṟshu** we will go
të ba lâṟshe you will go	**tâse ba lâṟshëy** you will go
hagha ba lâṟshi hc/she/it will go	**haghoy ba lâṟshi** they will go

—**"To like"** in its general sense is expressed with a possessive construction rather than a verb, e.g.

Hagha-me ḏer *khwas* day.   "I like it very much."

(literally: "It-my very nice is.")

Angur dë halëkâno ḏer *khwas* di.   "The boys like grapes very much."

(literally: "Grapes of boys very nice are.")   ∎

PRONUNCIATION GUIDE

Pashto letter	Pashto example	Approximate English equivalent
a	**akhbâr** "newspaper"	*a*pple
â	**âzâdî** "freedom"	f*a*ther, in South British English
b	**bâd** "wind"	*b*ox
ch	**chây** "tea"	*ch*urch
d	**dôkân** "shop"	*d*og
<u>d</u>	**<u>d</u>odëy** "bread; food"	like *d* but "retroflexive"
dz	**dzangal** "forest; wood"	a*dz*e
e	**s̤teshan** "station"	p*e*t
f	**fo̤tbâl** "soccer"	*f*at
g	**gâz** "gas"	*g*ot
gh	**gharb** "west"	—
h	**hokumat** "government"	*h*at
i	**lik** "letter"	h*ea*t
j	**jahân** "world"	*j*et
k	**kar** "agriculture"	*k*ick
kh	**khpëlwâki** "independence"	a*ch*, as in German
l	**lâs** "hand"	*l*et
m	**mô̤tar** "car"	*m*at
n	**na̤tëy** "world"	*n*et
<u>n</u>	**<u>n</u>ân** "bread"	like *n* but "retroflexive"
o	**obë** "water"	c*o*t, in South British English
p	**pulis** "police"	*p*et
q	**qâhwa** "coffee"	—
r	**râdyô** "radio"	*r*at, but "rolled' as in Scottish English
<u>r</u>	**<u>r</u>umbay** "first"	like *n* but "flapped" almost like an l

s	**sinamâ** "cinema"	_s_it
sh	**shamâl** "north"	_sh_ut
<u>sh</u>	**<u>sh</u>ë** "good"	like _sh_ but "retroflexive"
t	**tilifun** "telephone"	_t_en
<u>t</u>	**<u>t</u>aksi** "taxi"	like _t_ but "retroflexive"
ts	**tsalor** "four"	hi_ts_
u	**kutsa** "street"	sh_oo_t
w	**wakht** "time"	_w_orld
y	**yakh** "ice"	_y_es
z	**zëlzëla** "earthquake"	_z_ebra
zh	**zhwënd** "life"	a_z_ure
<u>zh</u>	**<u>zh</u>dën** "millet"	like _zh_ but "retroflexive"
'	**mâ'nâ** "meaning"	—

Nothing beats listening to a native speaker, but the following notes should help give you some idea of how to pronounce the following letters. Although Kandahar (**Kandahâr**), Kabul (**Kâbël**), Peshawar (**Peshawër**) and Quetta (**Kwëṯa**) are important centers for Pashto printing and broadcasting, no single standard of the language has been widely established as a spoken form. Like English, the spoken language has a range of variations in pronunciation that are not reflected in the written language. Most of the language in this book, however, is deliberately close to the written form thus enabling you to be understood clearly wherever you may be.

—Vowels

1) The combination **ay** is pronounced as the "y" in English "wh_y_", e.g. **paysa** "money".
2) The combination **ëy** is pronounced as the "ay" in English "s_ay_", e.g. **lârëy** "truck".
3) The combination **aw** is pronounced as the "ow" in English "h_ow_", e.g. **chawkëy** "chair".
4) There is widespread alternation of vowels, particularly **a** with **ë**, and **u** with **o**. This does not affect meaning or your ability to be understood.

—Consonants

d̲, **n̲**, **r̲**, and **t̲** are all *retroflexive* versions of **d**, **n**, **r**, and **t** respectively. This means that they are pronounced in each case with the tongue turned back to the roof of your mouth. For example, set your mouth up to pronounce a normal **d**, but then curl your tongue right up so that the bottom part of it touches the top part of your mouth. As you then try to pronounce the original **d**, you will feel your tongue "flapping" forward. Retroflexive consonants are a common feature of Urdu, Hindi and other languages spoken throughout the Indian sub-continent. Similar forms can also exist in American English (contrasting with their non-retroflexed British English forms), most commonly in the middle of words like "bid̲der", "han̲d", "hear̲t", and "bit̲ter", or at the ends of words like "bad̲", "ban̲", "butter̲", and "bat̲".

sh is a retroflex form of **sh**. In some areas it can be heard like a softer version of **kh** — for example, Scottish "loch"or, in German, where many speakers pronounce the "ch" in "ich" as less "rasping" than in "ach".

zh is a retroflex form of **zh**. In some areas it can be heard as **gh** or **g**.

gh is pronounced like a sort of growl in the back of your throat — like when you're gargling. Frequently transcribed into English for other languages that have this sound as "gh", the German or Parisian "r" is the easy European equivalent. [= Arabic غ]

kh is the rasping "ch" in German "ach", or the Spanish/Castillian "jota" in "jamás". This sound is frequently transcribed in English as "kh". [= Arabic خ]

q is pronounced like a **k**, but right back in your mouth at the throat end. Imagine you have a marble in the back of your throat and that you're bouncing it using only your glottis, and make a **k** sound at the same time. [= Persian or Arabic ق]

' represents the same pronunciation of two underlying sounds: the "glottal stop" — a simple stop of the breath instead of a consonant — or a representation of the pharyngal consonant *'ain* found in words of Arabic origin (it also occurs in Hebrew). In spoken Pashto, when it comes between vowels it usually becomes a connecting "**y**", e.g. **shâ'ir** "poet" is pronounced "**shâyir**". Before a consonant, it usually prolongs the preceding vowel, e.g. **mâ'nâ** "meaning" is pronounced "**mâ-ana**", or simply "**mânâ**". When it comes after a consonant, it is usually pronounced as a sort of stop or catch in the flow of breath before articulating the following vowel, e.g. **san'at** "industry" should be pronounced in two distinct segments as "**san-at.**" [= Turkish **ʼ**/Persian ﺀ or ﻉ]

—Spelling notes

1) Apart from the variations mentioned above, like English there are personal and regional alternations in Pashto of consonants and vowels in the spoken language that are not reflected in the spelling. These usually have no effect on meaning, and are easily picked up once you have found your 'Pashto ear.' Many speakers will vary their pronunciation of vowels without affecting meaning, particularly the substituion of **ë** for **a**, **o**, and **u**.

2) Likewise, **k** is a regular substitution in speech for the written **q**, and **p** for written **f**.

3) Other common sound changes depending on the speaker are: loss of h at the beginning of words, e.g. **alëk** for **halëk** 'boy', **alta** for **halta** 'there'; swapping the order of letters, e.g. **mzëka** for **zmëkë** 'land'; dropping of vowels, e.g. **zma** for **zëma** 'my', **zmunzh** for **zëmunzh** 'our'. Again these are pure sound changes and do not affect meaning.

4) In the rare cases where the letters **sh** represent the two separate sounds **s** and **h** in sequence, they are divided by an apostrophe, e.g. **es-hâl** 'diarrhea.' The same is done for **z + h**, e.g. **maz-hab** "sect".

5) Remember that **h**, as a separate letter, is usually pronounced in combinations like **mahsul** ("**mah-sul**") "product," **mashhur** ('**mash-hur**') "famous."

6) Abbreviations used are: *m* for "male" and *f* for "female". ∎

The Pashto alphabet

Pashto letter	Roman equivalent	Name of letter	Pashto letter	Roman Equivalent	Name of letter
ا، آ	a, â	alef	ش	sh	shin/khe
ب	b	be	ص	s	swât
پ	p	pe	ض	z	zwât
ت	t	te	ط	t	twe
ټ	t	te	ظ	z	zwe
ث	s	se	ع	'	ayn
ج	j	jim	غ	gh	ghayn
چ	ch	che	ف	f	fe
ځ	dz	dze	ق	q	qâf
څ	ts	tse	ك، ک	k	kâf
ح	h	halwa he	ګ، گ	g	gâf
خ	kh	khe	ل	l	lâm
د	d	dâl	م	m	mim
ډ	d	dâl	ن	n	nun
ذ	z	zâl	ڼ	n	nun
ر	r	re	و	w, u, o	wâw
ړ	r	re	ه	h	gër dë he
ز	z	ze	ي، ی	y, i	ma'rufa ye
ژ	zh	zhe	ې	e	majhula ye
ږ	zh	zhe	ئ	ëy	ta'nis ye
س	s	sin	ئ	ëy	fe'li ye
ش	sh	shin	ء	'	hamza

1. Since the Pashto alphabet is based on a consonantal system, note that the short vowels **a**, **e**, **ë**, **o** and **u** are not always indicated.
2. **Ayn** and **hamza** are not normally written in the transliteration used in this book, and they are rarely pronounced in conversational Pashto.

Numbers

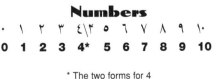

۰	١	٢	٣	٤\٥	٥	٦	٧	٨	٩	١۰
0	**1**	**2**	**3**	**4***	**5**	**6**	**7**	**8**	**9**	**10**

* The two forms for 4 are interchangeable.

PASHTO
Dictionary

Like French, Spanish, Arabic or Urdu, Pashto has various masculine and feminine forms, and where possible these have been noted. The feminine form is not given for masculine nouns or adjectives with the common ending **-ay**. Simply replace this with **-ëy** to create the feminine form, e.g. **Pâkistânay** "Pakistani man", **Pâkistânëy** "Pakistani woman".

PASHTO–ENGLISH
PASHTO–ANGREZI

A/Â

abâ father
âbâdawël to build
abadi eternal
âb aw hawâ climate
âbël parun the day before yesterday
âbi blue
achawël to pour
adâ pay; payment; **adâ kawël** to pay
âdâb etiquette
adabyât literature
adâlat justice; *(Pakistan)* law court
ade mother
âdi average; normal
âdras address
Afghân Afghan
afghânëy afghani *currency*
Afghâni Afghani
Afghânistân Afghanistan
afsâna legend
afsar officer *military*
afuni septic
afuni-zid antiseptic
aghostël to dress; to put on; to wear *clothes*
aghshël to make bread/dough
aghustël *see* aghostël
aghzay thorn
ahamiyat importance
âhangar blacksmith
ahli domestic; tame
ajib-o-gharib strange
ajir mercenary
akâdimi academy
akâs photographer
akâsi photography

akhbâr newspaper
âkhër end
akhistël to get; to receive; to buy
akhshël to knead
aks picture; photo
aksara most
aksariyat majority
âksijan oxygen
Aktobar October
alagula crisis
a'lâmya declaration
alâqa interest; **alâqa larël** to interest
âlim scientist
alkol alcohol *medical*
Allâh God
Almân Germany
Almânay *m* German
Almânëy *f* German
almârëy cupboard; shelf
âlobâlu berry
âlu potato(es)
âlubâlu cherry
alucha plum
âlugân potatoes(es)
alutaka; alwëtaka airplane; **alwëtaka tashtawël** to hijack *a plane*; **dë alwëtake tashtawël** hijacking; **Alwëtaka tsë wakht rawânezhi?** What time does the plane take off?
alwëtak-tashtawunkay hijacker
alwëtël to fly
ama aunt *father's sister*
âma wazhla genocide
amaliyat operation; surgery; **dë amaliyat kota** operating theater/room

ambolâns ambulance

amër order; **amer kawël** to command; to order

âmir boss

ammâ but

amniyat safety; security; peace

Amrikâ America; **dë Amrikâ Mutahida Ayâlatuna** United States of America

Amrikâyëy *f* American

Amrikâyi *m* American

amsâ walking stick

anâ grandmother

anâr pomegranate(s)

anârgëray pomegranate

andiwâl boyfriend

andiwâla girlfriend

andzorawël to draw *an image*

andzorgari painting

angër yard; courtyard

Angrez *m* Englishman; Briton

Angreza *f* Englishwoman; Briton

Angrezi; Angrizi English *language*; **Angrezi wayalay she/shëy?** Do you speak English?

angur grapes

anistityut institute

antibiyotik antibiotic

apârtmân apartment

apozisun opposition

apretar *m* operator; telephone operator

apretara *f* operator; telephone operator

April April

aqalyat minority

aqël intelligence; mind; wisdom; **dë aqël ghâsh** wisdom tooth

aqida faith; belief

âqil wise

ara saw *noun*

Arab *m* Arab

Araba *f* Arab

Arabi Arabic *language*

ârâm comfortable

arghawâni purple

arike relationship

ariza petition

arkh side *of body*

artiyâ need *noun*

arwâ soul

aryân puzzled

ârzân cheap

arzedël to cost

arzësht larël to value; to be worth

âs; as horse; **âs dzghâsta** horse racing; **âs sparli** horseback riding

asab nerve

asal origin

asâmblëy *(Pakistan)* assembly *government*

âsân easy; horses

âsânawël to ease

âsântiya ease *noun*

asâs basis

asâsi qânun constitution

asbâb equipment

âshnâ acquaintance

ashpâz cook

ashpâzi kawël to cook

asir prisoner-of-war

askar soldier; troops

askari military service

asli main; original; **asli chawk** main square

âsmân sky

aspa mare

aspirin aspirin

asrâr secrets

astawël to transmit

astâzay representative

astâzitob representation

astâzitob kawël represent

astër lining *of clothes*

Âstrâliyâ Australia

Âstrâliyâyay *m* Australian

Âstrâliyâyëy *f* Australian

Âsyâ Asia

atal hero

atar perfume

atë eight

atë-lës eighteen

a'tirâz protest; **a'tirâz kawël** to protest

atiyâ eighty

atkalawël to estimate

âtletik athletics

âtomi atomic

atrâf directions

aw and

awal first

awâra plain *noun*

awdas ablutions; **awdas kawël** to perform ablutions

awë<u>sh</u>tël to turn; to fall over

awredël to listen; to hear

awredunkay listener

aw<u>sh</u>âr waterfall

aw<u>sh</u>ay brother-in-law *sister's husband/wife's brother*

awyâ seventy

awzâr tools

âyâ whether

ayâlat state *federal*

âyina mirror

aynaki glasses; spectacles; sunglasses

Âyrlen<u>d</u> Ireland

Âyrlenday *m* Irish

Âyrlen<u>d</u>ëy *f* Irish

âys-krim ice cream

âzâd free; **âzâd matbu'ât** the free press

âzâdawël to liberate

âzâdi freedom

azala muscle; **azale** muscles

âzân Islamic call to prayer

azghën sim barbed wire

azmi<u>sh</u>t trial *test*

azmoyana test

âzuqa provisions

B

ba will; shall

bâbâ father

bâbâ grandfather

bachatawël to save *money*

bachay child

bachyân children

bâd wind *noun*

bad bad; **bad gumân** suspicion

ba<u>d</u>a waistband

badala song

bâdâm almond

badan body

badi feud

bâdi; bâdlarunke windy

badlawël to change; to exchange

badmëkhey unfriendly

badmërgh unfortunate

bâdrang cucumber

badtar worse

bâdurya blizzard

baga waistband

bagëy cart; carriage; tonga

bâgh garden; orchard

baghâwat riot

bâghi rebel

bâghu eczema

bâghwân gardener

bagri beans

bahar outside

bahedël to flow

bahër; bahira sea; ocean

bahranay foreign

bahs dicussion; **bahs kawël** to discuss

bâja brother-in-law *wife's sister's husband*

baje o'clock; **Sһ<u>ı</u>pa<u>zh</u> baje di.** It is six o'clock.; **Tso baje di?** What time is it?

bakës bag

bakh<u>sh</u>ël to forgive

bakh<u>sh</u>ëna! sorry!

bakht luck; destiny

baks bag

baksuna baggage

bâktaryâ bacteria

bal light *not dark*

bâl (*Pakistan*) ball

balawël to light

bale yes

balël to call; to invite

balëna invitation

bâlë<u>sh</u>t pillow; cushion

balki

balki but
baltëy *(Pakistan)* bucket
bam bomb; **dë bam pârcha** shrapnel; **bam shandawël** bomb disposal
bâm roof
bamba water pump; **bamba kawël** to pump water
bambâri bombardment
bambirak dragonfly
bampar bumper/fender
ban garden
bana form; shape
bânat bonnet; hood *of car*
band closed; blocked; dam; joint
bandar port
bandawël to close
bandâzh bandage *medical*
bânde on
bandi prisoner; **bandi kawël** to arrest; to take prisoner; **bandi khâna** prison
bândi above *upon*
bânë eyelashes
bâng Islamic call to prayer
bângi rooster
bânjën; tor bânjën aubergine/eggplant; **srë/rumi bânjën** tomato
bânk bank
bânk not bank note
bânkdâr banker
bansët foundation *building*
banyân jumper/sweater
bâr bar
barâbar equal; even; level; equivalent
barâbarawël to supply
baramta kawël to kidnap
baramtagar kidnapper
baramta-kawël kidnapping
bârân rain; **Bârân ori. It is raining.**
baranda veranda
baray success; victory
barband naked
bârëwël to load
barf koch avalanche

barjis pantyhose
bârkay ankle
barkha part; **barkha akhistël** to share
barkhlik destiny
barma kawël to drill
barq electricity
barqi jitka electric shock
Bartâniyâ Britain
Bartâniyâyi British
baryâlay kedël to pass an exam
baryâlitob success
bas bus; enough; **bas kedël** to be enough; **dë bas pë zariya** by bus; **dë basuno hada** bus station
bashar human; **bashar dustâna mrasta** humanitarian aid
bashari humanitarian; **bashari huquq/haquna** human rights; **bashari mrasta** humanitarian aid
bashpër complete
bâsi stale
bâskitbâl basketball
batwa wallet
bâwar kawël to believe
baya price
bâyad must; have to
bayân expression
bayânawël to explain; to state
baylël to lose; to be defeated
bâyskil bicycle
bâz falcon; hawk
bâzâr market
bazâzi clothes shop
be -less; without; **be lë** apart from; **be bure** no sugar; **be dzâya shaway** displaced person
be-adab(a) impolite
beda hay
befikra thoughtless
begâ last night; **begâ ta** this evening
be-gunâh innocent
behtar better
behtarin best
be-imân unbeliever

bekâr(a) unemployed
bekâri unemployment
be-khabëra uninformed
bekhatara safe
bekhwanda tasteless
be-kora homeless
bël other; another; separate; spade; **bël botal** another bottle
belawël to separate
belcha shovel
bëlmënga saltless
bël sabâ the day after tomorrow
bëluk group; platoon
bema *see* bima
bema'nâ insignificant
be-mâlye tax-free
be-mora motherless
bën co-wife
be-nazma disorderly
bënzay son *of co-wife*
bënzëy daughter *of co-wife*
beplâra fatherless
bera hurry; **bera kawa!** hurry up!; **Bera me da.** I'm in a hurry.
beral barrel *for storage*
bëramta hostage; **bëramta kawël** to take hostage
berawël to frighten
berëy ship; boat; ferry
be-roh lifeless
besâray unique
besawâd illiterate
bëshpër perfect
be-tiksa tax-free
betrëy battery *electric*
be-wasi failure
bëzërg holy man
bi'aqla silly
bide asleep
bikhi very
bil bill/check; different
biltun separation
bima insurance; **Zmâ jaydâd bima day.** My possessions are insured.; **Zë tibi bima laram.** I have medical insurance.
bir beer
birokrâsi bureaucracy

bistar; bistira sleeping bag
biyâ then
biyâti scissors
bizi *(Pakistan)* busy *telephone call*
bizo monkey
boluk platoon
bording kârt boarding pass
borqa chador; *woman's* veil
bors brush
bot shoe
botal bottle
botëy steak
botuna shoes; **dë botuno dukân** shoeshop
brastën duvet/quilt
brëj tower
bresh stitch *in one's side*
breshnâ electricity; lightning; **Breshnâ qata shawe da.** The electricity has been cut off.
breshnâlik e-mail
brëstën duvet/quilt
bret mustache
brid attack; ambush
brik brake; **brik niwël** to brake
brituna mustache(es)
buda old man
budëy old woman
budija budget
bukhâr deg cooker; stove
bukhârëy heating stove
bukht busy
bulbël nightingale
bura sugar
bus straw
butay herb
buti firewood
buy smell; **buy kawël** to stink
buy zida mawâd deodorant
byâ again
byâ-byâ often

CH

C.D. C.D.; **C.D. tep** C.D. player
châ who?

châbëk quick
châchi *(Pakistan)* aunt *father's brother's wife*
châdari chador; *woman's* veil
chaka cottage cheese
châklet chocolate
chakush hammer
chal tactic
châlâk quick
chalawël to drive; to operate
chalawunkay driver; editor
chamcha spoon
chamtu ready; **Chamtu yam.** I am ready.
chândzây refinery
changak hook *noun*
chap left *side*
chapa kedël to reverse
châpawël to print
châqu penknife
châra; chârë knife; dagger; machete
charbi fat *noun*
chârgol fastener *for clothes*
charm leather
chârpây cot
chars hashish
Chârshamba Wednesday
chârtarâsh beam; girder
chashme *(Pakistan)* eyeglasses
chasp kâli tights
chat ceiling
chatak quick; rapid; express
chatrëy umbrella
châwdana explosion; detonation
châwdël to blow up; to explode; to detonate; to burst
châwdunkay explosives
chawk town square; roundabout
chawkëy chair; seat; stool; bench
chawkidâr nightguard; nightwatchman
chây tea
châyjush kettle
châykhori kâchugha teaspoon

châynak(a) teapot
chaynal T.V. channel
che that *conjunction*
chëkotara grapefruit
chëprâs janitor
chërchërak cicada
dë chërg ghwasha chicken *meat*
chërg rooster
chërga hen
chërgân poultry
chërguray chicken
cheri? where?; **cheri day?** where is?; **cheri di?** where are?
chëwël to burst; to explode
chigha wahël to shout
chik *bank* check
chilam hookah
chilëmchi washbowl
chimcha spoon
Chin China
china spring *of water*
Chinâyay *m* Chinese
Chinâyëy *f* Chinese
chinchëna sparrow
chingâsh crab
chini; chini loshi chinaware
chinji worms
chips french fries
chirik guerrilla
chorkëy bayonet
chotëy kawël to braid
chungasha frog
chup silent
chuptiyâ silence
churledël to spin
chushkay tap; faucet

D/Ḍ/DZ

dâ she/it (is); this; **dâ pëkhpëla** herself
dabara stone
dablay can; canister
dâdâ father
dâda sure

dâfe hawâ top anti-aircraft cannon
daftar office
dâga beam; girder
dagar field
dagha this
dak full
dakawël to fill
dâkhil interior *noun*
dâkhila mamno no entry
dâkhili interior *adjective*
dâktar *m*; **dâktara** *f* doctor
dâku bandit
dâl lentils
dala group
dâlar dollar
dalayize rasunduye mass media
dâlëy present *gift*
dâlez corridor
dalil reason
dalta here
dâm trap *noun*
dama break *for refreshments*
damâgh brain
damâghi hamla epilepsy
damawël to brew; to infuse; to steam *food*
dâna grain; piece; boil *noun*
dand pond; pool
danda job; occupation; duty
dandar stem *noun*
dâne seeds
danëna inside
dangër thin
dangërwâlay thinness
danyâ coriander
daqiqa minute *noun*
dâr fear *noun*
dara valley
dara door; plank; stick
daraja degree
darawël to stop
dard pain
daredël to stand
dâredël to fear
dârël to bite
darghal treacherous

Dari Dari
darjan dozen
darlodël to contain; to own
darmaltun pharmacy
dars warkawël to teach
dâru medicine
darwâgh false; lie *noun*
darz fracture; **darz kawël** to split; to fracture
darzi tailor; dressmaker
dâsh oven
dashta desert
dâsi such
daskash glove(s)
dawâ medicine; drug
dawâm warkawël to continue
dawl kind; type; manner
dawlat state; **dë dawlat rayis** head of state
dawlatman rich
dawra reign *noun*
day he/it (is); this; **day pëkhpëla** himself
dâyemi eternal
dâyi midwife
daynamo dynamo
dâyra circle
dë of; **dë Shikspiyar drâme** the plays of Shakespeare
dëbândi out
deg pot
dehqân farmer
dënana râsha come in!
der many; much; more; (a) lot; very; **der dzali** often; **der lëzh** too little; **der na** not much; **der shë** excellent; **der ziyât** too much
dersh thirty
dërwâza door
dësband bracelet
dësmâl napkin; **dë poze dësmâl** handkerchief
dëstarkhân tablecloth
dewâl wall
dewâli bukharëy chimney
dewâlisât clock

di is
difa' kawël to defend
digri degree
dilchasp interesting
dilchaspi interest *noun*
dimokrâsi democracy
din religion
Dinmârkay *m* Dane
Dinmârkëy *f* Dane
Dinmârki Danish
dipârtmint department
diplumât diplomat
diplumâtike arike diplomatic ties
direwar driver
dirishi suit *of western clothes*
Disimbar December
dis-shway sink *noun*
diyâbit diabetes
diyâbiti diabetic
dizal diesel
do'â prayer; **do'â kawël** to pray; to bless
dobay summer
dobi laundry person
dod manner; mode; tradition
dod-dastur custom
dodëy bread; food; meal; **dë dodëy farmâysh warkawël** to order a meal; **dë dodëy kota** dining room; **dë dodëy lest** menu
dodiz traditional
dod-riwâj etiquette
doham second *adjective*; **doham lâs** secondhand
dokân store *shop*
dol drum *noun*
do-lës twelve
doshman enemy
dosiya file *paper*
dost friend
dosti friendship
doyam second *adjective*
dozakh hell
drâma play; drama
drana heavy
drâyi hairdryer

dre three
dresh! stop!
dre myâshte quarter *of year*
dre myâshtinëy quarterly
dreyam third
drund heavy
dubedël to sink
dughumra this much
dukân shop; store
dukândâr shopkeeper
dumra this much
durbin binoculars
Dushanba Monday
dushman enemy
duy they; them; these; **duy pakhpëla** themselves
dwa two; **dwa chanda** twice; **dwa fasla** half year; **dwa onëy** fortnight; **dwa pâwâ** half-hour; **dwa tarafa tikit** return ticket
dwâra both
dyârlës thirteen
dzaka che because of
dzal *an instance of* time
dzaledël to flash; to shine
dzân body
dzand delay
dzangal wood; forest
dzarawël to hang
dzarawunkay *clothes* hanger
dzawâb answer; **dzawâb warkawël** to answer
dzawâbawël to answer
dzây place; site; accommodation; **dzây badlawël** to replace
dzâyawël to place
dzëka because; therefore
dzghâstël to run
dzigar liver
dzinâwër animal
dzini some
dzirak intelligent
dziraki intelligence
dzmëka earth
dzwâk force

dzwâkuna troops
dzwân young; young person
dzwër slope

E

ebtidâ beginning
Edz AIDS
ejrâ'i administrative
elikoptar helicopter
emtihân exam
Enjil Bible; gospel
eqlim climate
es-hâl diarrhea
eshtihâ appetite
eyarkandeshan air conditioner; air conditioning

F

fâbrika factory
faks fax; **dë faks mâshin** fax machine
falajawël to paralyze
fanar spring *metal*
faqat only *ad*
faqir beggar
fâram (Pakistan) form *official*
Farânsaway Frenchman
Farânsawëy Frenchwoman
Farânsawi French
farnechar furniture
Fârsi Farsi/Persian *language*
fasël season; quarter year
fatah victory; **fatah kawël** to conquer
fawri urgent
fâyda gain; advantage
fâyl file *computer*
fâynal final *noun*
fazâ space
fëlm movie
fërij fridge
feshan fashion
Fibriwari February
fidrâsyun; **fidreshan**

(Pakistan) federation
fikir thought; mind; **fikir kawël** to think; **Fikir kawam che...** I think that...
fil elephant
fil; fi'l verb
filëm film; **dë filëm fistiwâl** film festival; **filëm jorawunkay** filmmaker
filiz metal *noun*
filizi metal *adjective*
filmorgh turkey
filtar filter
Firwari (Pakistan) February
fishâr pressure
fita tape
fizik physics
fizyutrâpi physiotherapy
flash *camera* flash
flet (Pakistan) apartment
folklor folklore
folkluri musiqi folk music
foqara vertebra
foqarât vertebrae
forma *official* form; **forma dakawël** to fill in a form
fotbâl football/soccer
frij refrigerator
fut foot *measurement*
futbâl football; soccer; **dë futbâl maych** soccer match
futokâpi photocopy; **futokâpi kawël** to photocopy; **dë futokâpi mâshin** photocopier

G/GH

gach plaster cast *medical*
gadawël to mix
gadedâ dance; dancing
gâdëy carriage; tonga
gâdëywân; gâdiwân carriage driver
gadula mixture
gadun kawël participate

gâm

gâm pace

gan several; **gan dzangal** thick forest

gandana gandana; leek

gandël to sew

gandunkay tailor

gangs dizzy; **Gangs yam.** I feel dizzy.

garâj garage

garam *see* garm

garandëy cockroach

gardzandoy tourism; **dë gardzandoy daftar** tourist office

gardzedël to hike

garëy wristwatch

garm hot

garma melon

garmi heat; **Garmi da.** It is hot.; **Garmi me kezhi.** I am hot.; **dë garmëy tsapa** heatwave

gârnizun garrison

gashniz coriander

gata stone; **gata kawël** to gain

gatawër useful

gatawërtiyâ usefulness

gatawërtub utility

gatël to win; to earn; to defeat

gâwanday neighbor

gaz yard *distance*

gâz gas

gâzëra carrot

gazma patrol

gëd sheep

geda stomach

gedawar paunchy

gëlam carpet *woven*

gelan gallon

ger gear *car*

gërdanëy cartridge belt

gërday round

gëre gëray sleet

gërzedël to walk

ges *(Pakistan)* gas

ghahidz morning

ghal thief; robber

ghala grain

ghalat wrong

ghalati mistake; **ghalati kawël** to make a mistake

ghâlëy carpet *knotted*

gham grief

ghamiza disaster

ghamjan sad

ghanamina bread *flat, wheat*

ghandël to condemn

ghanëm wheat

ghapël to bark

ghar mountain

ghâra neck; collar

gharagëy necklace

gharanëy lâr mountain pass

gharay member; organ *of body*

gharb west *noun*

gharma noon; **dë gharme dodëy** lunch

gharmanëy lunch

ghartsë stag

ghâsh tooth; **dë ghâsh dâktar** dentist; **ghâsh dard** toothache; **ghâsh khalay** toothpick; **dë ghâsho bors** toothbrush; **dë ghâsho krim** toothpaste

ghâshuna teeth

ghâsib dzwâk occupying forces

ghat big

ghata gwëta thumb

ghayr lë besides *preposition*

ghayri-qânuni illegal

ghâz gas

ghazël(a) love song

ghazh voice; sound

ghazhawël to play *a musical instrument*

ghazhedël to speak

ghazhedunkay speaker

ghbarg twins

ghbargawël to double

ghbargolay twins

ghëna spider

ghëri; dë badan ghëri limbs (of body)

ghërtsë gazelle

ghezh wrestling

ghlâ robbery; theft; **ghlâ kawël** to rob; to steal

ghlë thieves

ghobë cowherd

gholay floor *ground*

ghor nikë great-grandfather

ghora ganël to prefer

ghora kawël to elect

ghora nyâ great-grandmother

ghoray dish

ghumbasa wasp; hornet

ghundëy hill

ghurdzawël to throw

ghurfa kiosk; cashier's booth

ghusa angry

ghushtël to want

ghwâ cow; **dë ghwâ shode** cow's milk

ghwanda session; conference

ghwara kawël to select

ghwari ghee

ghwasha meat; **Ghwasha matakora shawe da.** This meat is tough.

ghwayay bull; ox; **dë ghwayi ghwasha** beef

ghwazh ear; **dë ghwazh parda** ear drum; **ghwazhuna** ears

gidër fox

gilâs *drinking* glass; cherry

gilgir fender *of car*

girâm gram

girâmar grammar

gobay cauliflower

gol goal; score; **gol kawël** to score a goal

golâbi pink

golëy tablet; bullet; ammunition

golpay cauliflower

goluband scarf

gor grave *noun*

goram herd

gota finger; **gote** fingers

gotma thimble

gowgal rib cage

gram blamed

gramawël to blame

grân hard; difficult; expensive

granday quick

grawi mortgage

grup lightbulb

gudâm store

gul kawël to switch off

gulâb rose

gulëy *see* **golëy**

gumruk *border* customs

gunda knee

gundi perhaps

gungay owl

gungri beans

gurdwâra temple *religious*

gwand party *political*

gwël flower; **gwël plorunkay** florist

gwëta ring

H

had limit

hadaf aim

hadera cemetery

hadukay bone

dë haduki mâghzë marrow *of bone*

hâfiza memory

hafta week

haftawâr weekly

hagëy egg

hagha; haghë he; she; it; that; those; **dë haghe** his; her; its **dë haghe kitâb** his/her book; **Haghe të me warkër.** I gave it to him/her.

haghasi such

haghe *see* **hagha**

hagho they; them; **dë hagho** their; theirs

haj pilgrimage *to Mecca*; **haj kawël** to go on pilgrimage

hâjat need; necessity

hâji pilgrim *to Mecca*

hakam referee

hal kawël to solve

halâl permitted *religiously*; halal

halâlawël to slaughter *an animal*

Hâlanday Dutchman

Hâlandëy Dutchwoman

Hâlandi Dutch *language*

hâlat state; condition; situation; Hâlat jidi di. The situation is serious.

halëk boy

halta there

halzun snail

ham too; also

hamaghë same

hamdâ os right now

hamdagha this (very)

hamesha always

hâmila pregnant; dë hâmilatob mëkhniway birth control

hamkâr colleague

hamla attack; hamla kawël to attack

haq legal right

haqiqat reality; truth

haquna rights

har each; every; har cheri anywhere; har tsë che whatever; Har tsë che ghwâre wâyekhla. Take whatever you want.

har tsuk anyone

harâm forbidden *religiously*

hâran horn *car*

harbi military; war *adjective*

harbi pohantun military university

harbi showundzay military school

harchâ everybody; everyone

harkala râshëy! welcome!

hartse everything

hartsok everybody; everyone

haryëw everybody; everyone

hasâs allergic; sensitive

hashara insect; hashara zid insecticide; hashare insects

hâsilkhez fertile

Haspânawi Spanish *language*

Haspâniyâyay *m* Spaniard

Haspâniyâyëy *f* Spaniard

Haspâniyâyi Spanish *thing*

hatâ even; hatâ kë even if

hatsa kawël to try

hawâ air; weather

hawâyi air *adjective*; **hawâyi chalan** aviation; hawâyi hamla air-raid; hawâyi adâ airbase; hawâyi chaland airline; hawâyi dagar airfield; hawâyi dagar airport; hawâyi dzwâk air force; hawâyi hamla air-raid; hawâyi post air mail; hawâyi sherkat airline

hawelëy yard; courtyard

hawz pool; swimming pool

hayânâk modest

haybatnâk terrible

hayrân surprised

hayrânedäl to be surprising

haywân animal; haywânât animals

hefzul-siha hygiene

her forgotten

herawël to forget

hesâb *see* hisâb

hewâd country; homeland

hidâyât instructions *on use*

hifzawël to learn by heart

hifzul-siha healthcare

hila hope; hila larël to wish; to expect

hilëy duck

Hind India

hindâra mirror

Hinday *m* Indian

Hindëy *f* Indian

Hindi Hindi

Hindu Hindu

Hindustân India

Hindutob Hinduism

hindwâna watermelon

hipâtit hepatitis

hisâb calculation; dë hisâb mâshin calculator

hits no; none; hits këla never

hitsuk nobody
ho yes
hokumat government; administration
hokumati government; administrative
hosâ kawël to relax
hoshyâr intelligent
hoshyâri intelligence
hudud limits
hukum order *noun*
hukumat rule *government*
hunar art
hunarman artist
huquq rights
hure there
husâ comfortable
husëy deer; gazelle
hutal hotel
huzha garlic

I

i'lân advert
i'lân kawël to advertise
ibâdat kawël to pray
idâptar adapter *electric*
idâra administration; department
idâri administrative
idrâr urine
igzâs exhaust *of car*
ihsâsawël to feel
ihtijâj protest; **ihtijâj kawël** to protest
ihtimâl larël to be likely; **Ihtimâl lari. It is likely.**
ihtimâl probability
ihtimâli probable
ihtirâm respect
ihtiyât caution
ijrâ performance
ijrâyi executive
ikar acre
iksre X-rays
ilarzhik allergic
ilëm knowledge; science

ilmi scientific
imâm imam
imân belief; faith
imândâr believer
imel e-mail; **dë imel âdras** e-mail address
imkân possibility; **imkân lari** maybe
imtihân test *academic*; **imtihân akhistël** to test
Inglisay *m* Englishman
Inglisëy *f* Englishwoman
Inglisi English *language*
Inglistân England
injin engine
injiniyar engineer
inqilâb revolution
insân human (being) *noun*
insâni human *adjective*
intarnit internet
intikhâbât election
intikhâbawël to choose
intizâr waiting
iqtisâd economy; **dë iqtisâd alam** economics; **iqtisâd pohana** economics
iqtisâdi châre finance; financial affairs
iqtisâdpoh economist
irâda larël to intend
Irân Iran
Irânay *m* Iranian; Persian
Irânëy *f* Iranian; Persian
irtibât connection; contact
iru euro *currency*
Isaway *m* Christian
Isawëy *f* Christian
Isawiyat Christianity
isedël to seem
isëm noun
ishâra indicator light; **dë ishâro zhaba** sign language *for the deaf*
ishodël to place
ishowël to plant
ishq love
ishtop stove
Islâm Islam

Islâmi

Islâmi Islamic
Isrâyil Israel
Isrâyilay *m* Israeli
Isrâyilëy *f* Israeli
istël to pull out; to take out; to extract
istimâl use
istimâlawël to use
istiqlâl independence
istirâhat rest; **istirâhat kawël** to rest
istri *(Pakistan)* iron *for clothes*
Iṭâlaway *m* Italian
Iṭâlawëy *f* Italian
Iṭâlawi Italian *language*
Iṭâliyâ Italy
itihâdiya union; trade union
iyarkandeshan air conditioner; air conditioning
izâfi extra; spare; **izâfi wakht** free time
izgâs silencer/muffler *of car*
iztirâri hâlat emergency
iztirâri khuruj emergency exit

J

ja'li counterfeit; **Dagha payse ja'li di.** This money is counterfeit.
jaba marsh; swamp
jabal lever
jaghal gravel
jagra argument; fight; battle
jahil lake
jak jack *of car*
jâkaṭ jumper/sweater
jakër thunderstorm
jâl n fishing net
jalâ separate *adjective*
Jalâlabâd Jalalabad
jâlëy mosquito net
jama' addition *maths*; **jama' kawël** to add
jâme clothes; dress; **jâme aghostël** to get dressed; **jâme istël** to get undressed
jâme jomât main mosque

jamhur rayis president *of country*; **dë jamhur rayis mrastiyâl** vice-president
jamhuriyat republic
janat heaven
jang battle; war; **jang achawunkay** warmonger; **jangawël** to wage war
jangedël fight
jangi bandi prisoner-of-war
jangyâlay fighter
janrâl general *noun*
jantari calendar
janub south *noun*
janubi south(ern)
Janwarëy January
Jâpân Japan
Jâpânay *m* Japanese
Jâpânëy *f* Japanese
Jâpâni Japanese *language*
jarâh surgeon
jarâhi surgery *subject*
jarëy shower *of rain*
jarima fine *of money*
Jarmanay *m* German
Jarmanëy *f* German
Jarmani Germany
jarobay waterfall
jarsaqil crane *machine*
jâru kawël to sweep
jârukash sweeper
jashën niwël to celebrate
jâsus spy
jawdër rye
jâynamâz prayer mat/rug
jâyza prize
jaz jazz
jâz *(Pakistan)* airplane
jazâ warkawël punish
jeb pocket
jëg tall; high; up
jëgwâlay height
jëkër thunderstorm
jel *(Pakistan)* prison
jidi serious
jihâd jihad
jinâza funeral; **dë jinâze lmundz** funeral prayer

jinëy girl
jins sex *gender*
jinsi muqâribat sex *act*
jinsi teray rape
jirga council
jismâni physical
jismi ya zihni zarba trauma
jiyâlojist geologist
joghrâfiya geography
Jom'a Friday
jora couple; pair; suit *of Afghan clothes*
jorawël to make; to create; to build; to establish
jorawunkay builder
jorësht structure
julâ spider
Julây July
jum'at mosque
jumla sentence *of words*
Jun June
jurâbe socks
jurum *(Pakistan)* crime
jus *(Pakistan)* fruit juice
jushkuray hedgehog
juz-o-tâm unit *military*
jwâl sack *noun*
jwâr corn; maize; **dë jwâr dodëy** bread *flat, maize*
jwâri kawël to gamble

K/KH

kab fish; **kab niwël** fishing; **dë kab niwëlo jâl** fishing net
kabâb kebab
Kâbël Kabul
kâbina cabinet *political*
kabisa kâl leap year
kachâlu potato(es)
kachar mule
kâchugha spoon
kadu pumpkin
kadwâl refugee(s); displaced person(s); **dë kadwâlo kamp** refugee camp
kâfer atheist

kâfi sufficient; coffee
kâfir unbeliever
kâghaz paper
kâghazbâd kite
kâghazi dusmâl tissues
kâhu lettuce
kâj buttonhole
kajir vulture
kâkâ uncle *father's brother*
kâkhti famine
kâl year
kala? when?; **kala che** when; **kala na kala** sometimes
kalâ castle
kalâband siege *blockade*
kalach clutch *of car*
kâlanay annual; yearly
kalawshe rubber boots
kalay countryside
kâli clothes; dress; **dë kâlo baks** suitcase; **dë kâlo gandalo mâshin** sewing machine; **dë kâlo mindzalo podar** washing powder; **dë kâlo mindzël** laundry
kâlij college
kalisâ church
kaliwâl villager
kâliza anniversary
kamarband belt
kamër rock
kameshan *(Pakistan)* commission; **Kameshan tsumra day?** What is the commission?
kamis shirt
kamisun commission
kamkhuni anemia
kamp camp
kampala blanket
kampanëy company *firm*
kampâyn campaign
kampyutar computer; **dë kampyutar progrâm** computer program; **dë kampyutar wirus** computer virus
kâmra camera
kamwâlay shortage

kamzoray weak

kân mine *mineral*; **dë kân kârgar** miner

kana *f* deaf

Kânâdâ Canada

Kânâdâyay *m* Canadian

Kânâdâyëy *f* Canadian

kânâl canal

kânay stone

kanda trench

Kandahâr Qandahar

kândam condom

kandu loft; wheat bin

kandwâle ruins

kandzël to swear; to curse

kanë if not

kanfrâns conference; **dë kanfrâns kota** conference room

kangal ice; freezing

kangalawël to freeze

kangalzâr glacier

kânge kawël to vomit; **Kânge kawëm.** I have been vomiting.

kâni mineral

kanisa synagogue

kansart concert; **dë kansart tâlâr** concert hall

kântinar container *freight*

kantrolawël to control

kapcha cobra

kâpi copy; **kâpi kawël** to copy

kapra *(Pakistan)* fabric

kâr job; work; **kâr kawël** to work

kara bracelet

Karâchëy Karachi

karakatana review *newspaper/ magazine*

karam cabbage

karana agriculture

karâr quiet *adjective*; **karâr karâr!** gently!; slowly!

kârbandiz strike *from work*; **kârbandiz kawël** to strike

karël to cultivate

kârgar worker

kârghë crow

karhana farming

kârk cork

kârtan carton

kârtus bullet; cartridge

kârubâr business *work*

karwanda farm

karwandgar farmer; agronomist

kas man

kâsa bowl

kashawël to pull

kashër junior

kasit cassette; tape

kat bed

katân cotton

katana meeting; **katana kawël** to visit

katandzay clinic

katara fence

katël to look; to check

katëwa; katwëy *cooking* pot

kâtib clerk; **sar kâtib** head clerk

katmël bug *insect*

katsora carrier bag

katwa *cooking* pot

kawa! continue!

kawday great-great-grandson

kawdëy great-great-granddaughter

kawël to do

kawshkan corridor

kâwtara pigeon

kazhedël to lean

kë if; **kë cheri** unless; **kë imkân lari** if possible; **kë tse ham** although

ke at

kebal cable

këchâlu potato(es)

kedël to become

kek cake

këkarëy skull

kela banana

këla këla sometimes

këlay village

këliwâl villager

kemp *(Pakistan)* camp

kenârâb toilet(s)

kenâstël to sit
kërboray lizard
kërkëy window
kërsha line
kërwasay great-grandson
kërwasëy great-grand-daughter
kësay pupil *of eye*
këshër youngest child
ketâb book
ketâbcha exercise book; notebook
kêtara dagger; bayonet
khabaruna news
khabëre kawël to talk; to converse
khabëri-atëri conversation
khalak people
Khâli Saturday
khâm raw; uncooked
khamak dozi kawël to embroider
khamira pasta
khânak bowl
khandâ laughter; **dë khandâ** funny
khandël laugh
khânl aunt *father's brother's wife*
khanzir boar
khapa unhappy
khapaska nightmare
khapër(a) handful
khar donkey
kharâb bad
kharâbawël to destroy
khârësht itch *noun*
khârijay foreigner
khartsawël to sell
khartsawunkay salesman
khartsawunke saleswoman
khartumay turkey
khasak bug *insect*
khat letter
khatâ kawël to miss *not hit*
khatâbâsël to deceive
khatar danger; risk; **khatar pë ghâra akhistël** to risk
khatarnâk dangerous

khate mud
khatëkay melon
khatël to climb; to mount; to rise
khatidz east; **dë khatidz** east(ern)
khatkash ruler *instrument*
Khâwënd God
khâwënd husband; owner *of building*; landlord
khâwra ground; earth; territory
khayât tailor; **dë khayâti mâshin** sewing machine
khayma tent
khayrât charity *action*
khayriya mwasisa charity *organization*
khazale; khazëli trash; rubbish
Khdây pâmân! good-bye!
khel relatives *blood*
khër gray; khaki
khëredël to snore
khërsâr dawn
khështa brick; **dë khështe tota** rubble
kheta stomach
khidmat service
khiran dirty
khish relatives *by marriage*
khiyâl imagination
khlâs open; finished
khlâsawël to open; to end
kho but
khob dream; sleep; **dë khob golëy** sleeping pill(s); **dë khob kota** bedroom; **khob lidël** to dream
khobawalay sleepy
khodkâr biro; pen
khor sister
khorâ very
khorâk food
khormânëy *(Pakistan)* apricot
khorye nephew *sister's son*
khorza niece *sister's daughter*
khosër father-in-law

khoshâla happy
khozh sweet *adjective*
khozhidël to hurt
khparawël to publish
khparawunkay publisher
khparedël to spread
khpël own; self; relative(s)
khpëlwâk independent; **khpëlwâk dawlat** independent state
khpëlwâki independence
khpëlwân *blood* relatives
khpëlwi *blood* relationship
khra *f* donkey
khreyël to shave
Khudây God
Khudây pâmân! good-bye!
khufya polis secret police
khuk pig
khuna room
khurin soft
khusâ septic
khusay calf
khushi kawël to free
khushtabi humorous
khususan especially
khwâ direction; side
khwâbaday unhappy
khwala sweat *noun*
khwalë secret
khwalëy hat
khwand taste *noun*
khwandawër tasty
khwandi safe
khwâr poor
khwar *see* khwër
khwarâ dër too many
khwârë food; **dë khwaro dzây** feeding station
khwarël to eat
khwash grateful; **Khwash yam** I am grateful.
khwashawël to like
khwashay kawël to release
khwâshe mother-in-law
khwashi pleasure
khwâshini sorrow
khwaynde sisters

khwâzhë candy; sweet(s); dessert; **khwâzhë welëni** aniseed
khwër mountain stream; torrent
khwërël to eat
khwëshay kawël to quit
khwëzh sore
khwlë mouth
khwrâki edible
kil furrow
kili key
kilogrâm kilogram
kilomitar kilometer
kimyâ chemistry
kimyâwi chemical
kin left; **kin lor ta wâwra!** turn left!; **kin lor ta** to the left
kin-arkh left-wing
kindël to dig
kinlasay left-handed
kinsilawël to cancel
kirâ kawël to rent *for oneself*
kirâ war-kawël to rent *to someone*
kirâya fare; **kirâya kawël** to hire; **Kirâya tsumra da?** What is the fare?; **kirâya warkawunkay** tenant
kirëray cricket *insect*
kisa story *tale*
kitâb plorandzây bookshop
kitâbkhâna library
kitâbtun library
kitseri nowhere
kizhdëy tent
klab club
klak hard; severe; tight
klâs *(Pakistan)* class
klinik clinic
kochay nomad
kod code
kohay well *of water*
kokuna stitches *surgical*
kolcha cake
komak help
komaki-qowa reinforcements
kometa committee

lârshowana

konj corner
koprëy skull
kor house; building; **dë kor kâr** homework
koranay internal; domstic; tame; **koranay kâr** homework; **koranëy jagra** civil war
koranëy family
korba host
kortëy jacket
korwâlâ owning a house
koshish kawël to try
kot fort; overcoat
kota room
kotband hangar
kraka hate; **kraka kawël** to hate
krâr see karâr
kridit credit; **kridit kârt** credit card
krikit cricket *game*
kuchnay little
kudatâ coup d'etat
kulâli ceramics; pottery
kulang pickax
kulara cholera
kulëp door lock
kulma intestine; gut; **kulme** guts
kultur culture
kum which; **kum yaw?** which (one)?; **kum cheri** somewhere; **dë kum dzây?** where from?; **Kuma neta da?** What's the date?
kumak see komak
kun *m* deaf
kunak pelvis
kunâtay hip
kunji key
kurtëy coat
kutël to chop
kutray puppy
kutsa street
kuza jug
kuzedël to descend; to alight
kwar grapes; vine

kwëch butter
kwënd widower
kwënda widow
kwëng owl
Kwëta Quetta

L

lâ still; yet; **lâ në** not yet; **lâ ârzân** cheaper; **lâ bad** worse;
lablabu beetroot
lâbrâtwâr laboratory
labsirin lipstick
lagawël to spend *money*; to switch on
lagedël to blow *wind*
lagiyâ busy *involved*
lahja dialect
lâket necklace
lâkin but
lâlâ elder brother
lâmbël to swim; to bathe
lâmbo swimming; **dë lâmbo kâli** swimsuit
lampa lamp
land short
landa f wet
lânde under *adverb*
lândi below; low; **lândi ishodël** to put down; **lândi kawël** to overcome
lânja dispute *noun*
lâr sha! go!
lâr road; way
lara fog; mist
lâre saliva
larël to have
larëm scorpion
lârëy lorry; truck
largay wood *substance*
larghunay ancient
larjan foggy
lârshod guide; **lârshod kitâb** guidebook; directory
lârshowana direction; **lârshowana kawël** to direct; to lead

lârs̲h̲owd kitâb guidebook; directory

lârs̲h̲uwēna *see* lârs̲h̲owana

lârway passer-by

las ten; **las perëy** millennium

lâs hand

lasam tenth

las̲h̲tay stream

lâsi baks handbag

lâsi bam grenade

lâsi barq *electric* light

lâsi kitâb manual; instruction book

lâsi san'at handicraft

lâsi tsirâgh flashlight; torch

lasiza decade

lâslik kawël to sign *a document*

lâslik signature

lâstay handle *noun*

lastonay sleeve

lat lazy; slow

latawël to seek

lâten lantern

lati laziness

lâtrëy lottery

law reaping; harvest

lawand single; not married

lawda fool

lâyiq able

layliya hostel

lâzim necessary

lë from; **lë mandza** through; ... **lë pâra** for ...

lecha forearm

lëka like *preposition*

lëmën hem

lemtsi carpet *felt*

lemu lemon; lime

lërëy series; radio series

leri far

lesans driver's license

lest list

letar liter

lewanay insane; **dë lewani spi dârël** to catch rabies

lewar brother-in-law *husband's brother*; **dë lewar s̲h̲ëdza** sister-in-law *husband's brother's wife*

lewë wolf

lëzh little; less

lëzhawël to decrease

lezhël to send

lëzh-o-der more or less

lëzh tar lëzha at least

lez-lez little by little

libârtri *(Pakistan)* laboratory

lidël to see; to meet

lift lift; elevator

lik letter

lika queue; line

likana writing

likchar lecture

likël to write

likwâl writer

linz lens; contact lenses

lisa high school

liyâqat ability

lmar sun; **dë lmar krim** sunblock; **lmar tsrak** sunrise; **lmar lwedë** sunset; **Lmar day. It is sunny.**

lmarsedzalay sunburn

lmasay grandson

lmasëy granddaughter

lmundz prayer; **lmundz kawël** to pray

loba game

lobedël to play

lobghâlay stadium

lor route; sickle; scythe

lora kawël to swear an oath

loshay pot; **dë losho almârëy** cabinet

loya jirga traditional parliament

loya lâr highway; motorway

loydrastiz chief of staff *military*

loystârnwâl attorney-general

lubyâ green beans

lugay smoke

lughat word

luma trap

lumranëy mrasta first aid

lumray first

lumray wazir prime minister

lumrey daraja first class

lund *m* wet; humid; damp
lune daughters
lungëy turban
lur daughter
luta lumps *of earth*
lutfan! please!
luts sim live wire
luy big; great; **luy war** gate
luyedël to grow up
lwast lesson
lwastël to read
lwedël to fall
lwedidz west; western
lwër high; loud
lwesht span
lwëst reading
lwëzha hunger

M

mâ I; me; **mâ pëkhpëla** myself
mablagh; mablëgh sum; amount
ma'dani mineral; **ma'dani obë** mineral water
madani civil; **madani huquq/ haquna** civil rights
madrasa madrasa
mâfi excuse *noun*
mafkura idea
magar but
mâghzë brain; marrow *of bone*
mahâjir immigrant; refugee
mahâjirat immigration; flight
mahâjirin refugees
mahâlwesh timetable
mahârat skill
mahâsib cashier
mâhi fish
mahkama law court
mahsul product; *customs* duty
majala magazine *printed*
makha niwël to prevent
makhta forward(s); in front
maktab school
maktub letter
mâl cattle; livestock; cargo

malaryâ malaria
malëk chief; headman
malëkh grasshopper
malesha mercenary
mâlga salt
malgaray companion
Malgari Milatuna United Nations
mâlgin salty
malham cream *ointment*
malika queen; monarch
mâlim teacher
mâlish cream; ointment
mâlta orange *fruit*
mâluch cotton wool
mâlumât information; **dë mâlumâto daftar** information office
mâlya tax; **dë mâlye wizârat** treasury *ministry*; **mâlya akhistël** to tax
mâmâ uncle *mother's brother*
mâmëy; mami aunt *mother's brother's wife*
mamiz raisins
ma'mulan; mâmulan normally
ma'muli; mâmuli normal
mâmur official; office worker
mâmurin officials; staff
mâmuriyat police station
mâmuriyat mission
mana apple
ma'nâ; mânâ sense; meaning
man'a forbidden; **man'a kawël** to forbid
manana kawël to thank
manana! thank you!; **manane** thanks
manay autumn
mândina wife
mandz center; middle
mânëy palace
manfi subtraction; **manfi kawël** to subtract
mangay jug
mangotay mug *noun*
mansabdâr officer *military*
manzël floor; story

manzil destination
maqâla essay; paper
maqsad destination
mâr chichël snakebite
mâr snake
mara *f* full up; satisfied
maraka interview
marakachi negotiator
marawël to feed
Mârch March
marëy bread
marëz quail
marg death
marghalëre pearl
ma'rifi kawël to introduce
markaz center
marmëy shell; ammunition; ordnance
marwënd wrist
masâla-dâr spicy *hot*
masalan for example
masâna bladder
mâsha mosquito
mâshâm evening; **dë mâshâm dodëy** dinner; supper
mashër boss
mashghul busy
mash-hur famous
mâshin machine
mâshindâr; mâshingan machine gun
mashora kawël to consult
mashq *school* exercise
mâshum infant; baby boy
mâshuma infant; baby girl; **dë mâshumâno dâktar** pediatrician; **dë mâshumâno nâroghëy** pediatrics; **dë mâshumâno tib** pediatrics
ma'sir contemporary
maslak profession
maslaki professional *person*
masno'i artificial; **masno'i gharay** artificial limb; **masno'i lâs** artificial arm; **masno'i psha** artificial leg; **masno'i starga** artificial eye
mâspashin afternoon

masruf busy *telephone call*
maste; mâstë yogurt
mâta defeat; to me; **mâta warkawël** to defeat
matakor tough *meat*
matal proverb
mâtaledël to wait for
matan text; inscription
mâtawël to break; to crash
matbu'a printer; press
matbu'ât the press
mâte: mâte payse change *money*; **mâte warkawël** to overturn
matër peas
mawâd material
mawqiyat position; situation
mawzo matter; subject
mayana *f* dear; loved
maych *football* match
maydân *sports* pitch
mâye liquid; **mâye ghwari** cooking oil
mayen *m* dear; loved
mâyn mine *explosive*; **mâyn larunke sima** minefield
mâyna wife
maynde mothers
mayra stepmother
mayranay wror half-brother
mayranëy khor half-sister
mayrezay stepbrother
ma'yub disabled
ma'yubiyat disability
maza taste *noun*
mazadâr tasty
mazdur servant
maz-hab religious sect
mâzi small
mazigar sunset
mazmun subject *academic*
mdzëka land; earth; **dë mdzëke shwayedâ** landslide
më...! do not...!; **më darezha!** don't stop!; **më wëla!** don't shoot!
Me May
me'da stomach; **dë me'de zakham** stomach ulcer

mëch fly *noun*

mecha size

mechawël to measure; to kiss

mechën flour mill

mëghshush confused

mëghshushawël to confuse

mehrabân kind *adjective*

mehtar groom; syce

mekhânik mechanic

mekap make-up *cosmetics*

mëkh face; cheek; *metal* nail;
mëkh kata/pëdzwër slope;
mëkh ke before

mëkhâmëkhedël to face

mela festival; gala; picnic

mëlakh locust

mëlgartub friendship

mëlgëray *m* friend

mëlgëre *f* friend

melma *m* guest

melmana *f* guest

melmapâl hospitable

melmastiyâ party; celebration;
feast

melmastun guesthouse

memâr architect

mena house; dwelling; homeland

mënay autumn

mëndzumay youngest child

mëngaray viper

menyu menu

mër dead; mër kedël die

merë husband

mëredël to be full

mërëy vertebra

mërghëy bird

mermën woman

Mermën Mrs.

mësâla spice

mëshëng lentils

mëshër head; boss; elder;
leader; senior

mëshrâno jirga parliament
Afghani upper house

mët arm; forearm

mëtër peas

mewa fruit; dë mewe obë fruit
juice

Mëy May

mez table; desk

mëzh ram

mëzha ewe; mole; rat

mezhay ant

mikrob germs

mil gun barrel; mile

milat nation

mili national; mili pëkhlâyana
national reconciliation

milyat nationality

milyon million

mina love; mina kawël to love

mindaka nut

mindë âs stallion

mindzël to wash

miqnâtisi magnetic

mirzâ clerk

mis copper

misâl example

mistri; mistari mechanic

mitër meter *measure*

mitro underground *subway*

mityâze urine

mlâ back; waist; dë mlâ tir
spine; dë mlâ dard backache;
Mlâ me khozhezhi. My back
hurts.

mlâtëre-qowa reinforcements

mlâwastënay belt

mo'akil client

mobârak holy; congratulations;
mobârak de sha! congra-
tulations to you!

mobâyl mobile phone; cell
phone

mochi cobbler

moda period *of time*

modim modem

mohâsera kawël to surround

mohasil student *university*

mohasira siege *blockade*

mojâhid Mojahed; mojâhidin
Mojahedin

mokhbir spy

monâsib proper

moqawâmat kawël to resist

mor mother

mor *m* full up; satisfied

morabâ jam; jelly

morghizari pheasant

morplâr parents

mosâfër passenger; traveler; mosâferin passengers; travelers

mosëm season

moshrek blasphemer

mo'taqed believer

motar car; dë motar asnâd car papers; motar pârkawël to park; dë motar râjistar car registration; Motar me panchar day. I have a flat tyre.; Motar mu kharâb shaway day. Our car has broken down.; Motar mu nshatay day. Our car is stuck.

motarwân driver; chauffeur

motërsâykël motorbike; motorcycle

mozâkira conversation

moze boots

mozhak mouse

mrasta help; co-operation; relief aid; mrasta kawël to help; Mrasta râsara kawalay she? Can you help me?

mrastiyâl helper; assistant; deputy

mrastiyâl wëlësmëshër vice-president *political*

mrastun orphanage

mrëch pepper

mrina death

mryay slave

mu'adab polite

mu'asisa foundation; organisation

mu'âyna kawël to examine *medically*

mu'jiza miracle

mubâriza campaign; struggle

mudir director; manager; administrator

mudiriyat director's office; directorship

muft free of charge

muhâkima trial *legal*

muhim important

muhimât ammunition

muhr stamp *official*

mujasima statue

mujrim criminal

mukarar frequently

mukhâbirât communication; telecommunications

mukhâlif opponent

mukhâlifat opposition

mulâ mullah

mulâqât meeting; mulâqât kawunkay visitor

mulëy radish

mulki civilian *noun/adjective*

mumkin possible; Mumkin day. It is probable.

munâra minaret

munâsib appropriate

mundël to find

munshi secretary

munzh we; us

muqâbil opposite

muraba square

murâm intention

musâbiqa contest

musakin painkiller

musakina tranquilizer

musala prayer mat/rug

mushâwir consultant

mushël rub

mushkil problem; difficult; mushkil na shta! no problem!; Mushkil tsë day? What's the trouble?

mushtamil included

musicha dove

musiqi music

mustaqil independent

msutaqim straight; Mustaqim ye rukh kawalay sham? Can I dial direct?

Musulmân *m* Muslim

Musulmâna *f* Muslim

mutakhasis specialist
mutâli'a study *noun*
mutasawif mystic *person*
mutawaje careful
mutawasit normal
mu<u>t</u>ay fist
muwasisa institute
muzâhira demonstration *political*
muzâhirachiyân demonstrators *political*
mu<u>zh</u> we; us
mu<u>zh</u>akprâng ferret; squirrel
muzik music
muzir harmful
muziyam museum
mwasisa foundation; organisation
myâsht month
myâshtënay monthly

N

na no; not
nâ-âshnâ strange
nâbaryâlay unsuccessful
nâ-binâ blind *adjective*
nâchâwdalay bam unexploded bomb
nafrat aversion
nahë nine
Nahe Tuesday
nahw syntax
najâr carpenter; joiner
nâjor(a) ill
nâjori illness
nâk pear
nâkâm unsuccessful
nâkarâri trouble *problems*
nakhod chickpeas
nâkhwa<u>sh</u> unhappy
nal pipe; catheter
nâlawël to shoe *a horse*
nâlbakëy saucer
nâmâlum unknown
namnâk wet; humid; damp
nâmtu well-known

nâ-mumkin impossible
namuna model; example
nana istël to put in
nânâ mint
nanawatël to enter
nanawatu lâr entrance
nandârdzay theater
nandâre theater
nandâridz stage *theater*
nandârtun exhibition; show
nândzëka doll
nânwâyi bakery
nâpezhanduy unknown; stranger
nâpoh unwise
naqsha map
nâr male *noun*
nârâm uncomfortable
nâ-rawâ illegal
naray randz tuberculosis
naray thin
nâray breakfast
na<u>r</u>ëy world
na<u>r</u>ëy lâr path
na<u>r</u>ëywâl international; **na<u>r</u>ëywâl âpre<u>t</u>ar** international operator; **na<u>r</u>ëywâl kod** international code; **na<u>r</u>ëywâl parwâz** international flight
nârina male *adjective*
nârinj orange *fruit*
nârinji orange *color*
narm soft
nârogh sick; *medical* patient; **Nârogh yam.** I am sick.
nâroghedël to be sick
nâroghi sickness; disease; infection; **dë nâroghëy na<u>sh</u>a** symptom *medical*
nars *m* nurse
narsa *f* nurse
Nârwe Norway
nas stomach; **nas dard** stomachache
nâsaka khor stepsister
nâsaka plâr stepfather
nâsaka wror stepbrother

nâsam wrong
nasha drunk
nasha evidence; proof; sign; nasha niwël to aim
nashayi drug addict
nashayiz mawâd drug *narcotic*
nâshir publisher
nashpâtay *(Pakistan)* pear
nashtedzël to squeeze
nâst seated
nâsta sitting
naswâri brown
natija result
natsâ dance; dancing
nâtsâpa suddenly
nâw ravine
naw *see* naway
nâwakhta late
Naway Zilând New Zealand
naway new; recent; **naway kâl** new year; **nawe miyâsht** new moon
nâwël novel
nawi ninety
nâwe bride
Nawruz New Year festival
naw-zezhay newborn child
nâyi barber
nâyt-klab nightclub
nazar eyesight
nazari theoretical
nazarya view; theory
nazhde *see* nëzhde
ndror sister-in-law *husband's sister*
në not; **në ... në** neither ... nor
negh straight
nëghështalay twisted
nëghështël to twist
neghwâlay straightness
nektây necktie
Nën kuma wradz da? What day is it?
nën today; **nën gharma/ maspashin** this afternoon; **nën mâshâm** this evening;

nën sahâr this morning; **nën shpa** tonight
nështwâlay lack
nesh wahël to sting
nësk lentils
neta date
nëzhde near; nearly; almost; **nazhde pandzos mila** about 50 miles
nikë grandfather
nikâh marriage
nim half; **nim sât** half-hour; **nima shpa** midnight
nimakhwâ unsuccessful
nimâyi half
nimbu *(Pakistan)* lime *fruit*
nimgëray incomplete
nisti poverty
niwël to hold; to catch; to seize; to beat; to conquer
niyâl plant; sprout
niyâlawël to plant
niyâlawëna planting
niyâlgay seedling
nizhdi *see* nëzhde
njëlëy girl
njune girls
no so; then
nobat turn
nolay weasel
nor other
noskha copy; edition; **dë dâktër noskha** prescription
not currency
nshëlawël to connect
nufus population
nuk fingernail; toenail
nukâra bruise
nukay small
nulës nineteen
num name; navel; umbilical cord; **Num de tsë day?** What is your name?; **Zmâ num Fred day.** My name is Fred.
numra number; score; **numra gatël** to score
nurmâl normal
nurs *m* nurse

Nuwâmbar November
nyâ grandmother
nzhor daughter-in-law

O

obdël to knit; to weave
obë water; **dë obo botal** bottle of water
odë kedël to go to sleep
om raw; uncooked
omedwâra pregnant; **Omed-wâra yam.** I'm pregnant.
omër age
omomi tilifun public phone
onëy week; **dë onëy pây** weekend
oniz weekly
ons ounce
oqâb eagle
or lagawël to light a fire
or fire
oray summer
orband ceasefire; truce
orë flour
orgâday train; **dë orgâdi mâshin** locomotive
orlagit matches *for fire*
ornay diaper; nappy
orsëy window
os now; **os-os** just now; **os wakht** the present *time*
osanay modern; present; **osanëy zamâna** the present *time*
osedël to live; to dwell
oshka tear *noun*
oske raisins
ostâz teacher
otu iron *for clothes*
owë seven
owëlas seventeen
ozgâr unemployed
ozha shoulder
ozhd long
ozhdawël to lengthen
ozhdwâlay length

P

pâchâ monarch; king
pagrëy turban
pâk clean; **pâk ruykashuna** clean sheets
pâkat envelope; package; packet
pâkawël to clean
pâkawunki mawâd detergent
pakay fan
pakha *f* ripe; cooked
pakhawël to cook
pakhawonkay cook
pakhlandzay kitchen
pakhta cotton wool
pâki razor; razor blade
Pâkistân Pakistan
Pâkistânay *m* Pakistani *person*
Pâkistânëy *f* Pakistani *person*
Pâkistâni Pakistani *thing*
pakol *Nuristani* hat
pal millstone
palak plug *electric*
palastar plaster *medical*
palâstik plastic
palatana enquiry
palatël to search (for)
palaw rice *cooked*
pâlawâni wrestling
pâlëk spinach
pâlël to raise; to foster; to care for
palet *(Pakistan)* plate
palëtana investigation
pâlez melon field
pâm care; **pâm kawël** to consider
pamp pump *noun*
pampawël to pump
pâna leaf; sheet *of paper*
panâ akhistël to take shelter
panâ dzây shelter
panchar puncture; flat tire
pand thick; **pand tukër** thick cloth
pandëy leg; tibia
pandzos fifty

pane shoes
paner cheese
panj shamba Thursday
panja fork
panjbolt fan belt
pâo quarter
parangay foreigner; English-man
parâshut parachute
paray rope; string
parda curtain
parhez diet
pârk park *noun*
parkatay son *of wife's first husband*
parkatëy daughter *of wife's first husband*
pârking car park
pârlimân parliament
parosazh kâl last year
parpus *(Pakistan)* lung
pârsal parcel
parsedël to swell
Pârsi Persian *language*
parsunal staff; personnel; **parsunal zid mâyn** anti-personnel mine
partala kawël to compare
pârtëy party *celebration*
partug trousers
partughâsh belt
parun yesterday
parunay yesterday's
parunay headscarf *woman's*
parwâ: Parwâ na lari! It doesn't matter!; No problem!
parwâz flight; **parwaz badlawël** to transfer flights; **Parwâz kinsil day.** The flight is canceled.
pâs top; up
pas lë gharme afternoon
pase after
Pashtana *f* Pashtoon
pâsport passport; **dë pâsport numra** passport number
pasta *f* soft; **pasta pandëy** calf *of leg*

patakay flask
patang butterfly
patâte potato(es)
patay field
pâte rest; remaining; **pâte kedël** to remain
patëy bandaid; plaster; bandage; dressing
patkay turban
patlëy railway
patlun trousers
patnus tray
patsedël to get up
patu headscarf *man's*
patun thigh
pawdz army
pawdzi military *adjective*; **pawdzi ada** military base
pawnd pound *weight/sterling*
pây end *noun*
payghâm message
payghambar prophet
payl beginning
paylawël to begin
pâyp pipe
payra patrol
paysa; payse money; currency; finance; **Payse badlawe?** Do you exchange money?; **Payse ye tsumra kezhi?** What is the charge?
pâytakht capital *city*; seat *political*
pë at; on; **pë (... ke)** in; **pë (zariya)** by; **pë ... bânde** onto; **pë mandz ke** among; **pë trëts ke** during; **pë mëkh ke** in front of; **pë bada** badly; **pë dzây** instead; **Pë bânk ke kâr kawëm.** I work in a bank.; **pë chatakëy** quickly; **pë dâd** sure *adverb*; **Pë Dari pohezhe?** Do you know Dari?; **pë har hâl** however; **pë karâra** quietly; **pë pâm** carefully; **pë këli ke** in the country; **pë psho** on foot; **pë tik wakht** on time
pech screw; dysentery

pechël to wind
pechkâri syringe; injection
pechkash; pechtâw screwdriver
peghla young girl
Peghla Miss; Ms.
pëke into
pëkhlâ reconciled
pëkhlâyana reconciliation
pëkhpëla self; **pëkhpëla zmunzh** ourselves
pëkhwâ ago; already; past
pëlaṭël to look for; to investigate
pëlay pedestrian
pensëlpâk eraser
për above; up; over
për beaten; defeated
perana buying
perël to weave
perëy century
përkha frost
përmëkhtag progress
perodël to sell; to buy
përsob edema
pësh blacksmith
Peshawër Peshawar
peshedël to happen
peshqâb plate
peshqawza bayonet
pështawërgay kidney
Pështo Pashto
Pështun *m* Pashtoon
Pështunistân Pashtunistan
pët secret; hidden
pëṭawël to hide; to camouflage; to rob
petay backpack
pëy *human* milk
pezhand kârt/pâna I.D.; pass
pezhandël to know; to recognise; **Pezhanam.** I know.
pezhandël shaway known
pezhandgalwi identification
pëzṛëpori interesting
pezwân fastener *for clothes*
pichkâri *see* pechkâri
piloṭ pilot

pindzë five
pindzëlas daqiqe quarter of an hour
pindzë-lës fifteen
ping safety pin
pinsël pencil
pinsëlpâk rubber *eraser*
pinsilin penicillin
pisho cat
pishqâb *see* peshqâb
piṭrol petrol; gas; **Piṭrol me khlâs shawi di.** I have run out of petrol.
piyâda waiter; waitress
piyâdaraw footpath
piyâno piano
piyâwaray strong
plâr father
plaruna fathers
plâstiki moze rubber boots
plâzmena seat *political*
plëndër stepfather
plën wide
pleṭfârm *railway* platform; **dë pleṭfârm shmera** platform number
plorël to sell
podar powder
podëri shode powdered milk
poh intelligent; wise
poha intelligence; wisdom
pohana knowledge
pohând professor
pohandzây college; faculty *of university*
pohantun university
pohedël to understand; to realize; **Pohezhe?** Do you understand?; **Pohezham.** I understand.
pokh *m* ripe; cooked
pokh shaway cooked
polâd steel
polis police; policeman
polis wâlâ *(Pakistan)* policeman
polo loba polo
pomba cotton wool

por debt; **por akhistël** to borrow; **por warkawël** to lend
pore kawël to shut *a door*
pori until; up to; to; **tar pindzo bajo pori** till five o'clock; **pë tâ pori ara lari** it's up to you
porikhwâ beyond *preposition*
poriwahël to push
poriwatël to cross
poriwahël to push
porta kawël to lift; to take off
poshël to wrap
poshtana question
poshtawërge kidneys
poshtëy rib(s)
post *m* soft
posta; post mail; **dë post pë zariya** by post
postakhâna post office
post-baks mailbox
postëkay skin
posti daftar post office
posti tikit *postal* stamp
postin *sheepskin* coat
postkârt postcard
powanda nomad
powël to tend *cattle*
poza nose
praday stranger
prâjiktar projector
prâkhtiyâ development
prâng leopard
prânistay open
prânistël to open; to undo
pranjay sneeze
pranjedël to sneeze
prata *f* situated; lying down
prata lë... except (for)...
prekawël to cut; to amputate
prekra decision; **prekra kawël** to decide
prekralik resolution
premâni excess
premindzël to wash
preshâna worried; **preshâna kedël** to be worried
preshodël to allow; to leave; to evacuate

prewân placenta
prewëtël to lay (down)
prewlalay washed
printar printer *computer*
prora straw
prot *m* situated; lying down
psarlay spring *season*
psë sheep; **dë psë ghwasha** mutton
psha foot; leg
pshay; pshëy cat
pudina mint
pukanëy condom
pukhwâ previously
pul bridge
pula frontier
pulis *see* **polis**
punda heel
pur floor; story
puri closed *door*
pushâk clothes
pushtël to ask
pyâla cup
pyâz onion(s)

Q

qâ'ida regulation
qâb plate
qâbila midwife
qabz constipated
qabziyat constipation; **Qabziyat ye?** Are you constipated?
qâchâqwrunkay smuggler
qadam step; pace
qadarman respected; esteemed
qadifa sanitary towel
qalam pen
qalami bam booby trap
qâlina carpet *knotted*
qâmus dictionary
qand diabetes
qandânëy sugar bowl
qandi diabetic
qâne' satisfied

qânun law; rule; regulation
qânuni legal
qaraquli Astrakhan fur hat
qarn century
qasâb butcher
qasam oath
qata kawël to cut
qatal killing; murder; assassination
qatâr queue; line; row
qatârawël to range
qâtil killer; murderer; assassin
qaychi scissors
qâz goose
qâzi judge *noun*
qir sarëk tarmac road
qirtâsiya stationery; **dë qirtâsiye dukân** stationer's shop
qishla barracks
qolba plow; **qolba kawël** to plow
qondâgh butt
Qorân Koran
qotbnomâ compass
qowat power
qudrat power
qulf lock; padlock
qulfawël to lock
qumanda command; **dë qumande markaz** headquarters
qomandân commander
qomandâni police headquarters
qawmi tribal
qunsilgari consulate
Qur'ân Quran
qurbâni victim
qurbâniyân victims
qurma gravy

R

Rab God
râdâr radar
râdiyâtor radiator

râdiyo radio; **râdiyo steshan** radio station
râdiyoyi: râdiyoyi khparawana radio broadcast; **râdiyoyi khparawëna** radio program; **râdiyoyi progrâm** radio program
rafiq friend
rag vein; artery
râgardzedël to return
raghawël to heal
râghë hillside
rahim uterus
rakbi rugby
râket rocket; **râket lënchar** rocket launcher
rama flock; **dë rame spay** sheepdog
ranâ light; bright
randawël to blind
rândë blind people
randzurpâla nurse
rang color; ink; paint
ranga qalam crayon
rangawël to paint
rangmâl painter
râniwël to buy
râniwunkey buyer
rânjë mascara
râpor report; **râpor warkawël** to report
râportar reporter
râportâzh story *news*
raqs dance; dancing
rasâma marmëy tracer bullet
rasanduye media
rasedël to arrive (at)
râshay avalanche
rasid receipt
rasmi official *adjective*
rasturân restaurant
râtlël to come
râtlunkay next; future; **râtlunke hafta** next week
raw path
rawâ permitted *religiously*
rawâj custom; tradition
rawânedâ departures

rawâq drawer
rawdël to suck
râwṟël to bring
râya vote; **râya achawël** to cast a vote; **râya warkawël** to vote
rayis head; boss; director; president
raywërkawunkay voter
râz secret; kind; sort
relkarsha railway
rel-steshan railway station
resâla brochure
rgharawël to roll up
rghaway palm *of hand*
rikârd record *noun*
rinch wrench *tool*
risâla pamphlet
risha root
rishtiyâ fact; true
rishtiyânay real
rishwatkhor corrupt
rishwatkhori corruption
risipshan reception *desk/area*
rizarf reservation; **rizarf kawël** to reserve
rizhim regime; diet
rob ketchup
rogh healthy
roghtiyâ health; **dë âme roghtiyâ wezârat** ministry of public health
roghtun hospital
rohâni priest
rojâyi sheet
rota bread *flat, barley*
rozha fast; fasting; **rozha niwël** to fast; **Rozha yam.** I am fasting.
Rozha Ramadan
ruh soul
rukh kawël to dial
rukhsatëy holidays
rukhsati holiday
rumbay first
rumi bânjân tomato
rumi tomato
run clear; bright; light
runawël to clear
Rus; Rusiya Russia
Rusay *m* Russian
Rusëy *f* Russian
Rusi Russian *language*
ryâzi mathematics; maths

S/SH/SH

sâ'at hour; watch; *school* period; **sâ'at teri** recreation; **sâ'ati bam** booby trap
sabâ tomorrow
sabab cause; reason; **sabab kedël** to cause
sâbandi asthma
sabar kawël to wait
sabâwon dawn *noun*
sabër kawël to wait for
sâbir patient *adjective*; **Sâbir osa!** Be patient!
sâbit constant
sâbitawël to prove
sabnâray breakfast
sabtawël to record
sâbun soap
sabzi *fresh* vegetables; **sabzi khartsawonkay** greengrocer; **dë sabzo dukân** vegetable shop
sabzi-khor(a) vegetarian; **Sabzi-khora yam.** I am a vegetarian.
sâda simple
sâdirât exports
sâdirawël to export
sadrëy waistcoat *jacket*
safar travel; **dë safar dalil** reason for travel; **safar kawël** to travel; **dë safar mahâlwesh** travel timetable
safârat embassy
safari chikuna traveler's checks
safir ambassador
sâg spinach
sâh soul; breath; **sâh istël** to breathe; **Sâh ye tarbatezhi!** He/She is choking!
sâha area

sahâr morning; **dë sahâr chây** breakfast

sahâranëy breakfast

sâhib gentleman

sahih right; correct

sâhil shore; coast

sahna stage *theater*

sakht difficult; **sakhta garmi** severe heat

salâkâr consultant

salâkot arsenal; magazine *of gun*

salâm! hello!

sâlandi asthma

salânsar silencer/muffler *of car*

salâta salad

salmân barber; hairdresser

saltanati royal; monarchy

sam true; right; correct;exact; straight; **Sam wâye.** You are right.

sâmân baggage

samandër; samandargay sea; ocean

samâwâr tea house

samawël to correct; to fix

sambol symbol

san'at industry

san'atkâr; san'atgër craftsman

sanad document; **sanad muhra-wël** to stamp a document

sandëra song; **sandëra wayal** to sing

sândiwich sandwich

sandoq box; chest

sandu brother-in-law *wife's sister's husband*

sânya second *noun*

sar head; **sar khlâsawonay** bottle-opener

sara fertilizer; together; with

sarak *see* **sarëk**

sara-sam according to

saratân cancer

saray man

sarbadâli concussion *medical*

sarbera besides; **sarbera për** in addition to

sarchina source

sardardi headache

sârë cold; **sare obë** cold water; **Sârë me kizhi.** I am cold.

sarëk road; street; **dë sarëk naqsha** road map; **dë sarëk nasha** road sign; **sarëk band** roadblock; **Sarëk khlâs day?** Is the road passable?

sarhad border; frontier

sarhadi askar border guard

sari men

sâri nârughi epidemic

sarkâtib head clerk

sarkhlâsawonay can opener; corkscrew

sarmâlim principal *school*

sarposh plug *bath*

sarshuwënkay principal *school*

sarwanza waistband

sarwe survey; **sarwe kawunkay** surveyor; **sarwe kawël** to survey

sarwes bus

sâs sauce

sâsij sausage

satal basket; bucket

sâtalay safe

sâtana protection

sâtël to keep; to guard; to protect

satilayt satellite; **satilayt tilifun** satellite phone

satranj chess

sâtunkay guard *noun*

sawdâ shopping

sawdâgari itihâdiya trade union

sawdâgari nandârtun trade show

sawdâgër businessman; trader

sawdâgëra businesswoman; trader

sawghât gift

sawka slow

sayl sightseeing; trip

sâyns science

sâynspoh scientist

sâz music; **dë sâz mela** music festival

sazh; sazhkâl this year
sâzusâmân supplies
sehat health
sek(a) strength
sël hundred
sel flood
sëra manure
serlay goat *kid*
Seshamba Tuesday
sëta trunk *of tree*
sëzhay lung
shâ back *noun*
shabnam dew
shâdo monkey
shaftâlu peach(es)
Shâghalay Mr.
shâgird *school* pupil
shâhen sparrowhawk
shâhi royal; monarchy
shahid martyr
shâhid witness
shâhidi warkawël to testify
shâ'ir poet
sha'iri poetry
shak doubt; suspicion
shakal shape
shâkh branch
shakhawël to bury
shakhs person
shakman doubtful; suspicious
shal paralyzed
shâl shawl
shama candle
shamadân candlestick
shamâl north
shamâli north(ern)
Shamâli Âyrland Northern Ireland
Shamba Saturday
shame candles
shâmpu shampoo
shân way *manner*
shâperak bat
shâqul level *noun*
shâr town; city; dë **shâr** chawk town square; dë **shâr** lëman suburb; dë **shâr** markaz city center; dë **shâr** nandâre city

hall; dë **shâr** naqsha city map; **shâr** ta nazhde about town
sha'r poem
sharâb alcohol; wine
sharâbkhâna bar
sharam shame *noun*
sharbat syrup
sharël to throw out; to expel
sharëy headscarf *woman's/man's*
shâri urban; civic
sharmawël to shame
sharmedalay ashamed
sharq east *noun*
sharsham rape seed
shart condition *term*
shârwâl mayor
shârwâli municipality
shât honey
shâta behind; **shâta** tlël to go backwards
shâtag kawël to retreat
shâwar shower *bath*
shawtal clover
shay right; **shay** lâs right hand; **shay** arkh right-wing
shay thing; item
shâyad; shâyi perhaps
shâysta pretty
shaytân devil
shâzâda prince
shë good; well; nice; **shë** aw bad good and evil; **shë** kawël to improve
sheba moment; storm
shëdza woman; wife; female; **shëdze** women; dë **shëdzo** huquq/haquna women's rights
shëdzina female *adjective*
shëga sand
shël twenty
sherkat business; company; firm
shëy edge; bank
shide milk
shikanja torture; **shikanja**

kawël to torture

shikâyat complaint; **shikâyat kawël** to complain

shin blue; green; **shin chây** green tea; **shin kadël** to grow crops

shina sister-in-law *wife's sister*

shindël to scatter

shirini candy; sweet(s)

shiryakh ice cream

shisha glass; window pane

shishapâk windshield; windscreen

shkâr hunting; **shkâr kawël** to hunt

shkâra evident; **shkâra kedël** to appear

shkâredël to seem

shkata below

shkëlay pretty

shkër horn

shkhëra fight; argument

shkhwand wahël chew

shkulâ beauty

shkun porcupine

shkwalay beautiful

shlumbi buttermilk

shmera number

shmerël to count

shna-zarghuna rainbow

shode milk

shodël to place; to show

shole rice *raw*

shor noise

shorawël to move; to shake; to stir

shornakhod chickpeas

shorwâ soup

showundzay school

showunkay school teacher

shpa night; evening; **shpa (mu) pë khayr!** good night!

shpana *f* shepherdess; shepherd's wife

shpârës sixteen

shpazh six

shpazham sixth

shpelkay whistle

shpetë sixty

shpun *m* shepherd

... shta there is/are ...

shtaman rich

shtapni spare; **shtapni tâyr** spare tire

shtring steering wheel

shudë milk

shudo chây tea with milk

shuk shock *medical*

shunda lip

shuro beginning

Shuro Wednesday

shwaya smooth; slippery

shwayedël to slip

sifar zero

sifat adjective

sigret cigarette(s); **sigret mamno** no smoking

sigret-letar lighter; **Sigret-letar lare?** Do you have a light?

sihat health; **dë sihat bema** medical insurance

sika coin; **sike** coins

sil tuberculosis

silëy gale; gust(s)

siltirâj underwear

sim wire

sima area; district; region

sin river; **dë sin ghâra** river bank

sina chest *of body*

sinaband bra; brassiere

sind river

sinëmâ movie theater

sinimâ; sinamâ cinema

sink sink *noun*

sipëy shell *snail/sea*

Siptambar September

sirf only

sirka vinegar

siryâl TV series

sistëm system

sit seat *in vehicle*

siw *(Pakistan)* apple

siyâli competition

siyuray shade *noun*

skârë

skârë coal; charcoal(s)

Skâtland Scotland

Skâtlanday *m* Scot

Skâtlandëy *f* Scot

Skâtlandi Scottish

skhër father-in-law

skhondar calf

ski kawël to ski

skolël to shear

slet slate

smëtsa cave

soba victory; *(Pakistan)* province

sokrëk bread *flat, maize*

sola peace; **dë sole khabëre atëre** peace talks; **sola sâtay dzwâk** peace-keeping troops; **sola kawël** to make peace; **sola râwëstël** to bring peace

somi'a monastery

sond ginger

soparmârket supermarket

sor *m* cold; cool; fresh

sorp lead *noun: metal*

sorsak maize bread

sotak hammer *noun*

sotri stars

soy *m*; **soya** *f* rabbit; hare

spanj sponge

sparedël to get in *to a vehicle*; to board *a plane*; to mount *a horse*; to ride *a horse*

spârël to hand over; to extradite

spay dog

speda châwd dawn *noun*

spëk light *not heavy*; **spëk khwârë** snack

spetsalay holy; **spetsalay saray** saint; holy man

spëzha louse; lice

spin white; **spin zar** silver; **spina mulëy** radish

spinchak whitish

spinsare old woman

spinzhiray village elder; old man

spoghz bladder

sport sports

spozhmëy moon

spring *metal* spring

sra *f* red

Sra Miyâsht Red Crescent

sra mulëy radish

srë zar gold

srish glue

srishawël to stick

stâ your; yours *singular*

starling pawnd sterling

stâso; stâsi your; yours *plural*

stâyël to praise

stëdyum stadium

stej stage *theater*

stën needle; pin; **Stën aw târ lare?** Do you have needle and thread?

stëra mahkama supreme court

stëray tired; **stëray kedël** to get tired

stërga eye; **stërge** eyes

steshan station

stitiskop stethoscope

stomân tired

stomâni exhaustion

storay star

stunay throat; trachea; **dë stuni khwëzh** sore throat

stunza problem

subut proof

sud interest *financial*

suk fist; **suk loba** boxing

sultân sultan

suluk behavior

sur *m* red

Sur Salib Red Cross

sur'at speed

surang *(Pakistan)* tunnel

suray hole

surlanday jackal

swadzedël to burn

swadzedunkay inflammable

swâlgër beggar

swan burn *medical*

swarlëy riding

swëdzedël to run out (of)

swën fuel

swëy *m* hare; rabbit

swich switch *electric*
syâsat politics
syâsatwâl politician
syâsi political

T/T̲/TS

ta; tâ at
tâ you *singular*
t̲ab tub
tab'a citizen
taba fever; Taba lar̲am. I have a temperature.
tabar ax
tabâshir chalk
tabdil change
t̲abër clan
tabiyat nature
tâbiyat nationality; citizenship
tabiyi natural; tabiyi nâwrin natural disaster; tabiyi sarchine natural resources
tabsira commentary
tadâwi cure; medication; tadâwi kawël to cure
tâdi: tâdi kawa! hurry up!; Tâdi me da. I'm in a hurry.
tâdiya pay; payment
tafri(h) recreation; recess
taftish inquiry
tag departure
t̲ag treacherous
tahsil kawël to study
tâjër trader
tak vine
t̲akar accident
t̲akawël to knock
t̲akey point
takhalus nickname; penname
takhnik technique
takhniki technical
takht throne
takhta plank
taklif trouble *inconvenience*
takra skilled
takrârawël to repeat
t̲aksi taxi

tâktik tactic
tâktikuna tactics
tal base; bottom
talafuz pronunciation
talafuzawël to pronounce
tâlânawël to loot
tâlanda thunder
talâq divorce *noun*
talâshi check-in; dë talâshëy dzây check-in counter
talay sole
tâlay bowl
tâ'le destiny
tâlëy bowl
ta'lim; tâlim education; instruction
tamâțër *(Pakistan)* tomato
tamba door
tambâku tobacco
tâmbu tent
tamdzay bus stop
tamrin exercise; dë tamrin ketâbcha exercise book
tamsil performance; play
tan body
t̲an ton; tonne
tâṇa *(Pakistan)* police station
tanâsuli: tanâsuli sistëm genitals; tanâsuli nârughëy venereal disease
tanday forehead
tandër lightning
tanëy button
tang narrow
tanhâ alone
tânk armored car
t̲ânk tank; armored car; dë t̲ânk zandzir caterpillar track; t̲ânk zid mâyn anti-tank mine
t̲ânkar tanker
tankay tender
tanur oven
t̲ap sore; ulcer; injury
t̲api injured
t̲api kawël to injure
t̲apus vulture
tâq single
tâqat power

taqâtu

taqâtu crossing
taqdir destiny
taqibawël to follow; to chase
taqriban approximately
taqsim division
taqsimawqât timetable
tar than; **tar dë ziyât** more than that; **tar osa** yet
târ thread; wire; **târ pechël** to wind thread
tarâfik traffic; traffic police
tarâfiki ishâra traffic lights
taraktur tractor
tarâs balcony
tarbatedël to choke
tarël to tie; to fasten
târikh history; dsate; **târikh likunkay** historian
tarkâri vegetables *ready to eat*
tarmâmetar thermometer
tarmandz between
tarmim repair *noun*
tarmimawël to repair
tarsara kawël perform
tartib order; arrangement
tartibât arrangements; preparations
tarun agreement; contract; treaty
taryâk opium
tasbe rosary
tashadud violence
tashawël to empty
tashkhis diagnosis *medical*
tashnâb bathroom; toilet(s); **dë tashnâb kâghaz** toilet paper
tashreh; tashri(h) explanation; **tashrih kawël** to describe
tashriyât; tashrihât explanations
tasht basin
tashtedël to run; to escape
tâsi you *plural*
taslimawël to surrender
tâso you *plural*; **tâso pakhpëla** yourselves
taswir image; picture
tatar chest; thorax

tato pony
tâtubay territory
tâ'us peacock
tâw trikhwâlay violence
tâwân compensation
tâwawël to bend
tawda warm
tawdawël to heat
tawde obë hot water
tawpir difference
tay breast
tayâr ready
tayâra airplane
tayârawël to prepare
tayâri preparation
tâyp typewriter
tâypawël to type
tâyprâytar typewriter
tayr tire; **Tâyr me panchar day.** I have a flat tire.
tâza fresh *food*
tâzi hound; Agfhan hound
tazkira stretcher *hospital*; I.D.
të to
të you *singular*; to; **të pakhpëla** yourself
tëba fever; **Tëba laram.** I have a temperature.
tël always; eternal
tel oil; petrol; **dë telo dabay** oilcan; **dë telo maydân** oilfield; **dë telo pamp/tânk** fuel dump; **dë telo pâyplin** oil pipeline; **dë telo tsâh** oil well; **Tel wogora.** Check the oil.
teliwizun television
tëmâncha pistol
tënda thirst
tënda forehead
tendâr aunt *father's brother's wife*
tep tape
tepër turnip
teprikârdër tape recorder
tër to; until; **tër ... lânde** under; **tër mez lânde** under the table; **tër de che** until;
ter past; **tera shpa** last night; **tera hafta** last week; **ter kâl**

last year; **tera per<u>ë</u>y** the past century

terawël to swallow

teray invasion; **teray kawël** to invade

terbâsöl to mislead

tërbur cousin *distant*

tërbur cousin *father's brother's son*

terë sharp; **terë kawël** to sharpen

teredël to pass; to cross

tërla *f* cousin

tësh empty

tëshawël to evacuate

tështedël to flee

tët pale; dark

tez quick

tëzhay thirsty; **Tëzhay yam.** I'm thirsty.

tibi medical *adjective*

tijârati sherkat enterprise

tijâri itihâdiya trade union

tikâla bread

tike *(Pakistan)* kebab

tikhor child

tiki<u>t</u> ticket; **tiki<u>t</u> plorandzây** travel agency; **dë tikit khartsawëlo daftar** ticket office

tikitpull; tiki<u>t</u>âna interest *financial*

tikray headscarf *woman's*

til gasoline

tilifun telephone; **dë tilifun ghurfa** pay-phone; **dë tilifun narëywâl kod** international dialing code; **tilifun kawël** to telephone; **Tilifun kâr në kawi.** The phone doesn't work.; **Tilifun me qata shu.** I've been cut off.

tilifunchi telephone operator

tiligrâm telegram

tiliks telex

tiliskop telescope

tim team

tinga shorwâ thick soup

tingawël to press

tinis tennis

tis<u>t</u>awël to test

ti<u>t</u> short

tit-parakwâlay diaspora

tiwâl mammal

tiyâra dark; darkness *noun*

tiyâtër theater

tiyori theory

tiyub inner-tube

tizha stone

tlël to go

tod hot; warm

toka humor

toka joke

tol all

tolana; tolëna society; community; institute; academy

tolaniz social

tolawël to collect

tolbaks boot; trunk *of car*

tolëna *see* tolana

tolgay class

tolya towel

top ball; cannon

topak gun; rifle

topchi gunman

topëy *(Pakistan)* hat

topkhâna artillery

topwahël to leap

tor black; **tor bânjân** aubergine; **tor bâzâr** black market; **tor chây** black tea; **tor lagawal** to accuse; **tora khëra** dawn; **tora takhta** blackboard

toray pancreas

torbakhun blackish

toray letter *of alphabet*

torist tourist; **toristân** tourists

torizëm tourism

tormrëch pepper *black*

toshak mattress

tos<u>t</u> shawe do<u>d</u>ëy toast *bread*

to<u>t</u>a piece; loaf

totakëy swallow *bird*

toyedël to spill

transfârmar transformer

trânsme<u>t</u>ar transmitter

trânsport transport *noun*
trë uncle *father's brother*
trewal travel; **trewal chikuna** traveler's checks; **trewal ijinsëy** travel agency
trikh bitter
trikhay gall bladder
triw sour
tror aunt
tsâ(h) well *of water*; **tsâ barma kawël** to drill a well
tsâdër cloak *woman's/man's*
tsakël to taste
tsalor four
tsaloram fourth
tsalorama barkha quarter *area*
tsalorlâre; tsalorlâri crossroads; intersection
tsalwesht forty
tsamtsëy ladle
tsanda suburb
tsang side; **tsang ta** to the side
tsanga *see* **tsënga**
tsânga section; branch; department
tsangël elbow
tsaplëy sandals
tsaponay scarf
tsaranga? what kind?
tsârël to watch
tsarkh chawkëy wheelchair
tsârunkay observer
tsârway animal
tsâsht noon
tsatël to lick
tsë (shay)? what?; **tsë ranga** how?; **tsë wakht** when; **Tsë ghwâre?** What do you want?; **Dë tsë mânâ lari?** What does this mean?
tsëkawël to drag
tsëmlastël to go to bed; to lie down
tsënga how?
tsera portrait
tserana research; **tserana kawël** to research

tsërmën leather
tsëshâk drink; **dë tsëshâk obë** drinking water
tsëshël to drink
Tsështën God
tseshtën owner; husband
tsët nape *of neck*
tsëtsedël to leak
tsikawël to smoke
tsikawunkay smoker
tsirâgh lamp
tsirël to tear
tsok (che) who
tsparkay chapter
tsrak track
tsu how many; how much; several
tsuk pase ghushtël to search a person
tsuka peak; summit
tsumra? how much/many?; **tsumra leri?** how far?
tsuwârlasama spozhmëy full moon
tswâr-lës fourteen
tswërb fat *adjective*
tufân storm
tufâni windy
tughanday missile
tuhfa present *gift*
tuk volume; book
tukar cloth
tukay material; cloth
tukël to spit
tukër fabric
tukhay cough
tukhël to cough
tukhum seeds
tunal tunnel
Turk Turk
turshi pickles
turyâlay brave
tush felt-tip pen
tut mulberry
tutëy strawberry
tuti parrot
twânedël to be able
tyup tube

U

ufunat infection
umayd hope
umuman generally
umumi general *adjective*
urdu army
Urdu Urdu
u<u>r</u>ë kawël to grind
Urupâ Europe
Urupâyi European
Urupâyi Itihâdiya European Union
ush *m*; **u<u>sh</u>a** *f* camel
u<u>sh</u>ba camel driver
uzhd big; long

V

V.C.R. *(Pakistan)* video player

W

wada kawël to grow
wadânëy building
wâdë marriage; wedding
wahël to hit
wâhid unit *military*
wahshi wild
waja cause
wakht time; **dë wakhta day** He is early.; **wakht terawël** to spend time; **Wakht në larëm.** I don't have time.
wakhti early
wakhtnâwakht occasionally
wakil lawyer
wâkman ruler *person*
wâksin kawël to vaccinate; **Wâksin shaway yam.** I have been vaccinated.
wâksinâsun vaccination
wâlëy earrings
walwër dowry
wâlyum volume *size*
waqfa interval
wâqi'an indeed

war door
wâr turn; time
wâ<u>r</u> able; suitable
wa<u>r</u>akây *m*; **wa<u>r</u>a** *f* little; child; **wa<u>r</u>a gwëta** little finger; **wa<u>r</u>a njëlëy** girl
wa<u>r</u>ëy wool
wâ<u>r</u>idawël to import
wa<u>r</u>in woolen
warkawël give
warsho meadow
warta same; similar
wartlël to go *over there*
warukay boy
wa<u>r</u>yâ free of charge
warzish sports
warzishkâr sportsman
wasâyl tools
wa<u>sh</u>ay bracelet
wâ<u>sh</u>ë grass
wâs<u>k</u>at waistcoat; vest
wasla arms; weapon
watan country
watël to go out; to exit
wâwra snow; **dë wâwre potsënay** snow flakes; **Wâwrâ ori.** It is snowing.
wayând speaker *radio, etc.*
wayël to say; to tell
wazën weight
wâzga fat *animal*
wazhana murder *noun*
wazhay hungry; **Wazhay yam.** I'm hungry.
wazhël to execute
wazhël to kill
wazhla killing
wazhunkay killer
wazir minister
wëbakh<u>sh</u>a! excuse me!
wëch dry; arid; **wëche shode** powdered milk
wëchwâlay dryness
wedyu video player; **wedyu kasit** video cassette
wëhël to hit
wëlay shoulder blade
welënay mint

wëlësmëshër president; **dë wëlësmëshër gârd** presidential guard
wëli why
wëna tree; **wëne** trees
wena termite
wërbëshe barley
wërghumay kid *goat*
wërma wradz the day before yesterday
wërmezh neck
wesh frontier; division
weshël to divide
weshtë hair *singular/collective*; **dë weshto bors** hairbrush
weto veto; **weto kawël** to veto
wëy egg
wëza goat
wëzhay hungry
wëzhunkay killer
widë asleep; **widë kedël** to fall asleep
widedël to sleep; to go to bed
wijarawël to demolish
wikâlat legal profession
wil wheel
wilâyat province
wina blood; **wine kedël** to bleed; **dë wine badlun** blood transfusion; **dë wine fishâr** blood pressure; **dë winë ghuta kedâ** thrombosis; **dë wine grup** blood group; **dë wine luwër fishâr** high blood pressure; **dë wine tit fishâr** low blood pressure; **dë wine tist** blood test
wirus virus
wish awake
wishawël to be awake; to wake up
wishtël to shoot
witâmin vitamins
wiyâla stream
wiyâr pride; honor
wiyâralay proud; honorable
wiza visa
wizârat ministry
wobâ *(Pakistan)* cholera

wojud body
wolisi jirga assembly *government*
wradz day
wradzanay daily
wradzpâna *daily* newspaper; **dë wradzpâno ghurfa** newsstand
wrânawël to destroy
wrândi front; **wrândi kawël** to submit; **wrândi kedël** to overtake *by car*
wrândiz proposal
wrârë nephew *brother's son*
wrasta *f* rotten
wray lamb
wredz cloud
wrëkawël to lose *mislay*
wrël to carry; to take away; to transport
wrëlkedunkay tiliwizun portable T.V.
wrendâr sister-in-law *brother's wife*
wrera niece *brother's daughter*
wreshëm silk
wreshmin silken
wretawël to roast
wrëy gum
wrëzh flea
wridza eyebrow
wriji rice *hulled*
wro slow; **wro wro!** slowly!; carefully!
wror brother
wrost *m* rotten
wrudze eyebrows
wrumbanay; wrumbay first
wrun thigh
wruna brothers
wrusta lë since
wrusta after(wards); behind; then
wrustanay; wrustay last; recent
wulës nation; people
wulësi atan folk dancing
wulësi jirga; wulisi jirga Afghani parliament *lower house*; **dë wulisi jirge rayis** speaker *of parliament*
wulëswâl governor *of district*
wut *(Pakistan)* vote *noun*

Y

ya no
yâ or; yâ ... yâ either ... or
yabli pshe barefoot
yâbu mule; packhorse
yâd memory
yâdgâr monument
yâghi rebel *noun*
Yahud *m* Jew
Yahud(a) Jewish
Yahuda *f* Jew
Yahuday *m* Jew
Yahudëy *f* Jew
Yahudiyat Judaism
yakh cold; icy; yakh wahalay frostbite; Yakh day. It is cold.
yakhchâl refrigerator
yakhni cold *noun*
yakh-zid anti-freeze
Yakshamba Sunday
yana liver
yaqinan certainly
yaqini certain
yarghal invasion; yarghal kawël to invade
yatim orphan
yaw; yawa one; yaw dzal once; yaw dzây together; yaw kasiza koṭa single room; yaw ḏawl somehow; yaw shay something; yaw shân same; yaw tarafa kutsa one-way: one-way street; dë yawe khwâ ṭikiṭ one-way ticket
yawâzi only *alone*
yawdzây all together
yawtsok somebody
yazh bear
yëshawël to boil
yëshedële hagëy boiled egg
yëw; yëwa *see* yaw
yëwâzi alone
yiwe plow
yiwo-lës eleven
yor sister-in-law *husband's brother's wife*
yum spade

Yunân Greece
Yunânay *m* Greek
Yunânëy *f* Greek
Yunâni Greek *language*
yunifârm uniform

Z/ZH/ZH

zad *see* zid
zafrân saffron
zahr poison
zakham sore; hurt; injury; wound
zakhira store *for storage*
zakhmi kawël to injure
zaki intelligent
zâlim cruel
zalmay teenager *boy*
zamâna time
zâmën sons
zâna wild goose
zandzir chain; zipper
zang rust; bell; zang wahël to ring
zangdâr sât alarm clock
zângo cradle
zangun knee
zara *f* old
zarb multiplication
zarbawël to multiply
zardâlu apricot
zargar jeweler
zargari jewelry
zariza millennium
zarukay headscarf *woman's*
zarurat larël to need
zaruri necessary; zaruri day it's necessary
zawab: Zawab ye këray. It is infected.
zâya kawël to spoil
zda kawël to learn
zdakawunkay school pupil
zdakra kawël to study : *academic*
zë I; me
zeb zipper

zëkha boil *noun*

zëlândz placenta

zëlzila earthquake

zem drain *noun*

zëna chin

zër thousand

zer yellow

zërâ'at agriculture

zere posh armored car

zërka partridge

zerkhâna cellar

zerma spare

zërurat necessity

zezhantun maternity hospital

zezhawël to give birth (to)

zezhedël to be born; **Të cheri zezhedalay ye?** Where were you born?; **Zë pë Niw Yârk ke zezhedalay yam.** I was born in New York.

zghargâday armored car

zhaba tongue

zhabpoh linguist

zhabpohana linguistics

zhagh voice; sound

zhâla ice cream

zhalëy hail *noun*

zhâma jaw

zhar early

zharël to cry; to weep

zhawartiya depth

zhawër deep

zhâwla chewing gum

zhbâra interpretation; translation

zhbârël to interpret; to translate

zhbârën interpreter; translator

zhbârunkay translator

zhdën millet

zhëba language

zhebawar eloquent

zhëmay winter

zhër soon; quick; **zhër kawa!** hurry up!

zher yellow

zhëwërtob depth

zhghorël to save *rescue*

zhira beard; **dë zhire krim** shaving cream

zhmundz comb

zhoban zoo

zhobël injured; wounded

zhobla injury; wound

zhoblawël; zhobledël to injure; to wound

zhornâlist journalist

zhowël to chew

zhranda mill; watermill

zhwand *see* **zhwënd**

zhrandagaray miller

zhwanday alive

zhwandun life

zhwënd life; **dë zhwand tariqa** way of life; **zhwënd kawël** to live

zhwenday alive

zilzila earthquake

zina ladder; stairs; **barqi zine** escalator

zira cumin

ziyârat pilgrimage; **ziyârat kawunkay** pilgrim; **ziyârat kawël** to go on pilgrimage

ziyât many; too; very

ziyâtawana addition

ziyâtawël to add

zizh coarse; rough

zmâ my

zmaray lion

zmëka land; ground; soil

zmunzh our

zokra birth; **dë zokre kâliza** birthday; **dë zokre tasdiq** birth certificate

zor *m* old; **zor shâr** old city

zoy son

zrë heart; **dë zrë hamla** heart attack

zrëwartiyâ courage

zrëwër brave

zukâm flu; cold; **Zukâm shaway yam.** I have a cold.

zum son-in-law; bridegroom

zyârat tomb *of saint*

ENGLISH—PASHTO
ANGREZI—PASHTO

A

ability liyâqat
able lâyiq; **to be able** twânedël
ablutions awdas; **to perform ablutions** awdas kawël
about nazhde; taqriban; **about 50 miles** nazhde pandzos mila; **about town** shâr ta nazhde
above up për; upon bândi
absence nështwâlay
academy tolëna; akâdimi
accident takar
accommodation dzây
according to sara-sam
accuse tor lagawal
acquaintance âshnâ
acre ikar
adapter electric idâptar
add ziyâtawël; maths jama' kawël
addition ziyâtawana; maths jama'
address âdras
adjective sifat
administration organisation idâra; hokumat
administrative idâri; hokumati
administrator mudir
advantage fâyda
advert i'lân
advertise i'lân kawël
Afghan Afghân
afghani currency afghânëy
Afghani Afghâni
Afghanistan Afghânistân
after wrusta; pase
afternoon mâspashin; pas lë gharme; **this afternoon** nën maspashin

afterwards wrusta
again byâ
age omër
ago pëkhwâ; **a week ago** yawa hafta pëkhwâ; **two days ago** dwa wradze pëkhwâ
agreement tarun
agriculture karana; zërâ'at
agronomist karwandgar
aid mrasta
AIDS Edz
aim nasha niwël
air hawâ
airbase hawâyi adâ
air conditioner; air conditioning iyarkandeshan
airdrop lë hawâ ghurdzawël
airfield hawâyi dagar
air force hawâyi dzwâk
airline hawâyi sherkat; hawâyi chaland
air mail hawâyi post
airplane alutaka; jâz (Pakistan)
airport hawâyi dagar
air-raid hawâ'i hamla
alarm clock zangdâr sât
alcohol sharâb; medical alkol
alight kuzedël
alive zhwanday
all tol; **all together** yawdzây
allergic hasâs; ilarzhik
allow preshodël
almond bâdâm
almost nazhde; taqriban
alone tanhâ; yëwâzi
already pëkhwâ
also ham
although ke tse ham
always tël; hamesha

ambassador

ambassador safir
ambulance ambolâns
ambush hamla
America Amrikâ
American *m* Amrikâyi
American *f* Amrikâyëy
ammunition marmëy
among së mandz ke
amount mablëgh
amputate prekawël
ancient larghunay
and aw
anemia kamkhuni
anesthetic *general* dë behushëy dawâ; *local* dë kërakhtawëlo pichkâri
angry ghusa
animal haywân; **animals** haywânât
aniseed khwâzhë welëni
ankle dë pshe tiqay; bârkay
anniversary kâliza
annual kalanay
another bël; **another bottle** bël botal
answer *noun* dzawâb; *verb* dzawâbawël
ant mezhay
anti-aircraft cannon dâfe hawâ top
antibiotic antibiyotik
anti-freeze yakh-zid
antiseptic afuni-zid
anyone har tsuk
anywhere har cheri
apart from be lë
apartment apârtmân; flet *(Pakistan)*
appear shkâra kedël
appetite eshtihâ
apple mana; siw *(Pakistan)*
appropriate munâsib
approximately taqriban
apricot zardâlu; khormânëy *(Pakistan)*
April April
Arab *m* Arab; *f* Araba
Arabic *language* Arabi

architect memâr
argument *row* jagra
area sima
arid wëch
arm mët
armored car tânk; zere posh
arms wasla
army pawdz
arrangement tartib; **arrangements** tartibât
arrest bandi kawël
arrive rasedël
arsenal salâkot
art hunar
artery rag
artificial masnoyi; **artificial limb** masnoyi gharay; **artificial leg** masnoyi psha; **artificial arm** masnoyi lâs; **artificial eye** masnoyi starga
artillery topkhâna
artist hunarman
ashamed sharmedalay
Asia Âsyâ
ask pushtël
asleep widë
aspirin aspirin
assassin qâtil
assassination qatal
assault hamla
assembly *government:* wolisi jirga *(Afghanistan)*; asâmblëy *(Pakistan)*
asthma sâbandi
astonished hayrân
at së; ke; ta
atheist kâfer
athletics âtletik
atomic âtomi
attack *noun* hamla; brid; *verb* hamla kawël
aubergine tor bânjyân
aunt *father's sister* ama; tror; *father's brother's wife* châchi *(Pakistan)*; *father's brother's wife* tendâr; *mother's sister* tror; *mother's brother's wife* dë mâmâ shëdza; mâmëy

Australia Âstrâliyâ
Australian *m* Âstrâliyâyay
Australian *f* Âstrâliyâyëy
author likwâl
autumn mënay
avalanche râshay; barf koch
average *adjective* âdi
aversion nafrat
aviation hawâ'i chalan
awake wish; **to be awake**
  wishawël
ax tabar

B

baby *boy* mâshum; *girl* mâshuma
back *noun* mlâ
backache dë mlâ dard
backpack petay
backwards: to go backwards
  shâta tlël
bacteria bâktaryâ
bad bad; kharâb
badly pë bada
bag bakës; baks
baggage baksuna
bakery nânwâyi
balcony tarâs
ball top; bâl *(Pakistan)*
ballpoint qalam
banana kela
bandage *medical* patëy
Band-Aid *plaster* patëy
bandit dâku
bank bânk
banker bânkdâr
bar bâr; sharâbkhâna
barbed wire azghën sim
barber nâyi; salmân
barefoot yabli pshe
bark ghapël
barley wërbëshe
barrel *of gun* mil; *storage* beral
base *bottom* tal; **military base**
  pawdzi ada
basin tasht
basis asâs

basket satal
basketball bâskitbâl
bat shâperak
bathe lambël
bathroom tashnâb
battery *electric* betrëy
battle jagra
bayonet barcha
be *see page 16.*
beam *girder* chârtarâsh
beans bagri; **green beans** lubyâ
bear yazh
beard zhira
beat wahël; *to overcome* niwël
beaten për
beautiful shkwalay
beauty shkulâ
because dzeka; **because of**
  dzaka che
become kedël
bed kat; **to go to bed** tsëmlastël
bedroom dë khob kuta
bee dë shato mëchëy
beef dë ghwayi ghwasha
beer bir
beetroot lablabu
before mëkh ke
beggar swâlgër
begin paylawël
beginning payl
behavior suluk
behind tar shâ; wrusta
belief imân
believe bâwar kawël
believer imândâr; mo'taqed
bell zang
below lândi
belt mlâwastënay; **cartridge**
  belt gërdanëy
bench chawkëy
bend *verb* tâwawël
berry âlobâlu
besides *adverb* sarbera;
  preposition be lë
best behturin
better behtar; **I feel**
  better. *health* Shëwâlay/ëy
  ihsâsawam.

between tarmandz

beyond *preposition* porikhwâ; **beyond the river** dë sin porikhwâ

biannual shpazh myâshtënay

Bible *Gospel* enjil

bicycle bâyskil

big *large* luy; *long* uzhd

bill *check* bil

binoculars durbin

bird mërghëy

biro khodkâr

birth zokra; **to give birth to** zezhawël; **birth certificate** dë zokre tasdiq; **birth control** dë hâmilatob mëkhniway

birthday dë zokre kâliza

bit tota

bite *verb* dârël

bitter trikh

black tor

blackboard tora takhta

blackish torbakhun

black market tor bâzâr

blacksmith pësh

bladder spoghz; masâna

blanket kampala

blasphemer moshrek

bleed wine kedël

bless do'â kawël

blind *adjective* rond; nâbinâ; **blind people** rândë; *verb* randawël

blizzard bâdurya

blocked band; **The toilet is blocked.** Tashnâb band day.

blood wina; **blood group** dë wine grup; **blood pressure** dë wine fishâr; **blood test** dë wine tist; **blood transfusion** dë wine badlun

blow *verb: wind* lagedël

blow up *to explode* chawdël

blue shin

boar khanzir

board *a plane* sparedël

boarding pass bording kârt

body dzân; tan; badan

boil *noun* zëkha; dâna; *verb* yëshawël

bomb bam; **bomb disposal** bam shandawël

bombardment bambâri

bone hadukay

bonnet *of car* bânat

booby trap qalami bam; sâ'ati bam

book ketâb

bookshop kitâb plorandzây

boot *of car* tolbaks

boots moze; **rubber boots** kalawshe

booth: cashier's booth ghurfa

border sarhad; **border crossing** lë sarhada teredâ; **border guard** sarhadi askar

born: to be born zezhedël; **Where were you born?** Të cheri zezhedalay ye?; **I was born in New York.** Zë pë Niw Yârk ke zezhedalay yam.

borrow por akhistël

boss mëshër

both dwâra

bottle botal; **bottle of water** dë obo botal

bottle-opener sar khlâsawonay

bottom *level* tal

bowl kâsa; tâlëy; **sugar bowl** qandânëy

box sandoq

boxing suk loba

boy halëk; warukay

boyfriend andiwâl

bra; brassiere sinaband

bracelet dësband; washay

braid chotëy kawël

brain mâghzë

brake *noun* brik; *verb* brik niwël

branch tsânga

brave turyâlay

bread dodëy; **to make bread** aghshël

break *for refreshments* dama; *verb* mâtawël

break down: Our car has broken down Moṭar mu kharâb shaway day.
breakfast sabnâray
breast tay
breathe sâh istël
brew damawël
brick khështa
bride nâwe
bridge pul
bridegroom zum
briefly pë land dawël
bright *light* run *m*; ranâ *f*; *intelligent* zaki
bring râwrël
Britain Bartâniyâ
British Bartâniyâyi
Briton *m* Angrez; *f* Angrcza
brochure resâla
brother wror; **brothers** wruna
brother-in-law *sister's husband* awshay
brother-in-law *husband's brother* lewar; **brother-in-law** *wife's brother* awshay; **brother-in-law** *wife's sister's husband* sându; bâja
brown naswâri
bruise *noun* nukâra
brush bors
bucket satal; balṭëy (*Pakistan*)
budget budija
bug *insect* khasak; kaṭmël
build jorawël
builder jorawunkay
building kor; wadânëy
bull ghwayay
bullet golëy
bumper *fender* bampar
bureaucracy birokrâsi
burn *medical* swan; *verb* swadzedël
burst chëwël
bury shakhawël
bus saïwes; bas
bus station dë basuno haḍa
bus stop tamdzay
business *enterprise* sherkat;

work kârubâr
businessman sawdâgër
businesswoman sawdâgëra
busy mashghul; *telephone call* masruf; bizi (*Pakistan*)
but lâkin; kho; balki
butcher qasâb
butt qondâgh
butter kwëch
butterfly patang
buttermilk shlumbay
button taṇëy
buttonhole kâj
buy râniwël
buyer râniwunkay
buying perana
by pë (zariya); **by bus** dë bas pë zariya; **by post** dë post pë zariya

C

cabbage karam
cabinet *cupboard* dë losho almârëy; *political* kâbina
cable kebal
cage: rib cage gowgal
cake kek
calculation hesâb
calculator dë hisâb mâshin
calendar jantari
calf skhondar; *leg* pasta paṇḍëy
call balël; **Call the police!** Pulis khabër kra!; **What are you called?** Të tsë balal kezhe?
camel ush *m*; usha *f*
camel driver ushba
camera kâmra
camouflage pëṭawël
camp kamp; kemp (*Pakistan*); **Can we camp here?** Dalta kamp darawalay shu?
campaign mubâriza; kampâyn
campus dë puhantun sâha
can *noun* ḍablay; **I can...** Zë ... sham.; **Can I eat?** Khwaralay sham?

can opener sarkhlâsawonay
Canada Kânâdâ
Canadian *m* Kânâdâyay
Canadian *f* Kânâdâyëy
canal kânâl
cancel kinsilawël
canceled: The flight is canceled. Parwâz kinsil day.
cancer saratân
candle shama; **candles** shame
candlestick shamadân
candy shirini; khwâzhë
canister dabay
cannon top
capital *city* pâytakht; *financial* payse
car motar; **car papers** dë motar asnâd; **car park** pârking; **car registration** dë motar râjistar
care pâm
careful mutawaje
carefully! wro wro!
cargo mâl
carpenter najâr; tarkân
carpet *felt* lemtsay; *knotted* ghâlëy; qâlina; *woven* gëlam
carriage gâdëy
carriage driver gâdëywân
carrier bag katsora
carrot gâzëra
carry wrël
cart bagëy
carton kârtan
cartridge belt gërdanëy
cartridge kârtus
cashier mahâsib
cassette kasit
cast: plaster cast *medical* gach
castle kalâ
cat pisho
catch niwël
caterpillar dë wënes chinjay; **caterpillar track** dë tank zandzir
catheter nal
cattle mâl
cauliflower gobay

cause *noun* sabab; *verb* sabab kedël
caution ihtiyât
cave smëtsa
C.D. C.D.
C.D. player C.D. tep
ceasefire orband
ceiling chat
celebrate jashën niwël; lmândzël
cell phone mobâyl
cellar zerkhâna
cemetery hadera
center markaz; mandz
century perëy
ceramics kulâli
certain yaqini
certainly yaqinan
chador *woman's* châdari; borqa
chain zandzir
chair chawkëy
chalk tabâshir
change *noun* tabdil; *money* mâte payse; *verb* badlawël; **I want to change some dollars.** Ghwâram yaw tsë dâlar badal kram.
channel: T.V. channel chaynal
chapter tsparkay; fasël
charcoal(s) skârë
charge: What is the charge? Payse ye tsumra kezhi?
charity *action* khayrât; *organization* khayriya mwasisa
chase *verb* tâqibawël
chauffeur motarwân
cheap ârzân
cheaper lâ ârzân
check *bank* chik; *verb* katël; **Check the oil.** Tel wogora.
check-in talâshi; **check-in counter** dë talâshëy dzây
cheek bârkho
cheese paner; **cottage cheese** chaka
chemical kimyâwi
chemistry kimyâ
cherry gilâs

chess satranj

chest *box* sandoq; **chest** *of body* sina

chew shkhwand wahël

chewing gum zhâwla

chicken chërguray; *meat* dë chërg ghwasha

chickpeas nakhod

chief *of village* malëk

child *boy* warukay; *girl* wara; **youngest child** këshër; mëndzumay

children bachyân

chimney dewâli bukhârëy

chin zëna

China Chin

chinaware chini; chini loshi

Chinese *m* Chinâyay

Chinese *f* Chinâyëy

chocolate châklet

choke tarbatedël; **He/She is choking!** Sâh ye tarbatezhi!

cholera kulara

cholera wobâ *(Pakistan)*

choose intikhâbawël

chop kutël

Christian *m* Isaway; *f* Isawëy

Christianity Isawiyat

church kalisâ

cicada chërchërak

cigarette(s) sigret

cinema sinimâ; sinamâ

circle dâyra

citizen tab'a

citizenship tâbi'at

city shâr; **city center** dë shâr markaz; **city hall** dë shâr nandâre; **city map** dë shâr naqsha

civil rights madani huquq

civil war koranëy jagra

civilian *noun/adjective* mulki

clan tabër

class *academic* tolgay; klâs *(Pakistan)*

clean *adjective* pâk; **clean sheets** pâk ruykashuna; *verb* pâkawël

clear *adjective* run; *verb* runawël

clerk kâtib; mirzâ; **head clerk** sar kâtib

client mo'akil

climate âb aw hawâ; eqlim

climb *verb* khatël

clinic katandzay; klinik

cloak *woman's/man's* tsâdër

clock dewâlisât

close (to) *adjective* nizhde

close *verb* bandawël; **to close a door** pore kawël

closed band; *door* puri

cloth tukar; tukay

clothes jâme; kâli; **clothes shop** bazâzi

cloud wredz

clover shawtal

club klab

clutch *of car* kalach

coal skârë

coarse zizh

coast sâhil

coat kurtëy; *sheepskin* postin

cobbler mochi

cobra kapcha

cock; cockerel chërg

cockroach garandëy

code kod; **international dialing code** dë tilifun narëywâl kod

coffee kâfi; **coffee with milk** kâfi aw shide

coin sika; **coins** sike

cold *adjective* sor; *noun* sârë; *medical* zukâm; **cold water** sare obë; **It is cold.** Yakh day.; **I am cold.** Sâre me kezhi; **I have a cold.** Zukâm shaway yam.

collar ghâra

colleague hamkâr

collect tolawël

college pohandzây; kâlij

color rang

comb zhmundz

come râtlël; **come in!** dënana râsha

comfortable

comfortable ârâm; This car seat is comfortable. Dâ siṭ ârâm day.

command amer kawël

commentary tabsira

commission kamisun; kameshan (*Pakistan*); What is the commission? Kameshan tsumra day?

committee komeṭa

communications mukhâbirât; dë mukhâbirâto wizârat ministry of communications

community ṭolana

companion malgaray

company *firm* sherkat; kampanëy

compare partala kawël

compass qotbnomâ

compensation tâwân

competition siyâli

complain shikâyat kawël

complaint shikâyat

complete bashpër

computer kampyuṭar; computer program dë kampyuṭar progrâm; computer virus dë kampyuṭar wirus

concert kansart; concert hall dë kansart tâlâr

conciliated pëkhlâ

concussion *medical* sarbadâli

condemn ghandël

condition *state* hâlat; *term* shart

condom kândam; pukaṇëy

conference kanfrâns; ghwanḍa

conference room dë kanfrâns koṭa

confirm: I want to confirm my flight. Ghwâṛam che ṭikiṭ me kanfaram shi.

confuse mëghshushawël

confused mëghshush

to connect nṣhëlawël

connection irtibât

conquer fatah kawël; niwël

consider pâm kawël

constant sâbit

constipated qabz

constipated: Are you constipated? Qabziyat ye?

constipation qabziyat

constitution asâsi qânun

consulate qunsilgari

consult mashora kawël

consultant salâkâr; mushâwir

contact irtibât

contact: I want to contact my embassy. Ghwâṛam che lë khpël safârat sara tamâs wënisam.

contact lenses linz

contain darlodël

container *freight* kântinar

contemporary ma'sir

contest musâbiqa

continue dawâm warkawël; continue! kawa!

contract taṛun

control *verb* kanṭrolawël

conversation mozâkira; khabëri-atëri

converse khabëre kawël

cook *noun* ashpâz; *verb* ashpâzi kawël

cooked pokh shaway

cooker bukhâr deg

cooking pot kaṭëwa

cool *adjective* soṛ

cooperation mrasta

copper mis

copy *noun* kâpi; *edition* noskha; *verb* kâpi kawël

coriander daṇyâ; gashniz

cork kârk

corkscrew sarkhlâsawonëy

corn jwâr

corner konj

correct *adjective* sam; *verb* samawël

corridor dâlez

corrupt rishwatkhor

corruption rishwatkhori

cost *verb* arzedël

cot chârpây

cottage cheese chaka
cotton wool pakhta; katan
cough *noun* ṯukhay; *verb* ṯukhël
council jirga
count shmerël
counterfeit ja'li; **This money is counterfeit.** Dagha payse ja'li di.
country hewâd; watan
countryside kalay
coup d'etat kudatâ
courage zṛëwartiyâ
court *law* mahkama; adâlat (Pakistan)
cousin *female* tërla; *aunt's daughter* dë tror lur; *aunt's son* dë tror zoy; *father's brother's daughter* dë trë lur; *father's brother's son* dë trë zoy; *mother's brother's daughter* dë mâmâ lur; *mother's brother's son* dë mâmâ zoy; *distant* tërbur
cow ghwâ
cowherd ghobë
co-wife bën
crab chingâsh
cradle zângo
craftsman san'atkâr; san'atgër
crane *machine* jarsaqil
crash *verb* mâtawël
crayon ranga qalam
crazy lewanay
cream *ointment* malham; mâlish
create joṛawël
credit kriḏiṯ; **credit card** kriḏiṯ kârt
cricket *game* krikiṯ; *insect* krëṛay
crime jurum
criminal mujrim
crisis alagula
cross *verb* teredël
crossing taqâtu
crossroads tsalorlâre
crow kârghë
cruel zâlim
cry *to weep* zhaṛël

cucumber bâdrang
cultivate karël
culture kultur
cumin zira
cup pyâla
cupboard almârëy
cure *noun* tadâwi; *verb* tadâwi kawël
currency paysa; noṯ
curtain parda
cushion bâlësht
custom dod-dastur; *border* gumruk
to cut *verb* qata kawël
cut off: I've been cut off. Ṯilifun me qata shu.; **The electricity has been cut off.** Breshnâ qata shawe da.

D

dagger châra
daily wradzanay
dairy dë labanyâto fârm
dam band
damp namnâk
dance; dancing natsâ; gaḏeḏâ
Dane Ḏinmârkay *m*; Ḏinmârkëy *f*
danger khatar
dangerous khatarnâk
Danish Ḏinmârki
Dari Dari; **Do you know Dari?** Pë dari pohezhe?
dark *adjective* tët
dark; darkness *noun* tiyâra
date *time* neṯa; **date of arrival** dë râraseḏo neṯa; **date of departure** dë rawâneḏo neṯa; **date of birth** dë zezheḏo neṯa; **What's the date?** Kuma neṯa da?
daughter lur; *of co-wife* bënzëy; *of wife's first husband* parkaṯëy; **daughters** lune
daughter-in-law nzhor
dawn *noun* speda châwd

day

day wradz; **What day is it?**
Nën kuma wradz da?
dead mer
deaf _m_ kun; _f_ kana
dear _loved m_ mayen; _f_ mayana
death mrina; marg
debt por
decade lasiza
deceive khatâbâsël
December Disimbar
decide prekra kawël
decision prekra
declaration a'lâmya
decrease _verb_ lëzhawël
deep zhawër
deer husëy
defeat _noun_ mâta; _verb_ mâta
warkawël
defeated për
defend difa' kawël
degree _grade_ daraja; _academic_
digri
delay _noun_ dzand
delayed: The plane is delayed.
Alwutaka wadzandeda.
democracy dimokrâsi
demolish wijârawël
demonstration _political_
muzâhira
demonstrators _political_
muzâhirachiyân
denounce ghandël
dentist dë ghâsh dâktar
deodorant buy zida mawâd
department tsânga; idâra;
dipârtmint
departure tag
departures rawânedâ
depth zhëwërtob
descend kuzedël
describe tashreh kawël
desert _noun_ dashta
desk mez
dessert khwâzhë
destination manzil
destiny bakht
destroy kharâbawël
detergent pâkawunki mawâd

detonate châwdël
detonation châwdana
development prâkhtiya
devil shaytân
dew shabnam
diabetes diyâbit; qand
diabetic diyâbiti; qandi
diagnosis _medical_ tashkhis
dial _verb_ rukh kawël; **Can I dial
direct?** Mustaqim ye rukh
kawalay sham?
dialect lahja
diaper ornay; **I need to
change my baby's diaper.**
Pëkâr da che dë khpël
mâshum ornay badal kram.
diarrhea es-hâl
diaspora tit-parakwâlay
dictionary qâmus
die mër kedël
diesel dizal
diet parhez;
difference tawpir
different bel
difficult sakht
dig kindël
dining room dë dodëy kota
dinner dë mâshâm dodëy
diplomat diplumât
diplomatic ties diplumâtike
arike
direct _adjective_ negh; _verb_
lârshowana kawël
direction _to a place_ khwâ; _act of_
lârshowana
directions atrâf
director mudir; **director's
office** mudiriyat
directorship mudiriyat
directory lârshowd kitâb
dirty khiran
disability ma'yubiyat
disabled ma'yub
disaster ghamiza
discover mundël
discuss bahs kawël
dicussion bahs
disease nâroghi

dish ghoray
disorderly be nazma
displaced person kadwâl; be-dzâya shaway
dispute *noun* lânja
distant leri
distinct bil
distinction tawpir
district sima
divide weshël
division taqsim
divorce *noun* talâq
dizzy gangs; **I feel dizzy.** Gangs yam.
do kawël; **do not...!** më...!
doctor dâktar *m*; dâktara *f*
document sanad
dog spay
doll nândzëka
dollar dâlar
domestic *animal* ahli
donkey *m* khar; *f* khra
door dara
door darwâza; war; **door lock** kulëp
double *verb* ghbargawël
doubt *noun* shak
dough: to make dough aghshël
dove musicha
down lândi
dowry walwër
dozen darjan
drag tsëkawël
dragonfly bambirak
drain *noun* zem
draw *an image* andzorawël
drawer rawâq
drawing *picture* taswir
dream *noun* khob; *verb* khob lidël
dress *noun* kâli; jâme; *verb* aghostël
dressed: to get dressed jâme aghostël
dressing *medical* patëy
dressmaker darzi
drill *verb* barma kawël; **to drill a well** tsâ barma kawël
drink *noun* tsëshâk; *verb* tsëshël

drinking water dë tsëshâk obë
drive *verb* chalawël
driver chalawunkay; direwar
driver's license lesans
drug *medical* dawâ; *narcotic* nashayiz mawâd; **drug addict** nashayi
drum *noun* dol
drunk: to be drunk nasha
dry wëch
dryness wëchwâlay
duck hilëy
during pë trëts ke
Dutch *language* Hâlandi
Dutchman Hâlanday
Dutchwoman Hâlandëy
duty *customs* mahsul; *obligation* danda
duvet brastën
dynamo daynamo
dysentery pech

E

each har
eagle oqâb
ear ghwazh; **ear drum** dë ghwazh parda
early wakhti; **He is early.** Dë wakhta day
earn gatël
earrings wâlëy
ears ghwazhuna
earth mdzëka; dzmëka
earthquake zilzila
ease *noun* âsântiya; *verb* âsânawël
east *noun* khatidz; sharq
east(ern) *adjective* dë khatidz
easy âsân
eat khwarël
economics iqtisâd pohana
economist iqtisâdpoh
economy *of country* iqtisâd
eczema baghu
edema përsob
edible khwarâki

editor

editor chëlawunkay
education ta'lim; tâlim
egg hagëy; **boiled egg** yëshedële hagëy
eight atë
eighteen atë-lës
eighty atiyâ
either ... or yâ ... yâ
elbow tsangël
elder brother lâlâ
elder mëshër
elect ghora kawël
election intikhâbât
electric shock barqi jitka
electricity breshnâ; barq
elephant fil
elevator lift
eleven yiwo-lës
eloquent zhëbawar
e-mail breshnâlik; imel; **e-mail address** dë imel âdras
embassy safârat
embroider khamak dozi kawël
emergency iztirâri hâlat
emergency exit iztirâri khuruj
empty *adjective* tësh; *verb* tëshawël
end *noun* âkher; pây; *verb* khlâsawël
enemy dushman
engine injin
engineer injiniyar
England Inglistân
English *language* Inglisi; Angrezi
Englishman Angrez; Inglisay
Englishwoman Angreza; Inglisëy
enough bas; **to be enough** bas kedël
enquiry palatana
enter nanawatël
enterprise tijârati sherkat
entire tol
entrance nanawatu lâr
envelope pâkat
epidemic sâri nârughi
epilepsy damâghi hamla

equal barâbar
equipment asbâb
equivalent barâbar
eraser pinsëlpâk
escape tashtedël
especially khususan
essay maqâla
establish jorawël
estimate atkalawël
eternal dâyimi
etiquette dod-riwâj
euro *currency* iru
Europe Urupâ
European Urupâyi
European Union Urupâyi Itihâdiya
evacuate preshodël; tëshawël
even hatâ **even if** hatâ kë
evening mâshâm; shpa; **this evening** nën mâshâm
every har
everybody; everyone hartsok
everything hartsë
evidence nasha
evident shkâra
ewe mezha
exact sam
exam emtihân
examine *medically* mu'âyna kawël
example misâl; **for example** masalan
excellent der shë
except (for)... prata lë...
excess premâni
exchange badlawël; **Do you exchange money?** Payse badlawe?
excuse *noun* mâfi; **excuse me!** wëbakhsha!
execute *verb* wazhël
executive ijrâyi
exercise *noun: activity* tamrin; *school* mashq; **exercise book** dë tamrin ketâbcha
exhaust *of car* igzâs; salânasar
exhaustion stomâni
exhibition nandârtun
exit *noun* dë wato lâr; *verb* watël

expect hila larël
expel sharël
expensive grân
explain tashrih kawël; bayânawël
explanation tashri(h); **explanations** tashriyât; tashrihât
explode châwdël; chëwël
explosion châwdana
explosives châwdunkay
export *verb* sâdirawël
exports sâdirât
express *fast* chatak
expression bayân
extra izâfi
extract istël
extradite spârël
eye stërga; **eyes** stërge
eyebrow wridza; **eyebrows** wrudze
eyeglasses aynaki; chashme *(Pakistan)*
eyelashes bânë
eyesight nazar

F

fabric tukër; kapra *(Pakistan)*
face *noun* mekh
to face *verb* mëkhâmëkhedël
fact rishtiyâ
factory fâbrika
faculty *of university* pohandzay
failure be-wasi
faith imân
falcon bâz
fall *autumn* manay; *verb* lwedël; **to fall over** awështël
false darwâgh
family koranëy
famine kâkhti
famous mash-hur
fan pakay; **fan belt** panjbolt
far leri
fare kirâya; **What is the fare?** Kirâya tsumra da?
farm karwanda

farmer karwandgar; dehqân
farming karhana
Farsi *language* Fârsi
fashion feshan
fast *quick* tez; *verb* rozha niwël; **I am fasting.** Rozha yam.
fast; fasting *noun* rozha
fasten tarël
fastener *for clothes* chârgol
fat *adjective* tswërb; *noun* charbi; *animal* wâzga
father abâ; plâr; **fathers** plaruna
father-in-law skhër; khosër
fatherless beplâra
faucet chushkay
fax faks; **fax machine** dë faks mâshin
fear *noun* dâr; *verb* dâredël
feast milmastiyâ
February Fibriwari; Firwari *(Pakistan)*
federation fidrâsyun; fidreshan *(Pakistan)*
feed *verb* marawël
feeding station dë khwaro dzay
feel ihsâsawël
felt-tip pen tush
female *adjective* shëdzina; *noun* shëdza
femur dë wrâna hadukay
fence katara
fender *of car* gilgir
fennel tomna
ferret muzhakprâng
ferry berëy
fertile hâsilkhez
fertilizer sara
festival mela; fistiwâl
feud badi
fever tëba
field dagar; patay
fifteen pindzë-lës
fifty pandzos
fight *verb* jangedël
fight; fighting jagra; *argument* shkhëra

fighter

fighter jangyâlay
file *computer* fâyl; *paper* dosiya
fill dakawël; **to fill in a form** forma dakawël
film *movie/camera* filëm; **film festival** dë filëm fistiwâl
filmmaker filëm jorawunkay
filter *noun* filtar
final *adjective* wrustay; *noun* fâynal
finance *money* payse; *financial affairs* iqtisâdi châre
find mundël
fine *adjective/adverb* shë; *of money* jarima
finger gota; **fingers** gote
fingernail nuk
finish *verb* khlâsawël
fire or
firewood buti
firm klak
first wrumbanay; lumray; **first aid** lumranëy mrasta; **first class** lumray daraja
fish kab; mâhi
fishing kab niwël
fishing net dë kab niwëlo jâl
fist mutay; suk
five pindzë
fix samawël
flash *camera* flash; *verb* dzaledël
flashlight lâsi tsirâgh
flask patakay
flat tire panchar; **I have a flat tire.** Tâyr me panchar day.
flea wrëzh
flee tështedël
flight *plane* parwâz; *escape* mahâjirat
flock rama
flood *noun* sel
floor *ground* gholay; *story* manzel; pur
florist gwël plorunkay
flour orë; **flour mill** mechën
flow bahedël
flower gwël
flu zukâm
fly *noun* mëch; *verb* alwëtël

fog lara
foggy larjan
folk *noun* wulës
folk dancing wulësi atan
folklore folklor
folk music folkluri musiqi
follow taqibawël
food dodëy
fool *noun* lawda
foot psha; *measurement* fut
football fotbâl
footpath piyâdaraw
for ... lë pâra; **for the sake of** dë ... lë pâra
forbid man'a kawël
forbidden man'a
forbidden *religiously* harâm
force dzwâk
forearm mët
forehead tanday
foreign bahranay
foreigner khârijay; parangay
forest dzangal
forget herawël
forgive bakhshël
forgotten her
fork panja
form *official* forma; fâram (*Pakistan*); *shape* bana
fort kot
fortnight dwa onëy
forty tsalwesht
forward(s) makhta
foundation *building* bansët; *organisation* mwasisa
four tsalor
fourteen tswâr-lës
fourth tsaloram
fox gidër
fracture *noun* darz; *verb* darz kedël
fragrance atar
free *liberated* âzâd; **free of charge** waryâ; muft; **free time** izâfi wakht; **Is this seat free?** Dâ chawkëy khâli da?; *verb* âzâdawël
freedom âzâdi

glue

freeze kangalawël
freezing kangal
freight *noun* dâr
french fries chips
French Farânsawi
Frenchman Farânsaway
Frenchwoman Farânsawëy
frequently mukarar
fresh *food* tâza; *cool* sor
Friday Jom'a
fridge fërij
friend dost; *male* mëlgëray; *female* mëlgëre
friendship dosti; mëlgartub
frighten berawël
frog chungasha
from lë
front *noun* wrândi
frontier sarhad
frost përkha
frostbite yakh wahalay
fruit mewa; **fruit juice** dë mewe obë; jus *(Pakistan)*
fry *something* srë kawël
fuel swën; **fuel dump** dë telo pamp/tânk
full dak; **full moon** tsuwâr-lasama spozhmëy; **to be full** mëredël
full up *satisfied* mor *m*; mara *f*; **I am full up!** Zë mor/mara yam!
funeral jinâza
funny dë khandâ
furniture farnichar
furrow kil
future râtlunkay

G

gain *noun* fâyda; *verb* gata kawël
gala mela
gale tufân
gall bladder trikhay
gallon gelan
gamble jwâri kawël
game loba

gandana *leek* gandana
gangrene gazak
garage garâj
garden ban; bâgh
gardener bâghwân
garlic huzha
garrison gârnizun
gas gâz; ghâz; ges *(Pakistan)*; *petrol* pitrol; **gas bottle/canister** dablay
gasoline tel
gate luy war
gather tolawël
gazelle husëy
gear *car* ger
general *adjective* umumi; *noun* janrâl
generally umuman
genitals tanâsuli sistëm
genocide âma wazhla
gentleman sâhib
gently! wro wro!
geography joghrâfiya
geologist jiyâlojist
German *m* Almâny; Jarmanay; *f* Almânëy; Jarmanëy
Germany Almân; Jarmani
germs mikrob
get akhistël; **to get in** *to a vehicle* sparedël; **to get up** patsedël
ghee ghwari
gift sawghât
ginger sond
girder dâga
girl jinëy; (wara) njëlëy; **girls** njune
girlfriend andiwâla
give warkawël; **give me...** ... mâ ta râkra; **to give oneself up** taslimedël; **to give birth (to)** zezhawël
glacier kangalzâr
glass *substance* shisha; *drinking* gilâs; **glass of water** dë obo gilâs; **glasses** *spectacles* aynaki
gloves diskâshe
glue srish

go tlël; **to go** *over there* wartlël; **to go out** watël; **to go to bed** widedël; **go!** lâr sha!

goal *aim* hadaf; *football* gol

goat wëza; *kid* serlay; *meat* dë wuze ghwasha

God Khudây; Allâh

gold srë zar

good shë; **good and evil** shë aw bad

good night! shpa (mu) pë khayr!

good-bye! khudây pâmân!

goose qâz; **wild goose** zâna

government hokumat

governmental hokumati

grain dâna

gram girâm

grammar girâmar

granddaughter lmasëy

grandfather bâbâ; nikë

grandmother anâ; nyâ

grandson lmasay

grapefruit chëkotara

grapes angur

grasp niwël

grass wâshë

grasshopper malëkh

grateful khwash; **I am grateful. Khwash yam**

grave *noun* gor

gravel jaghal

gravy qurma

gray khër

great luy

great-granddaughter kërwasëy

great-grandfather ghor nikë

great-grandmother ghora nyâ

great-grandson kërwasay

great-great-granddaughter kawdëy

great-great-grandson kawday

Greece Yunân

Greek *language* Yunâni

Greek *m* Yunânay

Greek *f* Yunânëy

green shin

greengrocer sabzi khartsawonkay

grenade lâsi bam

grey khër

grief gham

grind *verb* urë kawël

groom *horses* mehtar

ground zmëka

group dala

group bëluk

grow wada kawël; **to grow crops** shin kedël; **to grow up** luyedël

guard *noun* sâtunkay; *verb* sâtël

guerrilla chirik

guest *m* melma; *f* melmana

guesthouse melmastun

guide *noun* lârshod; *verb* lârshuwëna kawël

guidebook lârshod kitâb

gum wrëy

gun topak; **gun barrel** mil

gunman topchi

gust silëy

gut kulma; **guts** kulme

gynecologist dë nisâyi châro dâktar

H

hail *noun* zhalëy

hair weshtë

hairbrush dë weshto bors

haircut: I want a haircut please. Lutfan weshtë me râkam kra.

hairdresser salmân

hairdryer drâyi

hajj haj

hajji hâji

half nim; **half year** dwa fasla

half-brother mayranay wror

half-hour dwa pâwâ; nim sât

half-sister mayranëy khor

hammer *noun* sotak

hand *noun* lâs; **to hand over** spârël

handbag lâsi baks

handful khapër(a)

handicraft lâsi san'at

handkerchief dësmâl (dë poze)
handle *noun* lâstay
hang dzaṟawël
hangar koṭband
hanger *clothes* dzaṟawʊnkay
happen peshedël
happy khoshâla
hard *difficult* grân; *not soft* klak
hardware store gudâm
hare swëy
harmful muzir
harvest law
hashish chars
hat khwalëy; ṭopëy *(Pakistan)*;
  Nuristani pakol; **fur hat**
  Astrakhan qaraquli
hate kraka
hate *verb* kraka kawël
have larël; **to have to** bâyad...
hawk bâz
hay beda
he haghë; day
head sar; *boss* mëshër; **head
  clerk** sarkâtib; **head of state**
  dë dawlat rayis
headache sardardi
headman malëk
headmaster sarmo'alim
headquarters dë qumande
  markaz
headscarf *woman's* paṟunay
heal raghawël
health sihat; roghtiyâ
healthcare hifzul-siha
healthy rogh
hear awredäl
heart zṟë; **heart attack** dë zṟë
  hamla; **heart condition** dë
  zṟë waziyat
heat *noun* garmi; *verb* tawdawël
heatwave dë garmëy tsapa
heaven janat
heavy drund
hedgehog ziᶎhgay
heel punda
height jëgwâlay
helicopter elikoptar
hell dozakh

hello! salâm!
help *noun* mrasta; *verb* mrasta
  kawël; **help!** kumak!; **Can
  you help me?** Mrasta râsara
  kawalay she?
hem lëmën
hen chërga
hepatitis hipâtit
her hagha; **I told her.** Mâ
  haghe të wëwayël.; **her book**
  dë haghe kitâb
herb buṭay
herd goram
here dalta
hero atal
hers dë haghe
herself dâ pëkhpëla
hidden pëṭ
hide pëṭawël
high lwër; **high blood
  pressure** dë wine lwër fishâr
high school lisa
highway loya lâr
hijack alwëtaka tashtawël
hijacker alwëtak-tashtawunkay
hijacking dë alwëtake
  tashṟawël
hike *verb* gardzedël
hill ghundëy
hillside râghë
him haghë; **I told him.** Mâ
  haghë ta wëwayal.
himself day pëkhpëla
Hindi Hindi
Hindu Hindu
Hinduism Hindutob
hip kunâṭay
hire kirâya kawël
his dë haghë
historian târikh likunkay
history târikh
hit wëhël
hold niwël
hole suray
holiday rukhsati
holidays rukhsatëy
holy mobârak; **holy man**
  bëzërg

homeland hewâd
homeless be-kora
homework koranay kâr
honey shât
honor wiyâr
hood *of car* bânaṭ
hook *noun* changak
hookah chilam
hope umayd
horn shkër; *car* hâran
hornet ghumbësa
horse âs; as; **horses** asân; **horse racing** âs dzghâsta
horseback riding âs sparli
hospitable melmapâl
hospital roghtun
host korba
hostage bëramta; **to take hostage** bëramta kawël
hostel layliya
hot garm; tod; **hot water** tawde obë; **I am hot.** Garmi me kezhi.; **It is hot.** Garmi da.
hotel huṭal
hound: **Agfhan hound** tâzi
hour sâ'at
house kor
how? tsë ranga; tsënga; **how far?** tsumra leri?; **How far is the next village?** Bël kalay tsumra leri day?; **how many?** tsumra?; **how much?** tsumra?; **how much is it?** pë tsu day?; **How much does this cost?** Dë dagha baya tsu da?
however pë har hâl
human (being) *noun* bashar; insân; *adjective* bashari; insâni; **human rights** bashari huquq
humanitarian bashari; **humanitarian aid** bashari (dustâna) mrasta
humid namnâk
humor ṭoka
humorous khushtabi
hundred sël
hunger lwëzha
hungry wëzhay; **I'm hungry.**

Wëzhay yam.
hunt shkâr kawël
hunting shkâr
hurry: **I'm in a hurry.** Tâdi me da; **hurry up!!** tâdi kawa!
hurt *noun* zakham; *verb* khozhedël; **It hurts here.** Dâ dzây dard kawi.; **My back hurts.** Mlâ me khozhezhi.
husband khâwand
hygiene hefzul-siha

I

I zë
ice kangal
ice cream âys-krim
icy yakh
I.D. pezhand pâna/kârt; tazkira
idea mafkura
identification pezhandgalwi
if kë; **if not** kane; **if only** kë cheri; **if possible** kë imkân lari
ill nârogh; **to be ill** nâroghedël; **I am ill.** Nârogh yam.
illegal ghayri-qânuni; nâ-rawâ
illiterate besawâd
illness nâroghi; nâjori
image taswir
imagination khiyâl
imam imâm
immediately zhër
immigrant mahâjir
immigration mahâjirat
impolite be-adab
import *verb* wâridawël
importance ahamiyat
important muhim
impossible nâ-mumkin
improve shë kawël
in pë (... ke); **in addition to** sarbera për; **in front of** pë mëkh ke; **in the country** pë këli ke
included mushtamil
incomplete nimgëray

indeed wâqi'an
independence khpëlwâki; istiqlâl
independent khpëlwâk; **independent state** khpëlwâk dawlat
index finger dë shahâdat gwëta
India Hind; Hindustân
Indian m Hinday; f Hindëy
indicator light ishâra
indigestion dë hâzime kharâbi
industry san'at
infant mâshum m; mâshuma f
infected: It is infected. Zawab ye këray.
infection ufunat
inflammable swadzedunkay
influenza zukâm
information mâlumât; **information office** dë mâlumâto daftar
infuse damawël
injure ṭapi kawël
injured ṭapi
injury zhobla
ink rang
inner-tube ṭiyub
innocent be-gunâh
inquiry taftish
insane lewanay
inscription matan
insect hashara; **insects** hashare
insecticide hashara zid
inside danëna
insignificant bema'nâ
instance: for instance masalan
instead pë dzây
institute ṭolana; anistiyut
instruction *teaching* ta'lim
instructions *on use* hidâyât
insurance bema; **I have medical insurance.** Zë tibi bema laram.
insured: My possessions are insured. Zmâ jaydâd bema day.
intelligence poha
intelligent poh

intend irâda larël
intention murâm
interest *noun* dilchaspi; *financial* sud; *verb* alâqa larël
interesting dilchasp
interior *adjective* dâkhili; *noun* dâkhil; **ministry of the interior** dë kuranëyo châro wizârat
internal koranay
international naṟëywâl; **international operator** naṟëywâl âpreṭar; **international code** naṟëywâl kod; **international flight** naṟëywâl parwâz
internet inṭarniṭ
interpret zhbârël
interpreter zhbârën
intersection tsalorlâri
interval waqfa
interview maraka
intestine kulma
into pëke
introduce ma'rifi kawël
invade yarghal kawël
invasion yarghal
investigate pëlaṭël
investigation palëṭana
invitation balëna
invite balël
Iran Irân
Iranian m Irânay; f Irâney
Ireland Âyrlenḏ
Irish m Âyrlenḏay; f Âyrlenḏëy
iron *for clothes* otu; istri *(Pakistan)*
Islam Islâm
Islamic Islâmi
Israel Isrâyil
Israeli m Isrâyilay
Israeli f Isrâyilëy
it m/f hagha
Italian m Iṭâlaway; f Iṭâlawëy
Italian *language* Iṭâlawi
Italy Iṭâliyâ
itch *noun* khârësht
item shay
its dë haghë

J

jack *of car* jak
jackal surlanday
jacket kortëy
Jalalabad Jalâlabâd
jam; jelly morabâ
janitor chëprâs
January Janwarëy
Japan Jâpân
Japanese *m* Jâpânay; *f* Jâpânëy; *language* Jâpâni
jaw zhâma
jazz jâz
Jew *m* Yahud(ay); *f* Yahuda; Yahudëy
jeweler zargar
jewelry zargari
Jewish Yahud(a)
jihad jihâd
job danda; kâr
joiner najâr
joint band
joke *noun* toka
journalist zhornâlist
Judaism Yahudiyat
judge *noun* qâzi
jug kuza; mangay; jag
juice: fruit juice dë mewe obë; jus *(Pakistan)*
July julây
jumper banyân; jâkat
June Jun
junior kashër
just now os-os
justice adâlat

K

Kabul Kâbël
Kandahar Kandahâr
Karachi Karâchëy
kebab kabâb; **kebab** tike *(Pakistan)*
keep sâtël
ketchup rob
kettle châyjush
key kili

khaki khër
kid *goat* wërghumay
kidnap baramta kawël
kidnapper baramtagar
kidnapping baramta-kawël
kidney pështawërgay; **kidneys** poshtawërge
kill wazhël
killer wëzhunkay; qâtil
killing wazhla
kilogram kilogrâm
kilometer kilomitar
kind *adjective* mehrabân; *noun* dawl
king pâchâ(h)
kiosk ghurfa
kiss mëchawël; shkulawël
kitchen pakhlandzay
kite kâghazbâd
knead akhshël
knee gunda
kneel pë gundo kedël
knife chârë
knit obdël
knock takawël
know pezhandël; I know. Pezhanam.; I don't know. Në ye pezhanam.; Do you know him/her? Hagha pezhane?
knowledge pohana
known pezhandël shaway
Koran Qor'ân

L

laboratory lâbrâtwâr; libârtri *(Pakistan)*
lack *noun* nështwâlay
ladder zina
ladle tsamtsëy
lake jahil
lamb wray; *meat* dë wri ghwasha
lamp lampa; tsirâgh
land *noun* zmëka; *verb (airplane)* pë mdzëka kenastël

landlord khâwënd

landslide dë mdzëke shwayedâ

language zhëba

lantern lâten

laptop *computer* dë ghezhi kampyutar

large luy

last wrustanay *m*; wrustay *f*; **last night** begâ; **last week** tera hafta; **last year** last year ter kâl

late nâwakhta; **I am late.** Pë mâ nâwakhta shaway day.

laugh khandël

laughter khandâ

laundry dë kâlo mindzël; **laundry person** dobi

law qânun; **law court** mahkama

lawyer wakil

lay (down) prewëtël

laziness lati

lazy lat

lead *noun: metal* sorp

lead *verb* lârshowana kawël

leader mëshër

leaf pâna

leak tsëtsedël

lean *adjective* dangër; *verb* kazhedël

leap topwahël; **leap year** kabisa kâl

learn zda kawël; **to learn by heart** hifzawël

leather charm

leave preshodël

lecture *noun* likchar

left *side* kin; chap; **to the left** kin lor ta

left-handed kinlâsay

left-wing kin-arkh

leg psha

legal qânuni; **legal profession** wikâlat

legend afsâna

lemon lemu

lend por warkawël

length ozhdwalay

lengthen ozhdawël

lens linz

lentils dâl

leopard prâng

less lëzh; **-less** be-

lesson lwast

let: Let's go! Râdza che dzu!

letter lik; *of alphabet* toray; **letters** *of alphabet* tori

lettuce kâhu

level *adjective* barâbar; *noun* shâqul

lever jabal

liberate âzâdawël

liberty khpëlwâki; âzâdi

library kitâbtun; kitâbkhâna

lice spëzha

lick tsatël

lie *noun* darwâgh

lie down tsëmlastël

life zhwënd

lifeless be-roh

lift *elevator* lift; *verb* porta kawël

light *noun* ranâ; *electric* lâsi barq; *torch* lâsi tsirâgh; *adjective: bright* run; *color* bal; *not heavy* spëk; *verb* balawël; **to light a fire** or lagawël; **Do you have a light?** Sigret letar lare?

lightbulb grup

lighter sigret-letar; **lighter fluid** dë sigret-letar tel

lightning tandër; *bolt* breshnâ

like *preposition* lëka; *verb* khwashawël; **I like... ...** zmâ khwashezhi.; **I don't like... ...** me në khwashezhi.

likely: to be likely ihtimâl larël

limbs (of body) (dë badan) ghëri

lime *fruit* lemu; nimbu *(Pakistan)*

limit had; **limits** hudud

line kërsha

linguist zhabpoh

linguistics zhabpohana

lining *of clothes* astër

lion zmaray

lip shunda

lipstick labsirin

liquid

liquid mâye
liquor sharâb
list lest
listen awredël
listener awredunkay
liter letar
literature adabyât
little *small* warakây *m*; wara *f*; *less* lëzh; **little finger** wara gwëta; **little by little** lez-lez
live: live broadcast negh pë negha khparawana; **live wire** luts sim
live *verb* zhwënd kawël; *to dwell* osedël
liver dzigar
livestock mâl
lizard kërboray
load bârëwël
loaf tota
local: a local shop for local people dë mahale dukân dë mahale dë khalko lapâra
location mawqiyat
lock *noun* qulf; *verb* qulfawël
locomotive dë orgâdi mâshin
locust mëlakh
loft kandu
loins mlâ
long ozhd
look katël; **to look for** pëlatël
loot *verb* tâlânawël
lorry lârëy
lose *to mislay* wrëkawël; *to be defeated* baylël; **I have lost my key.** Kili râna wraka shawe da.
lost: I am lost. Lë mâ lâra wraka da.
lot; a lot der
lottery lâtrëy
loud lwër
loudly pë zota
louse spëzha
love *noun* mina; ishq; *verb* mina kawël
low lândi; **low blood pressure** dë wine tit fishâr
lower *verb* lëzhawël

luck bakht
luggage baksuna
lumps *of earth* luta
lunch dë gharme dodëy
lung sëzhay; parpus *(Pakistan)*

M

machete châra
machine mâshin
machine gun mâshingan
madrasa madrasa
magazine *printed* majala; *gun* salâkut
magnetic miqnâtisi
mail posta; post
mailbox post baks
main asli; **main square** asli chawk
maintain sâtël
maize jwâr
majority aksariyat
make jorawël
make-up *cosmetics* mekap
malaria malaryâ
male *noun* nâr; *adjective* nârina
mammal tiwâl
man saray
manager mudir
manner *mode* dod
manual *book* lâsi kitâb; lârshod kitâb
manure sëra
many der; ziyât
map naqsha; **map of Kabul** dë Kâbël naqsha
March Mârch
mare aspa
mark nasha
market bâzâr
marriage nikâ(h)
married: I am married. *said by a man* Mâ wâdë karay day.; *said by a woman* Zë wâdë shawe yam.
marrow *of bone* dë haduki mâghzë
marry *see* married

marsh jaba
martyr shahid
mascara rânjë
mat: prayer mat jâynamâz
match *football* maych
matches *for fire* orlagit
material mawâd; *cloth* ṭukay
mathematics; maths ryâzi
matter *subject* mawzo; **It doesn't matter!** Parwâ na lari!
mattress toshak
May Me; Mëy
maybe imkân lari
me mâta; zë
meadow warsho
meal doḏëy
mean: What does this mean? Dâ tsë mânâ lari?
meaning ma'nâ; mânâ
measure *verb* mechawël
meat ghwaṣha
mechanic mistari; mekhânik
media rasanduye; **mass media** ḏalayize rasanduye
medical *adjective* tibi; **medical insurance** dë sihat bema
medication tadâwi
medicine dawâ
meet lidël
meeting mulâqât
melon khaṭëkay
member gharay
memory hâfiza; yâd
men sari
menu menyu; dë doḏëy lest
mercenary malesha
message payghâm
metal *noun* filiz; *adjective* filizi
meter; metre *measure* mitër
metro miṭro
mid; middle mandz
midday gharma
middle mandz
midnight nima shpa
midwife dâyi; qâbila
mile mil
military *adjective* pawdzi;

military service askari
milk shode; **human milk** pëy; **cow's milk** dë ghwâ shode; **goat's milk** dë wze shode; **powdered milk** poḏëri shode
mill zhranda
millennium las perëy
miller zhrandagaray
millet zhḏën
million milyon
millstone pal
minaret munâra
mind *noun* aqël
mine *adjective* zmâ; *mineral* kân; *explosive* mâyn; **anti-personnel mine** parsunal zid mâyn; **anti-tank mine** ṭânk zid mâyn
minefield mâyn larunke sima
miner dë kân kârgar
mineral kâni; **mineral water** ma'dani obë
minister wazir
ministry wizârat
minority aqalyat
mint welënay; nânâ
minute *noun* daqiqa
miracle mu'jiza
mirror hindâra; âyina
mislead khaṭâbâsël
miss *verb: not hit* khatâ kawël
Miss Peghla
missile tughanday
mission mâmuriyat
mist lara
mistake ghalati; **to make a mistake** ghalati kawël
mix gaḏawël
mixture gaḏula
mobile phone mobâyl
mode dod
model *ekhample* namuna
modem moḏim
modern osanay
modest hayânâk
Mojahed mojâhid
Mojahedin mojâhidin
mole mezḥa

mollah mullâ
moment sheba
monarch pâchâ *m*; malika *f*
monarchy saltanati; shâhi
monastery somi'a
Monday Dushanba
money payse
monkey bizo
month myâsht
monthly myâshtënay
monument yâdgâr
moon spozhmëy
more der; **more or less** lëzh-o-der; **more than that** tar dë ziyât
morning sahâr; **this morning** nën sahâr
mortgage grawi
mosque jum'at
mosquito mâsha; **mosquito net** jâlëy
most aksara
mother mor; **mothers** maynde
mother-in-law khwâshe
motherless be-mora
motorbike; motorcycle motërtsâykël
motorway loya lâr
mount khatël; *a horse* sparedël
mountain ghar; **mountain pass** gharanëy lâr; **mountain stream** khwër
mouse mozhak
mouth khwlë
move shorawël
movie fëlm; **movie theater** sinëmâ
Mr. Shâghalay
Mrs. Mermën
Ms. Peghla
much der; **not much** der na
mud khate
muffler *of car* salânsar
mug *noun* mangotay
mulberry tut
mule kachar
mullah mulâ
multiplication zarb

multiply zarbawël
munitions golëy; marmëy
murder *noun* wazhana; qatël; *verb* wazhël
murderer wazhunkay; qâtil
muscle azala; **muscles** azale
museum muziyam
music muzik; musiqi; sâz; **music festival** dë sâz mela
Muslim *m* Musulmân; *f* Musulmâna
must bâyad
mustache bret; **mustaches** brituna
mutton dë psë ghwasha
my zmâ
myself mâ pëkhpëla
mystic *person* mutasawif

N

nail *of finger/toe* nuk; *metal* mekh
naked barband
name num; **What is your name?** Num de tsë day?; **My name is Fred.** Zmâ num Fred day.
nape *of neck* tsët
napkin dësmâl
nappy ornay; **I need to change my baby's nappy.** Pëkâr da che dë khpël mâshum ornay badal kram.
narrow tang
nation milat
national milli
nationality milyat; tâbiyat
natural tabiyi; **natural disaster** tabiyi nâwrin; **natural resources** tabiyi sarchine
nature *the natural world* tabiyat
navel num
near; nearby nëzhde
nearly taqriban
necessary lâzim

necessary zaruri; **it's necessary** zaruri day
necessity zërurat
neck ghâra
necklace lâket
necktie nektâ'i
need *noun* hâjat; **to need** *verb* zarurat larël; **I need...** Zë ... ta zarurat larëm.
needle stën; **Do you have a needle and thread?** Stën aw târ lare?
negotiator marakachi
neighbor gâwanday
neither ... nor në ... në
nephew *brother's son* wrârë; *sister's son* khorye
nerve asab
net: fishing net jâl; **mosquito net** jâlëy
never hits këla
new naway; **new moon** nawe miyâsht; **new year** naway kâl; **New Year festival** Nawruz
New Zealand Naway Zilând
newborn child naw zezhay
news khabaruna
newspaper akhbâr; *daily* wradzpâna; **newspaper in English** Angrezi wradzpâna
newsstand dë wradzpâno ghurfa
next râtlunkay; **next week** râtlunke hafta
nice shë
nickname takhalus
niece *brother's daughter* wrera; *sister's daughter* khorza
night shpa
nightclub nâyt-klab
nightguard; nightwatchman chawkidâr
nightingale bulbël
nightmare khapaska
nine nahë
nineteen nulës
ninety nawi
no na; ya

no; none hits; **no entry** dâkhila mamno; **no problem!** parwâ na lari!; **no smoking** sigret mamno; **no sugar** be bure
nobody hitsuk
noise shor
nomad kochay; powanda
none hits
noon gharma; tsâsht
normal âdi; nurmal
normally ma'mulan
north *noun* shamâl
north(ern) *adjective* shamâli
Northern Ireland Shamâli Âyrland
Norway Nârwe
nose poza
not në; **not yet** lâ në
note: bank note bânk not
notebook ketâbcha
nothing hits
nought sifar
noun isëm
novel nâwël
November Nuwâmbar
now os
nowhere hicheri
number shmera; numra
nurse nurs *m*; narsa *f*
nut mindaka

O

o'clock baje; **It is six o'clock.** Shpazh baje di.
objective hadaf
observer tsârunkay
occasionally këla këla
occupation *job* danda
occupy a country dë yawë hewâd niwël
occupying forces ghâsib dzwâk
occur peshedël
ocean bahër; samandër
October Aktobar

of dë; *the plays of Shakespeare* dë Shikspiyar drâme

office daftar; **office worker** mâmur

officer *military* afsar

official *adjective* rasmi; *noun* mâmur; **officials** mâmurin

often byâ-byâ

oil *cooking* mâye ghwari; *engine* tel; **oil pipeline** dë telo pâyplin; **oil refinery** chândzây; **oil tanker** tânkar; **oil well** dë telo tsâh

oilcan dë telo dabay

oilfield dë telo maydân

ointment mâlish

old woman spinsare

old *m* zor; *f* zara; **old man** buda; **old woman** budëy; **old city** zor shâr; **How old are you?** Tsu kalan yâst?; **I am ... years old.** Zë ... kalan yam.

on bânde; pë; **on foot** pë psho

once yaw dzal

one yaw(a)

oneself pëkhpëla

one-way: one-way street yaw tarafa kutsa; **one-way ticket** dë yawe khwâ tikit

onion(s) pyâz

only *alone* yawâzi; *adverb* faqat

onto *preposition* pë ... bânde

open *adjective* prânistay; khlâs; *verb* prânistël; khlâsawël

operating theater/room dë amaliyat kota

operation *surgical* amaliyat

operator; telephone operator apretar *m*; apretara *f*

opium taryâk

opponent mukhâlif

opposite muqâbil

opposition mukhâlifat; apozisun

or yâ

orange *fruit* nârinj; *color* nârinji

orchard bâgh

order *command* amër; *arrange-ment* tartib; *to command* amër kawël; **to order a meal** dë dodëy farmâysh warkawël

ordinary ma'muli

organ *of body* gharay

origin asal

original asli

orphan yatim

orphanage mrastun

other bël

ounce ons

our zmunzh

ourselves pëkhpëla zmunzh

out dëbândi

outside bahar

oven tanur; dâsh

over për; ter

overcoat kot

overcome gatël

overtake *by car* wrândi kedël

overturn mâte warkawël

owl gungay; kwang

own *adjective* khpël; *verb* darlodël

owner tseshtën; *of building* khâwand

ownership *of property* korwâlâ

ox ghwayay

oxygen âksijan

P

pace gâm

packhorse yâbu

package; packet pâkat

padlock qulf

page mëkh; safha

pain dard

painkiller musakin

paint *noun* rang; *verb* rangawël

painter rangmâl

painting andzorgari

Pakistan Pâkistân

Pakistani *person* Pâkistânay *m*; Pâkistânëy *f*; *thing* Pâkistâni

palace mânëy

pale tët

palm *of hand* rghaway
pamphlet risâla
pancreas toray
pane shisha
pantyhose barjis
paper *substance* kâghaz; *newspaper* akhbâr; wradzpâna; *article* maqâla
parachute parâshut
paradise janat
paralyze falajawël
paralyzed shal
parcel pârsal
parents morplâr
park *noun* pârk; *verb* motar pârkawël
parliament pârlimân; *Afghani lower house* wulësi jirga; *Afghani upper house* mëshrâno jirga
parrot tuti
part barkha
participate gadun kawël
partridge zërka
party *celebration* melmastiya; pârtëy; *political* gwand
Pashto Pështo
Pashtoon Pështun *m*; Pashtana *f*
Pashtunistan Pështunkhwa
pass *I.D.* pezhand pâna; *mountain pass* gharanëy lâr
pass *verb* teredël; **to pass an exam** baryâlay kedël; **to pass time** wakht terawël
passable: Is the road passable? Sarëk khlâs day?
passenger mosâfër
passer-by lârway
passport pâsport; **passport number** dë pâsport numra
past *adjective* ter; *noun* pëkhwâ; **some years past** tsu kâla pëkhwâ; **the past century** tera perëy
pasta khamira
oath narëy lâr
patient *adjective* sâbir; **Be patient!** Sâbir osa!

patient *medical* nârogh
patrol payra; gazma
paunchy gedawar
pay *noun* adâ; *verb* adâ kawël
payment adâ
pay-phone de tilifun ghurfa
peace sola; **peace talks** dë sole khabëre atëre; **to make peace** sola kawël; **to bring peace** sola râwëstël
peace-keeping troops sola sâtay dzwâk
peach(es) shaftâlu
peacock tâ'us
peak tsuka
pear nâk; nashpâtay *(Pakistan)*
pearl marghalëre
peas mëtër
pebble wara dabara
pedestrian pëlay
pediatrician dë mâshumâno dâktar
pediatrics dë mâshumâno tib
pelvis kunak
pen qalam
pencil pinsël
penicillin pinsilin
penknife châqu
penname takhalus
people khalak
pepper mrëch
perfect bëshpër
perform tarsara kawël
performance tamsil
perfume atar
perhaps shâyi; shâyad
period *of time* moda; *class* sâ'at; *menstrual* miyâshtanay âdat
permitted *religiously* halâl; rawâ
Persian Irânay *m*; Irânëy *f*; *language* Fârsi; Pârsi
person shakhs
Peshawar Peshawër
petition ariza
petrol pitrol; **I have run out of petrol.** Pitrol me khlâs shawi di.

pharmacy

pharmacy darmaltun
pheasant dashti chërg
phone *noun* ṯilifun; *verb* ṯilifun kawël; **Please phone me.** Lutfan ṯilifun râ ta wëkṟa.
photo aks
photocopier dë fuṯokâpi mâshin
photocopy *noun* fuṯokâpi; *verb* fuṯokâpi kawël
photographer akâs
photography akâsi
physical jismâni
physics fizik
physiotherapy fizyutrâpi
piano piyâno
pickax kulang
picnic mela
picture aks
piece ṯota; dâna
pig khuk
pigeon kâwtara
pilgrim ziyârat kawunkay; *to Mecca* hâji
pilgrimage ziyârat; *to Mecca* haj; **to go on pilgrimage** ziyârat kawël; *to Mecca* haj kawël
pill gulëy
pillow bâlësht
pilot piloṯ
pin stën
pink golâbi
pipe pâyp
pipe nal
pistol tëmâncha
pitch *football* maydân
place *noun* dzây; *verb* ishodël; **place of birth** dë zezhedo dzây
placenta prewân; zëlândz
plain *noun* awâra
plane alwutaka; jâz
plank takhta
plant *noun* niyâl; *verb* niyâlawël
planting niyâlawëna
plaster *medical* palastar
plastic palâstik

plate qâb; paleṯ *(Pakistan)*
platform *railway* pleṯfârm; **platform number** dë pleṯfârm shmera
platoon boluk
play *noun: theater* tamsil; drâma; *verb* lobedël; *a musical instrument* ghazhawël
please! lutfan!
pleasure khwashi
plow *noun* qolba; *verb* qolba kawël
plug *bath* sarposh; *electric* palak
plum alucha
p.m. tar gharme wrusta
poach *animals/game* pë ghlâ shkar kawël
pocket jeb
poem sha'r
poet shâ'ir; she'ir
poetry sha'iri
point ṯakay
poison zahr
police polis; pulis; **police station** mâmuriyat; tâṉa *(Pakistan)*
policeman polis; polis wâlâ *(Pakistan)*
polite mu'adab
political syâsi
politician syâsatwâl
politics syâsat
polo polo loba
pomegranate(s) anâr
pond dand
pony ṯaṯo
pool hawz; dand
poor khwâr
population nufus
porcupine shkun
pork dë khuk ghwasha
port bandar
portable T.V. wṟëlkedunkay ṯiliwizun
portion barkha
portrait tsera
position mawqiyat
possess larël

possibility imkân

possibly shâyad; shâyi

post office postakhâna; posti daftar

postcard postkârt

pot deg; **cooking pot** katwëy

potatoes âlu; patâte

pottery kulâli

poultry chërgân

pound *weight/sterling* pawnd

pour achawël; toyawël

poverty nisti

powder podar

power qowat

praise stâyël

pray lmundz kawël

prayer mat/rug jâynamâz

prayer lmundz

prayer: funeral prayer dë jinâze lmundz

prayers lmundz

prefer ghora ganël

pregnant omedwâra; hâmila; **I'm pregnant.** Omedwâra yam.

preparation tayâri; **preparations** tartibât

prepare tayârawël

present *adjective: time* osanay; *noun: time* os; *gift* dâlëy

president *of country* wëlësmëshër; jamhur rayis; *of organisation* rayis

presidential guard dë wëlësmëshër gârd

press: the press matbu'ât; **the free press** âzâd matbu'ât; *verb* tingawël

pressure fishâr

pretty shkëlay

prevent makha niwël

previously pukhwâ

price baya

pride wiyâr

priest rohâni

prime minister lumray wazir; sadri a'zam

prince shâzâda

principal *adjective* asli; *noun: school* sarshuwënkay; sarmâlim

print châpawël

printer *place* matbu'a; *computer* printar

prison bandi khâna; jel *(Pakistan)*

prisoner bandi; **to take prisoner** bandi kawël

prisoner-of-war asir; jangi bandi

prize jâyza

probability ihtimâl

probable ihtimâli; **It is probable.** Ihtimâl lari.

probably shâyi

problem stunza; mushkil

product mahsul

profession maslak

professional *person* maslaki

professor pohând

program: radio program râdiyoyi khparawëna; **computer program** dë kampyutar progrâm

progress përmëkhtag

projector prâjiktar

pronounce talafuzawël

pronunciation talafuz

proof nasha

proper monâsib

prophet payghambar

proposal wrândiz

prosthesis *see* artifical

protect sâtël

protection sâtana

protest *noun* a'tirâz; ihtijâj; *verb* a'tirâz kawël; ihtijâj kawël

proud wiyâralay

prove sâbitawël

proverb matal

province wilâyat; soba *(Pakistan)*

provisions âzuqa

public phone omomi tilifun

publish khparawël

publisher khparawunkay

pull kashawël; **to pull out** istël

pump

pump *noun* pamp; **water pump** bamba; *verb* pampawël; **to pump water** bamba kawël

pumpkin kadu

puncture panchar; **I have a puncture.** Moṭar me panchar day.

punish jazâ warkawël

pupil *school* shâgird; *of eye* kësay

puppy kutray

purple arghawâni

pursue taqibawël

push poriwahël

put ishodël; **to put down** lândi ishodël; **to put in** nana istël; **to put on** *clothes* aghostël

puzzled aryân

Q

Qandahar Kandahâr

quail maṛëz

quarrel jagṛa

quarter pâo

quarter *area* tsalorama barkha; **quarter of an hour** pindzëlas daqiqe

quarterly dre myâshtinëy

queen malika

question poshtana

Quetta Kwëṭa

queue *noun* qatâr

quick tez; chaṭak

quickly pë chaṭakëy

quiet *adjective* krâr

quietly pë karâra

quilt brëstën

quit khwëshay kawël

Quran Qur'ân

R

rabbit soy

rabies: to catch rabies dë lewani spi dâṛël

radar râdâr

radiator râdiyâtor

radio râdiyo; **radio broadcast** râdiyoyi khparawana; **radio program** râdiyoyi progrâm; **radio station** râdiyo steshan

radish mulëy

raid hamla; **air-raid** hawâyi hamla

railway relkarsha

railway paṭlëy

railway station rel steshan

rain bârân; **rain shower** jaṛëy; **rain storm** sheba; **It is raining.** Bârân ori.

rainbow shna zarghuna

raisins mamiz

ram mëzh

Ramadan Rozha

range qatârawël

rape *noun* jinsi teray

rape seed sharsham

rapid chaṭak

rapidly pë chaṭaka

rat mëzha

rate *speed* sur'at

ravine nâw

raw om

razor; razor blade pâki

reach *arrive at* rasedël

read lwastël

reading lwëst

ready tayâr; chamtu; **I am ready.** Chamtu yam.

real rishtiyânay

reality haqiqat

realize pohedël

reaping law

reason dalil; **reason for travel** dë safar dalil

rebel *noun* bâghi; yâghi

receipt rasid

receive akhistël

recent *adjective* wrustay

recently pë de wrustëyo ke

reception (desk/area) risipshan

recess *break* tafri(h)

recreation tafri(h)

recognize pezhandël

reconciled peëkhlâ
reconciliation pëkhlâyana; **national reconciliation** mili pëkhlâyana
record *noun* rikârd; *verb* sabtawël
red sur *m*; sra *f*
Red Crescent Sra Miyâsht
Red Cross Sur Salib
referee rifri; hakam
refinery châ<u>n</u>dzây
refrigerator yakhchâl; frij
refugee ka<u>d</u>wâl; mahâjir; **refugees** ka<u>d</u>wâl; mahâjirin; **refugee camp** dë ka<u>d</u>wâlo kamp
regime rizhim
region sima
regulation qâ'ida
reign *noun* dawra
reinforcements komaki-qowa
relationship a<u>r</u>ike; *blood* khpëlwi
relative khpël
relatives *blood* khpëlwân; khel; *by marriage* khi<u>sh</u>
relax hosâ kawël
release khwashay kawël
relief aid mrasta
religion din
religious: religious sect maz-hab
remain pâte kedël
remaining pâte
remember pë z<u>r</u>ë larël
rent *for oneself* kirâ kawël; *to someone* kirâ war-kawël
repair *noun* tarmim; *verb* tarmimawël
repeat takrârawël
replace dzây badlawël
reply *noun* dzawâb; *verb* dzawâb warkawël
report *noun: news* râpor; *verb* râpor warkawël
reporter râportar
represent astâzitob kawël

representation astâzitob
representative astâzay
republic jamhuriyat
research *noun* tse<u>r</u>ana; *verb* tse<u>r</u>ana kawël
reservation *ticket* rizarf
reserve *verb* rizarf kawël; **Can I reserve a place/seat?** Keday shi dzây/<u>t</u>iki<u>t</u> rizarf kram?
reside osedël
resist moqawâmat kawël
respect ihtirâm
rest *remainder* pâte; *relaxation* istirâhat; *verb* istirâhat kawël
restaurant rasturân
result natija
retreat *verb* shâtag kawël
to return *verb* râgardzedël; **return ticket** dwa tarafa <u>t</u>ikit
reverse *verb* chapa kedël
review *noun: newspaper* karakatana; tabsira
revolution inqilâb
rib cage gowgal
rib(s) po<u>sh</u>tëy
rice *raw* shole; *hulled* wriji; *cooked* palaw
rich dawlatman
ride *a horse* sparedël
riding swarlëy
rifle <u>t</u>opak
right *correct* sam; sahih; *side* <u>sh</u>ay; **legal right** haq; **to the right** <u>sh</u>i lâs ta; **right hand** <u>sh</u>ay lâs; **You are right.** Sam wâye.; **right now** hamdâ os
rights huquq; haquna; **civil rights** madani huquq/haquna; **human rights** bashari huquq/ haquna; **women's rights** dë <u>sh</u>ëdzo huquq/ haquna
right-wing <u>sh</u>ay arkh
ring *noun* gwëta; *verb: bell* zang wahël; *verb: phone someone* <u>t</u>ilifun kawël; **I want to ring Emma.** Emma ta <u>t</u>ilifun kawam.

riot

riot *noun* baghâwat
ripe pokh *m*; pakha *f*
rise *verb: prices etc.* khatël
risk *noun* khatar; *verb* khatar pë ghâra akhistël
river sin(d); **river bank** dë sin ghâra
road sarëk; lâr; **tarmac road** qir sarëk; **road map** dë sarëk naqsha; **road sign** dë sarëk nasha
roadblock sarëk band
roast wretawël
rob ghlâ kawël; **I've been robbed!** Lë mâ ghlâ wëshwa!
robber ghal
robbery ghlâ
rock kamër
rocket râket
rocket-launcher râket lënchar
roll up rgharawël
roof bâm
room kota
rooster bângi; chërg
root risha
rope paray
rosary tasbe
rose gulâb
rotten wrost *m*; wrasta *f*
rough *coarse* zizh
round gërday
roundabout *road* chawk
route lâr
row *argument* jagra
row *line* qatâr
royal saltanati; shâhi
rub mushël
rubber *eraser* pinsëlpâk
rubbish khazale
rubble dë khështe tota
rude be-adaba
rug *see* **carpet; prayer rug**
rugby rakbi
ruins kandwâle
rule *government* hukumat; *regulation* qânun
ruler *instrument* khatkash; *person* wâkman

run tashtedël; dzghâstël; **to run out (of)** swëdzedël
Russia Rusiya
Russia Rus
Russian Rusay *m*; Rusëy *f*; *language* Rusi
rust *noun* zang
rye jawdër

S

sack *noun* jwâl; *verb: dismiss* (lë kâra) istël
sacred mobârak; spetsalay
sad ghamjan
safe bekhatara; khwandi
safety amniyat; **safety pin** ping
saffron zafrân
saint spetsalay saray
salad salâta
salesman khartsawunkay
saleswoman khartsawunke
saliva lâre
salt mâlga
saltless bëlmënga
salty mâlgin
same hamaghë
sand shëga
sandals tsaplëy
sandwich sândiwich
sanitary towel qadifa
satchel bakër
satellite satilayt; **satellite phone** satilayt tilifun
satisfactory dë qinâ'at war
satisfied mor *m*; mara *f*
Saturday Shamba; Khâli
sauce sâs
saucer nâlbakëy
sausage sâsij
save *rescue* zhghorël; *money* bachatawël
saw *noun* ara
say wayël
scarf tsaponay
scatter shindël
school showundzay; maktab;

shelf

school pupil zdakawunkay; **school pupil** shâgird; **school teacher** ostâz; **school teacher** showunkay
science sâyns; ilëm
scientific ilmi
scientist sâynspoh; âlim
scissors qaychi
score *noun: sports* numra; *football* gol; *verb: sports* numra gatël; *football* gol kawël; **What's the score?** *in football* Tsu goluna shawi di?; **Who scored?** Châ gol wëwâhë?
scorpion larëm
Scot Skâtlanday *m*; Skâtlandëy *f*
Scotland Skâtland
Scottish Skâtlandi
screw *noun* pech
screwdriver pechtâw; pechkash
scythe lor
sea bahira; samandargay
search (for) palatël; **to search a person** tsuk pase ghushtël; **to search a house** kum kor pase ghushtël
season fasël
seat chawkëy; *in vehicle* sit; *political* plâzmena; pâytakht
seated nâst
second *adjective* doham; *noun* sânya
secondhand doham lâs
secret *adjective* pët; *noun* râz; **secrets** asrâr; **secret police** khufya polis
secretary munshi
section tsânga
security amniyat
see lidël
seedling niyâlgay
seeds dâne
seek latawël; palëtël
seem isedël; shkâredël
seize niwël
select gwara kawël
self pëkhpëla
sell khartsawël; plorël

send lezhël
senior *adjective* mëshër
sense *meaning* ma'nâ; mânâ
sentence *of words* jumla
separate *adjective* bël
separate *verb* belawël
separation biltun
September Siptambar
septic afuni
series: radio series lërëy; **TV series** siryâl
serious jidi; **The situation is serious.** Hâlat jidi di.
servant mazdur
service khidmat
session ghwanda
set ishodël
seven owë
seventeen owëlas
seventy awyâ
several gan
severe klak; **severe heat** sakhta garmi
sew gandël
sewing machine dë khayâti mâshin; dë kâlo gandalo mâshin
sex *gender* jins; *act* jinsi muqâribat
shade *noun* siyuray
shake shorawël
shall ba
shame *noun* sharam; *verb* sharmawël
shampoo shâmpu
shape bana
share *verb* barkha akhistël
sharp terë
sharpen terë kawël
shave khreyël
shaving cream dë zhire krim
shawl shâl
she hagha; dâ
shear skolël
sheep psë
sheepdog dë rame spay
sheet rojâyi; *of paper* pana
shelf almârëy

shell

shell *military* marmëy; *snail/sea* sipëy
shelter panâ dzây
shepherd shpun *m*
shepherdess shpana *f*
shine dzaledël
ship berëy
shirt kamis
shock *medical* shuk
shoe *noun* bot; *verb: a horse* nâlawël; shoes botuna
shoeshop dë botuno dukân
shoot wishtël; Don't shoot! Më wëla!
shop dukân
shopkeeper dukândâr
shopping sawdâ
shore sâhil
short land; tit
shortage kamwâlay
shoulder ozha; shoulder blade wëlay
shout *verb* chigha wahël
shovel belcha
show *noun: fair* nandârtun; trade show sawdâgari nandârtun; *verb* shodël
shower *bath* shâwar; *of rain* jarëy
shrapnel dë bam pârcha
shut pore kawël
sick narogh; I am sick. Nârogh yam.
sickle lor
side *direction* khwâ; tsang; *of body* arkh; to the side tsang ta
sidestreet kutsa
siege *blockade* kalâband
sight *eyesight* nazar
sign *noun* nasha; *verb* lâslik kawël
signature lâslik
sign language dë ishâro zhaba
silence chuptiyâ
silencer *of car* salânsar
silent chup
silk wreshëm; silk worms dë wreshëmo chimjay

silken wreshmin
silly bi'aqla
silver spin zar
similar warta
simple sâda
since wrusta lë; since Monday le Dushambe tsakha
sing sandëra wayal
single yaw; *not married* lawand; single room yaw kasiza kota
sink *noun* sink
sink *noun* dishway; *verb* dubedël
sister khor; sisters khwaynde
sister-in-law *brother's wife* wrendâr; *husband's brother's wife* dë lewar shëdza; yor; *husband's sister* ndror; *wife's sister* shina
sit kenâstël
sitting nâsta
situated prot *m*; prata *f*
situation mawqiyat
six shpazh
sixteen shpârës
sixth shpazham
sixty shpetë
size mecha
ski *verb* ski kawël
skiing dë ski loba
skill mahârat
skilled takra
skin postëkay
skull koprëy
sky âsmân
slate slet
slaughter *an animal* halâlawël
slave mryay
sleep *verb* widedël; to go to sleep widë kedël
sleeping bag bistar; bistira
sleeping pill(s) dë khob golëy
sleepy khobawalay
sleet gëre gëray
sleeve lastonay
slip shwayedël
slippery shwaya
slope mëkh shkata

slow wro; laṭ; sawka
slowly! wro wro!
small lëzh
smell *noun* buy
smoke *noun* lugay; *verb* tsikawël
smoker tsikawunkay
smoking sigreṭ tsikawël
smooth shwaya
smuggler qâchâqwṟunkay
snack spëk khwâṟë
snail halzun
snake mâr
snakebite mâr chichël
sneeze *noun* pranjay; *verb* pranjedël
snore khëredël
snow wâwra; **snow flakes** dë wâwre potsënay; **It is snowing.** Wâwrâ ori.
so no; **so much/many** ḏer
soap sâbun
soccer fuṭbâl; **soccer match** dë fuṭbâl maych
social ṭolaniz
society ṭolana
socks jurâbe
soft narm; post *m*; pasta *f*
soil khâwra; zmëka
soldier askar
sole talay
solve hal kawël
some dzini
somebody yawtsok
somehow yaw ḏawl
someone yawtsok
something yaw shay
sometimes këla këla
somewhere kum cheri
son zoy; *of co-wife* bënzay; *of wife's first husband* parkaṯay; **sons** zâmën;
son-in-law zum
song sandara; badala; **love song** ghazël(a)
soon zhër
sore ṯap; khwëẕh; **sore throat** dë stuni khwëẕh

sorrow khwâshini
sorry! bakhshëna!
sort *noun* râz
soul ruh
sound zhagh; ghaẕh
soup shorwâ
sour triw
source sarchina
south *noun* janub
south(ern) *adjective* janubi
sow karël
space fazâ
spade bel
span lwesht
Spaniard Haspâniyâyay *m*; Haspâniyâyëy *f*
Spanish *language* Haspânawi; *thing* Haspâniyâyi
spanner *wrench* achâr; turshi
spare izâfi; shṭapni; **spare tire** shṭapni ṭâyr
sparrow chinchëna
sparrowhawk shâhen
speak ghaẕhedël; **Do you speak English?** Angrezi wayalay she/shëy?; **I speak English.** Zë Angrezi wâyam.
speaker ghaẕhedunkay; *on radio, etc.* wayând; *of parliament* dë wulisi jirge rayis
specialist mutakhasis
spectacles aynaki
speed sur'at
spell: How do you spell that? Dâ tsënga likëy?
spend *money* lagawël; **to spend time** wakht terawël
spice mësâla
spicy *hot* masâla-dâr
spider ghëna
spill toyedël
spin churledël
spinach sâg; pâlëk
spinal column dë mlâ tir
spine dë mlâ tir
spit *verb* tukël
splint *medical* dë mât haḏuki daṟa

split

split *verb* darz kawël
spoil zâya kawël
sponge spanj
spoon kâchugha; chimcha
sports sport; warzish
sportsman warzishkâr
spread khparedël
spring *metal* spring; fanar; *of water* china; *season* psarlay
sprout *noun* niyâl
spy jâsus; mokhbir
square muraba; **town square** (asli) chawk
squeeze nashtedzël
squirrel muzhakprâng
stadium stëdyum; lobghâlay
staff parsunal; mâmurin
stag ghartsë
stage *theater* sahna; stej; nandâridz
stairs zina
stale bâsi
stallion mindë âs
stamp *postal* posti tikit; *official* muhr; **to stamp a document** sanad muhrawël
stand *verb* daredël
star storay; **stars** sotri
start *verb* paylawël
state *noun: condition* hâlat; *federal* ayâlat; *nation* dawlat; *verb* bayânawël
station steshan
stationer's shop dë qirtâsiye dukân
stationery qirtâsiya
statue mujasima
stay pâte kedël
steak botëy
steal ghlâ kawël
steam *food* damawël
steel polâd
steering wheel shtring
stem dandar
stepbrother mayrezay
stepfather nâsaka plâr
stepfather plëndër
stepmother mayra; nâ saka mor

sterling starling pawnd
stethoscope stitiskop
stick *noun* dara; **walking stick** amsâ; *verb* srishawël
still *yet* lâ
sting *verb* nesh wahël
stink *verb* buy kawël
stir shorawël
store *shop* dukân
stitch *in one's side* bresh
stitches *surgical* kokuna
stomach nas
stomachache nas dard
stone tizha; dabara
stool chawkëy
stop darawël; **stop!** dresh!; **don't stop!** më darezha!
store *shop* dokân; *for storage* gudâm
storm tufân; **rainstorm** sheba; **thunderstorm** jâkër
story *tale* kisa; *news* râportâzh; *floor* pur; manzël
stove ishtop; **heating stove** bukhârëy
straight nëgh
straightness nëghwâlay
strange nâ-âshnâ
stranger praday; nâ-pezhanduy
straw bus; prora
strawberry tutëy
stream lashtay; wiyâla; **mountain stream** khwër
street kutsa
strength sek(a)
stretcher *hospital* tazkira
strike *noun: from work* kârbandiz; *verb: hit* wahël; *from work* kârbandiz kawël
string paray
strong piyâwaray
structure jorësht
struggle mubâriza
stuck: **Our car is stuck.** Motar mu nshatay day.
student *university* mohasil
study *noun* mutâli'a; *verb* tahsil kawël; *academic* zdakra kawël

subject mawzo; *academic* mazmun

submachine gun mâshindâr

submit wrândi kawël

subtract manfi kawël

subtraction manfi

suburb dë shâr lëman

success baray; baryâlitob

such haghasi

suck rawdël

suddenly nâtsâpa

sufficient kâfi

sugar bura; **sugar bowl** qandânëy

suit *of Afghan clothes* jora; *of western clothes* dirishi

suitable war

suitcase dë kâlo baks

sultan sultân

sum mablagh

summer oray; dobay

summit tsuka

sun lmar

sunblock dë lmar krim

sunburn lmarsedzalay

Sunday Yakshamba

sunglasses (dë lmar) aynaki

sunny: It is sunny. Lmar day.

sunrise lmar tsrak

sunset lmar lwedë

supermarket soparmârket

supper dë mâshâm dodëy

supplies sâzusâmân

supply *verb* barâbarawël

sure *adjective* dâda; *adverb* pë dâd

surgeon jarâh

surgery *subject* jarâhi; *operation* amaliyat

surname *family name* dë koranëy num

surprised hayrân

surprising: to be surprising hayrânedâl

surrender taslimedël

surround mohâsera kawël

survey *noun* sarwe; *verb* sarwe kawël

surveyor sarwe kawunkay

suspicion bad gumân; shak

swallow *bird* totakëy; *verb* terawël

swamp jaba

swear *to curse* kandzël; **to swear an oath** lora kawël

sweat *noun* khwala

sweater banyân

sweep jâru kawël

sweeper jârukash

sweet *adjective* khozh; *noun* shirini; khwâzhë

swell parsedël

swim lâmbël

swimming lâmbo; **swimming pool** hawz

swimsuit dë lâmbo kâli

switch *noun: electric* swich; *verb* **to switch off** gul kawël; **to switch on** lagawël

syce mehtar

symbol sambol

symptom *medical* dë nâroghëy nasha

synagogue kanisa

syntax nahw

syringe pichkâri

syrup sharbat

system sistëm

T

table mez

tablecloth dëstarkhân

tablet golëy

tactic tâktik; **tactics** tâktikuna

tailor khayât; tailor gandunkay

take akhistël; **to take away** wrël; **to take off** *something* porta kawël; **to take out** istël; **to take shelter** panâ akhistël; **What time does the plane take off?** Alwëtaka tsë wakht rawânezhi?

talk *verb* khabëre kawël

tall

tall jëg
tame koranay
tank *military/petrol* ţânk
tanker ţânkar
tap *faucet* chushkay
tape ţep; fita; *cassette* kasit; **tape recorder** teprikârder
tarmac road qir sarёk
taste *noun* tsaka; *maza; verb* tsakёl
tasteless bekhwanda
tasty mazadâr; khwёndawёr
tax *noun* mâlya; *verb* mâlya akhistёl
tax-free be-mâlye; be-ţiksa
taxi ţaksi
tea chây; **black tea** tor chây; **green tea** shin chây; **tea with milk** shudo chây; **tea house** samâwâr
teach dars warkawёl
teacher mâlim; *primary school* showunkay
team ţim
teapot châynak(a)
tear *noun* oshka
tear *verb* tsirёl
teaspoon châykhori kâchugha
technical takhniki
technique takhnik
teenager *boy* zalmay; *girl* peghla
teeth ghâshuna
telecommunications mukhâbirât
telegram ţiligrâm
telephone *noun* ţilifun; **telephone operator** âpreţar; *verb* ţilifun kawёl
telescope ţiliskop
television teliwizun
telex ţiliks
tell wayёl
temperature dё tawdoshi daraja; **The temperature in summer is high.** Pё dobi dё tawdoshi daraja lwara wi.; **The temperature in winter is low.** Pё zhёmi dё tawdoshi

daraja ţita wi.; **I have a temperature.** Taba laram.
temple *religious* gurdwâra
ten las
tenant kirâya warkawunkay
tend *to the sick* pâm kawёl
tender tankay
tennis tinis
tent khayma; tâmbo
tenth lasam
termite wena
terrible haybatnâk
territory khâwra; tâtubay
test *noun* azmoyana; *academic* imtihân; **blood test** dё wine ţist; *verb* ţistawёl; *academic* imtihân akhistёl
testify shâhidi warkawёl
text matan
than tar; **This book is better than that one.** Dâ kitâb tar hagha shё day.
thank *verb* manana kawёl; **thank you!** manana!; **thanks** manane
that hâgha; *conjunction* che
theater tiyâtёr; nandâre; nandârdzay
theft ghlâ
their; theirs dё hagho
them hagho
themselves duy pakhpёla
then biyâ; wrusta; no
theoretical nazari
theory tiyori
there halta; **there is/are ...** shta
therefore dё de lёpâra
thermometer tarmâmetar
these; them; they duy
thick *wide* pand; **thick cloth** pand ţukёr; **thick forest** gan dzangal; **thick soup** ţinga shorwâ
thief ghal; **thieves** ghlё
thigh patun
thimble gotma
thin naray
thing shay

think fikir kawël; **I think that...** Fikir kawam che...

thinness ḏangërwâlay

third dreyam

thirst tënda

thirsty tëẕhay; **I'm thirsty.** Tëẕhay yam.

thirteen dyârlas

thirty dersh

this dâ; dagha; **this (very)** hamdagha; **this afternoon** nën gharma; **this morning** nën sahâr; **this much** dughumra; **this much** dumra; **this week** dâ onëy

thorax taṯar

thorn aghzay

those hagha

thought fikir

thoughtless befikra

thousand zër

thread târ

three dre

throat stunay

thrombosis dë winë ghuṯa kedâ

throne takht

through lë mandza; *by means of* dë ... pë zeri'a

throw ghurdzawël; **to throw out** sharël

thumb ghaṯa gwëta

thunder tâlanda

thunderstorm jëkër

Thursday panj shamba

tibia panḏëy

ticket ṯikiṯ; **ticket office** dë ṯikiṯ khartsawëlo daftar

tie *necktie* nektây; *verb* taṟël

tight klak

tights chasp kâli

time wakht; zamâna; *an instance* dzal; **at the same time** pë hamdagha wakht; **for a long time** dë ẕer wakht lëpâra; **on time** pë ṯik wakht; **I don't have time.** Wakht në larëm. **What time is it?** Tso baje di?;

Has the bus arrived on time? Bas pëkhpël wakht râghalay?

timetable mahâlwesh; **travel timetable** dë safar mahâlwesh

tire *noun* ṯayr; *verb* stëṟay kedël

tired stëṟay; **to get tired** stëṟay kedël

tissues kâghazi dusmâl

to të; tër; **I gave it to her.** Haghe të me warkëṟ.; **This is superior to that.** Dâ tër haghe shë day.

toast *bread* ṯosṯ shawe doḏëy

tobacco tambâku

today nën

toe dë pshe gwëta

together sara; yaw dzây

toilet(s) kenârâb; tashnâb; **toilet paper** dë tashnâb kâghaz

tomato rumi; ṯamâṯër *(Pakistan)*

tomb *of saint* zyârat

tomorrow sabâ; **the day after tomorrow** bël sabâ

tonga *carriage* bagëy; gâḏëy; **tonga driver** gâḏiwân

ton; tonne ṯan

tongue zhaba

tonight nën shpa

too *also* ham; *very* ziyât; **too little** der lëẕh; **too many** khwarâ ḏer; **too much** ḏer ziyât

tools wasâyl; awzâr

tooth ghâsh; **teeth** ghâshuna

toothache ghâsh dard

toothbrush dë ghâsho bors

toothpaste dë ghâsho krim

toothpick ghâsh khalay

top pâs

torrent sel

torture *noun* shikanja; *verb* shikanja kawël

tough *meat* maṯukor; **This meat is tough.** Ghwâsha matakora shawe da.

tourism torizëm; gardzandoy

tourist torist; **tourists** toristân; **tourist office** dë gardzandoy daftar

tow: tow rope paray; **Can you tow us?** Muzh kâzhalay she?

towel tolya

tower brëj

town shâr; **town center** dë shâr markaz; **town hall** dë shâr nandâre; **town square** dë shâr chawk

tracer bullet rasâma marmëy

trachea stunay

track tsrak

tractor taraktur

trade union sawdâgari itihâdiya; tijâri itihâdiya

trader sawdâgër; tâjër

tradition dod

traditional dodiz

traffic *noun* tarâfik; **traffic lights** tarâfiki ishâra; **traffic police** tarâfik

train *noun* orgâday; **train station** steshan

tranquilizer musakina

transfer flights parwaz badlawël

transformer transfârmar

transfusion: blood transfusion dë wine badlun

translate zhbârël

translation zhbâra

translator zhbârunkay

transmit astawël

transmitter trânsmetar

transport *noun* trânsport; *verb* wrël

trap *noun* luma; dâm

trash khazëli

trauma jismi ya zihni zarba

travel *noun* safar; *verb* safar kawël; **travel agency** trewal ijinsëy; tikit plorandzây

traveler mosâfër; **travelers** mosâferin

traveler's checks trewal chikuna; safari chikuna

tray patnus

treacherous darghal

treasury *ministry* dë mâlye wizârat

treaty tarun

tree wëna; **trees** wëne

trench kanda

trial *legal* muhâkima; *test* azmisht

troops dzwâkuna

trouble *inconvenience* taklif; *problems* nâkarâri; **What's the trouble?** Mushkil tsë day?

trousers patlun

truce orband

truck lârëy

true sam

trunk *box* sandoq; *of car* tolbaks; *of tree* sëta

truth haqiqat

try hatsa kawël

tube tyup

tuberculosis naray randz; sil

Tuesday Seshamba; Nahe

tunnel tunal; surang *(Pakistan)*

turban patkay

Turk Turk

turkey filmorgh; khartumay

turn *noun* wâr; *verb* awështël; **turn left!** kin lor ta wâwra!; **turn right!** shi lor ta wâwra!

turnip tepër

twelve do-lës

twenty shël

twice dwa chanda

twins ghbarg

twist nëghështël

twisted nëghështalay

two dwa

type *noun* dawl; *verb* tâypawël

typewriter tâyprâytar

tyre *noun* tayr

U

ulcer tap; **stomach ulcer** dë me'de zakham

umbilical cord num

umbrella chatrëy
unbeliever kâfir
uncle *father's brother* kâkâ; trë; *mother's brother* mâmâ
uncomfortable nârâm
uncooked om
under *adverb* lânde; *preposition* tër ... lânde; **under the table** tër mez lânde
underground *adjective/adverb* tër mdzëke lânde; *subway* mitro
understand pohedël; **Do you understand?** Pohezhe?; **I understand.** Pohezham.; **I don't understand.** Na pohezham.
underwear siltirâj
undo prânistël
undress: to get undressed jâme istël
unemployed bekâr(a)
unemployment bekâri
unexploded bomb nâchâw-dalay bam
unfortunate badmërgh
unfortunately lë bada mërgha
unfriendly badmëkhey
unhappy nâkhwash
uniform yunifârm
uninformed be-khabëra
union; trade union itihâdiya
unique besâray
unit *military* juz-o-tâm; wâhid
United Nations Malgari Milatuna
United States of America dë Amrikâ Mutahida Ayâlatuna
university pohantun
unknown nâpezhanduy
unless kë cheri
unsuccessful nimakhwâ
until tër; tër de che
unwise nâpoh
up pâs
upright negh
Urdu Urdu; **Do you speak Urdu?** Pë Urdu pohezhe?

urgent zaruri
urine mityâze
us muzh; munzh
U.S.A. dë Amrikâ Mutahida Ayâlatuna
use *noun* istimâl; *verb* istimâlawël
useful gatawër
usefulness gatawërtiyâ
usual mâmuli
usually mâmulan
uterus rahim
utility gatawërtub

V

vacation rukhsati
vaccinate wâksin kawël; **I have been vaccinated.** Wâksin shaway yam.
vaccination wâksinâsyun
valley dara
value *verb* arzësht larël
veal dë skhundër ghwasha
vegetable shop dë sabzo dukân
vegetables *fresh* sabzi; *ready to eat* tarkâri
vegetarian sabzi-khor(a); **I am a vegetarian.** Sabzi-khora yam.
veil *woman's* châdari; borqa; *and see* **headscarf**
vein rag
venereal disease tanâsuli nâroghëy
veranda baranda
verb fil; fi'l
vertebra mërëy
very der
veto *noun* weto; *verb* weto kawël
vice-president *of country* mrastiyâl wëlësmëshër; dë jumhur rayis mrastiyâl
victim qurbâni; **victims** qurbâniyân; **the victims of the earthquake** dë zilzile qurbâniyân

victory soba
video cassette wedyu kasiṯ
video player wedyu; V.C.R. (Pakistan)
view *noun* nazarya
village këlay; **village elder** spinẕhiray; mëshër
villager këliwâl; kaliwâl
vine kwar; ṯâk
vinegar sirka
violence tashadud; ṯâw trikhwâlay
viper mëngaray
virus wirus
visa wiza
visit *verb* katana kawël
visitor mulâqât kawunkay
vitamins wiṯâmin
voice zhagh; ghaẕh
volume *size* wâlyum; *book* ṯuk
vomit kânge kawël; **I have been vomiting.** Kânge kawëm.
vote *noun* râya; wuṯ (Pakistan); *verb* râya warkawël; **to cast a vote** râya achawël
voter râywërkawunkay
vulture ṯapus

W

wage war jangawël
waist mlâ
waistband baḏa
waistcoat *vest* wâskaṯ; *jacket* sadrëy
wait sabër kawël; **to wait for** mâtaledël; **wait a moment!** lëẕh sabër wëkṟa!
waiter; waitress piyâda
waiting intizâr
to wake up wiẕhawël; **Please wake me up at ...** Lutfan mâ pë ... wiẕh kṟa.
walk gërzedël
walking stick amsâ
wall dewâl
wallet baṯwa
want ghuẕhtël; **What do you want?** Tsë ghwâṟe?; **I want ...** ... ghwâṟëm.; **I don't want ...** ... në ghwâṟëm.
war jang
warm garam
warmonger jang achawunkay
wash mindzël
washbowl chilëmchi
washed prewlalay
washing powder dë kâlo mindzalo poḏar
wasp ghumbasa
watch *clock* sâ'at; **to watch** tsârël
water obë; **Is there drinking water?** Halta dë tsëẕhlo obë shta?
water bottle dë obo botal
waterfall awshâr; jarobay
watermelon hindwâna
watermill zhranda
way lâr
way *manner* ḏawl; **way of life** dë zhwand tariqa
we muẕh; munẕh
weak kamzoray
weapon wasla
wear aghustël
weasel nolay
weather hawâ
weave obdël
wedding wâdë
Wednesday Chârshamba; Shuro
week hafta; onëy
weekend dë onëy pây
weekly haftawâr; oniz
weep zhaṟël
weight wazën
welcome! harkala râshëy!
well *adjective/adverb* shë; *noun: of water* tsâ(h)
well-known nâmtu
west *noun* lwedidz; gharb
west(ern) lwedidz
wet lund *m*; landa *f*
what? tsë (shay)?; **what's that?** dâ tsë shay day?; **what kind?** tsaranga?

whatever har tsë che; **Take whatever you want.** Har tsë che ghwâ<u>r</u>e wâyekhla.

wheat ghanëm; **wheat bin** kandu

wheel wil

wheelchair tsarkh chawkëy

when tsë wakht; **when?** kala?

where cheri; **where is?** cheri day?; **where are?** cheri di?; **where from?** dë kum dzây?

whether âyâ

which kum; **which (one)?** kum yaw?

while pë trëts ke

whistle *noun* shpelkay

white spin

whitish spinchak

who tsok (che); **who?** châ

whole <u>t</u>ol

why wëli; **why?** pë tsë waja?

wide plën

widow kwën<u>d</u>a

widower kwën<u>d</u>

wife <u>sh</u>ëdza

wild *animal* wahshi

wild goose zâna

will *shall* ba

win ga<u>t</u>ël; **Who won?** Châ wëgo<u>t</u>?

wind *noun* bâd

to wind *verb* pechël; **to wind thread** târ pechël

window orsëy; kë<u>r</u>këy

window pane shisha

windpipe stunay

windshield; windscreen shishapâk

windy bâdi

wine sharâb

winter zhëmay

wire târ; sim

wisdom poha; **wisdom tooth** dë aqël ghâ<u>sh</u>

wise poh

to wish *verb* hila larël

with ... sara; **I went with him.** Zë lë haghe sara lâ<u>r</u>am.; **They fought with courage.** Duy

pë me<u>r</u>âna wëjangedël.

without be-; **without work** bekâra

witness shâhid

wolf lewë

woman <u>sh</u>ëdza

womb rahim

women <u>sh</u>ëdze

wood *substance* largay; *forest* dzangal

wool wa<u>r</u>ëy

woolen wa<u>r</u>in

word lughat

work *noun* kâr; *verb* kâr kawël; **I work in a bank.** Pë bânk ke kâr kawëm.; **The phone doesn't work.** <u>T</u>ilifun kâr në kawi.

worker kârgar

world na<u>r</u>ëy

worms chinji

worried preshâna; **to be worried** preshâna kedël

worse badtar; **I feel worse.** Lâ badwâlay ihsâsawëm.

worth: to be worth arzë<u>sh</u>t larël

wound *noun* <u>t</u>ap; zakham; *verb* zakhmi kawël

wrap po<u>sh</u>ël

wrench *tool* rinch

wrestling ghe<u>zh</u>

wrist ma<u>r</u>wënd

wristwatch sâ'at

to write likël

writer likwâl

writing likana

wrong ghalat

X

X-rays iksre

Y

yard *courtyard* hawelëy; *garden* bâgh; *distance* gaz

year kâl; **this year** sa<u>zh</u>kâl

yearly kalanay

yellow zhe<u>r</u>

yes ho; bale

yesterday parun; **the day before yesterday** âbël parun

yesterday's parunay

yet lâ

yogurt maste; mâstë

you

you *singular* tâ; të; *plural* tâso; tâsi

young dzwân; **young person** dzwân; **young girl** peghla; **youngest child** këshër

your; yours *singular* stâ; *plural* stâso; stâsi

yourself të pakhpëla

yourselves tâso pakhpëla

Z

zero sifar

zipper zib; zandzir

zoo zhoba<u>n</u>

PASHTO
Phrasebook

1. ETIQUETTE

Hello ...

Salâm! ("peace!") is the Pashto way of saying "hello!", to which the repsonse is simply **salâm!** This greeting, which means "peace on you", is also used for the other greetings of the day, corresponding to English "good morning," "good afternoon," "good evening," and "good night." An extension of this becomes the more traditional Muslim greeting **Assalâmu alaykom!** ("peace on you!") to which the formal response is **alaykom assalâm** ("[and] on you peace!"). Some other common greetings used during the day are given below.

Hello! *to a man*	**Staray më she!**
Hello! *to a woman*	**Starëy më she!**
Hello! *to a group*	**Stari më shëy!**
Response to a man:	**Salâmat osëy!**
Response to a woman:	**Salâmata ose!**
Response to a group:	**Salâmat osëy!**
See you tomorrow!	**Tar sabâ khudây pë âmân!**
Response:	**Pë mëkha di sha!**
	or **Khudây pë âmân!**
Good bye!	**Khudây pë âmân!**
Response:	**Khudây pë âmân!**
Welcome!	**Pë khayr râghle!**
Response:	**Khayr ose!**
Please eat!/Please sit down!	**Mehrebani wakrëy!**
Congratulations!	**Mobârak sha!**
Excuse me!	**Wabakhsha!**
Sorry!	**Bakhshana ghwâram!**
yes	**ho**
no	**na; ya**
please	**lutfan**
thank you	**manana; tashakor**

2. QUICK REFERENCE

I	**zë**
you *singular*	**të**
you *formal/plural*	**tâso; tâsi**
he; it *masculine*	**day**
she; it *feminine*	**dâ**
he/she/it	**hâgha**
we	**munzh; muzh**
they	**haghoy; duy/doy**

this	**dâ; dagha**
that	**hagha**
these	**dagha**
those	**hagha**
here	**dalta**
there	**halta**

where?	**cheri?; cherta?**
who?	**tsuk?; châ?**
what?	**tsë?; tsë shay?**
when?	**kala?**
which?	**kum?**
how?	**tsanga?; tsaranga?**
why?	**wali?**
how much?	**tsumra?**
how many?	**tsu?**

what's that?	**dâ tsë shay day?**
is/are there . . . ?	**. . . halta shta?**
where is . . . ?	**. . . cheri day?**
where are . . . ?	**. . . cheri di?**
here is . . .	**. . . dalta day**
here are . . .	**. . . dalta di**

what must I do?	**bâyad tsë wakram?**
what do you want?	**tsë ghwâre?**
very	**dër; der**
and	**aw**
or	**yâ**
but	**kho**
I like . . .	**. . . zmâ khwashezhi.**
I don't like . . .	**. . . zmâ na khwashezhi.**
I want . . . *something*	**. . . ghwâram.**
I want to . . .	**Ghwâram che . . .**
I don't want . . . *something*	**. . . në ghwâram.**
I don't want to . . .	**Në ghwâram che . . .**
I know.	**Pohezham.**
I don't know.	**Në pohezham.**
Do you understand?	**(Ta) pohezhe?**
I understand.	**(Zë) pohezham.**
I don't understand.	**Në pohezham.**
Sorry!	**Wëbakhsha!**
My condolences. *if someone dies*	**Dera bakhshana ghwâram.**
I am grateful.	**Khwshâla yam.**
It's important.	**Dâ muhim day.**
It doesn't matter.	**Muhima në da.**
You're welcome!	**Hila kawam!**
No problem!	**Parwâ në lari!**
more or less	**der yâ lëzh**
Is everything OK?	**Har shay sam barâbar di?**
Danger!	**Khatar!**

Could you repeat that?	**Keday shi yaw wâr biyâ wëwâyâst?**
How do you spell that?	**Tsanga likël ke<u>zh</u>i?**

I am . . .	**. . . yam.**
hot	**tod**
right	**sam**
sleepy	**khubawalay**
hungry	**wa<u>zh</u>ay**
thirsty	**ta<u>zh</u>ay**
angry	**ghusa**
happy	**khwa<u>sh</u>**
sad	**khapa**
tired	**sta<u>ra</u>y**
well	**<u>sh</u>ë**
I am cold.	**Yakh me ke<u>zh</u>i.**

—Colors

black	**tor**
blue	**shin; âbi**
sky blue	**âsmâni**
brown	**naswâri**
khaki; grey	**kh<u>ë</u>r**
green	**zarghun**
pink	**golâbi**
red	**sur**
white	**spin**
yellow	**ze<u>r</u>**

3. INTRODUCTIONS

What is your name?	**Stâ num tsë day?** *or* **Num di tsë day?**
My name is . . .	**Zmâ num . . . day.**
May I introduce you to . . .	**Keday shi tâso . . . ta ma'rifi kram.**
This is my . . .	**Dâ zmâ . . . day.**
friend	**malgaray** *m*/**malgare** *f*
companion	**andiwâl** *m*/**andiwala** *f*
colleague	**hamkâr** *m*/**hamkâra** *f*
relative	**khpël** *m*/**khpëla** *f*

> **TITLES** — "Mr." is **Shâghëlëy** (also **Sâhib**) and "Mrs." is **Merman**, both in much the same way as in English. Especially when you don't know someone's name, you can also use **Mohtaram** "Sir" and **Mohtarama** "Madame". Use **Peghla** for "Miss". You can use **Ostâz** for a professor or teacher.

—Nationality

Aghanistan	**Afghânistân**
—Afghan	**Afghân** *m*/**Afghâna** *f*
Pakistan	**Pâkistân**
—Pakistani	**Pâkistânay** *m*/**Pâkistânëy** *f*
Where are you from?	**Dë kum dzây yâst?**
I am from . . .	**Zë dë . . . yam.**
America	**Amrikâ**
Australia	**Âstrâliyâ**
Britain	**Inglistân; Bartâniyâ**
Canada	**Kânâdâ**
China	**Chin**
England	**Inglistân**
Europe	**Urupâ**
Germany	**Jarmani; Almân**
India	**Hindustân; Hind**
Iran	**Irân**
Ireland	**Âyrland**

Japan	**Jâpân**
the Netherlands	**Hâlând**
New Zealand	**Naway Zilând;**
	Niw Zilând
Northern Ireland	**Shamâli Âyrlând**
Russia	**Rusiya**
Scotland	**Skâtlând**
the USA	**dë Amrikâ Mutahida**
	Ayâlatuna
Wales	**Wilz**

I am . . .	**Zë . . . yam.**
American	**Amrikâyi** *m*/**Amrikâyëy** *f*
Australian	**Âstrâliyâyi/**
	Âstrâliyâyëy
British	**Angrez/Angreza;**
	Inglisay/Inglisëy
Canadian	**Kânâdâyi/Kânâdâyëy**
Chinese	**Chinâyi/Chinâyëy**
Dutch	**Hâlânday/Hâlândëy**
English	**Angrez/Angreza;**
	Inglisay/Inglisëy
German	**Jarmanay/Jarmanëy**
Indian	**Hinday/Hindëy**
Iranian	**Irânay/Irânëy**
Irish	**Âyrlanday/Âyrlandëy**
Israeli	**Isrâyilay/Isrâyilëy**
Japanese	**Jâpânay/Jâpânëy**
Russian	**Rusay/Rusëy**
Scottish	**Skâtlanday/Skâtlandëy**
Welsh	**Wilzay/Wilzëy**

| Where were you born? | **Cheri zezhedalay ye?** |
| I was born in . . . | **Pë ... ke zezhedalay yam.** |

—Regional nationalities

| Bangladesh | **Bangladesh** |
| —Bangladeshi | **—Bangâlay** *m*/**Bangâlëy** *f* |

Kirghizstan	**Qirghizistân**
—Kirghiz	**—Qirghiz(ay)** *m*/**Qirghiza** *f*
Nepal	**Nipâl**
—Nepali	**—Nipâlay** *m*/**Nipâlëy** *f*
Tajikistan	**Tâjikistân**
—Tajik	**—Tâjik** *m*/**Tâjika** *f*
Tibet	**Tibit**
—Tibetan	**—Tibitay** *m*/**Tibitëy** *f*
Turkmenistan	**Torkmanistân**
—Turkmen	**— Torkman** *m*/**Torkmana** *f*
Uzbekistan	**Ozbakistân**
—Uzbek	**—Ozbak** *m*/**Ozbaka** *f*

—Occupations

What do you do?	**Tâso tsë kâr kawëy?**
I am a/an . . .	**Zë . . . yam.**
accountant	**mahâsib**
administrator	**mâmur**
agronomist	**karwandgar**
aid worker	**mrastanduy**
architect	**me'mâr**
artist	**hunarmën**
blacksmith	**pësh; âyngër**
business person	**sawdâgër; tâjir**
carpenter	**najâr; tarkân**
consultant	**mushâwir**
dentist	**dë ghâsh dâktar**
diplomat	**diplumât**
doctor	**dâktar** *m*/**dâktara** *f*
economist	**iqtisâdpoh**
engineer	**injinyar**
farmer	**karwandgar; bazgër**
film-maker	**film jorawunkay**
joiner	**najâr; tarkân**
journalist	**zhornâlist**
judge	**qâzi**
lawyer	**wakil; huquqpoh**

mechanic	**mistari; mekhânik**
negotiator	**marakachi**
nurse	**narsa; nars;**
	randzurpâla
observer	**tsârunkay**
officer worker	**mâmur; kârmand**
pilot	**pelot**
political scientist	**siyâsatpoh**
scientist	**sâynspoh**
secretary	**mrastiyâl**
soldier	**askar**
student *school*	**zdakawunkay**
university	**muhasil**
surgeon	**jarâh**
tailor	**khayât**
teacher	**mo'alem; showunkay**
specialist	**mutakhasis**
tourist	**turist**
trader	**sawdâgёr; tâjёr**
writer	**likwâl**

I work in . . .	**Pё ... ke kâr kawёm.**
an aid agency	**khayriya mwasisa**
the hotel industry	**hotal**
industry	**sanat**
I.T.	**itlâti tiknâluzhi**
the media	**khabёri rasandoye**
telecommunications	**mukhâbirât(o)**
the tourist industry	**gardzandoy; torizёm**

—Age

How old are you?	**Tsu kalan yâst?**
I am . . . years old.	**Zё . . . kalёn yam.**

—Family

Are you married? *male*	**Wâdё mu karay day?**
female	**Wâdё shawe yâst?**

I am not married. *male*	**Mâ wâdë në day karay.**
female	**Wâdë shawe në yam.**
I am married. *male*	**Mâ wâdë karay.**
female	**Wâdë shawe yam.**
I am divorced. *female**	**Talâqa shawe yam.**
I am a widow.**	**Kwënda yam.**
Do you have a boyfriend?	**Andiwâl lare/larëy?*****
Do you have a girlfriend?	**Andiwâla lare/larëy?**
What is his/her name?	**Tsë numezhi?**
How many children do you have?	**Tsumra mâshumân lare/larëy?**
I don't have any children.	**Hita mâsum nê laram.**
I have a daughter.	**Yawa lur laram.**
I have a son.	**Yaw zuy laram.**
How many brothers do you have?	**Tsu wruna lare/ larëy?**
How many sisters do you have?	**Tsu khwandi lare/ larëy?**
How many brothers and sisters do you have?	**Tsu wruna aw khwandi lare/larëy?**

> **FAMILY TERMS** — Pashtoons have a highly developed sense of family ties and there is therefore a wide range of special words for relatives — distant as well as close. Only immediate family are outlined below. For details of aunts, cousins and in-laws, look up the relevant English term in the dictionary section of this book.

father	**plâr**
mother	**mor**
parents	**morplâr**
grandfather	**nikë**
grandmother	**nyâ; anâ**
granddaughter	**lmasëy**
grandson	**lmasay**
brother	**wror**

* A man would say **"Shëdza me talâqa karay da"** for "I am divorced", although you would not hear it said.
** "I am a widower" is **"Kwënd yam"**, although, again, men would tend not say this.
*** **Lare** is "you have" informal; **larëy** is "you have" formal/plural.

sister	**khor**
daughter	**lur**
son	**zoy**
twins	**ghbarg**
husband	**merẹ; khâwënd**
wife	**mândina; mayna**
co-wife	**bën**
family	**koranëy**
man	**sa̱ray**
woman	**sh̲ëdza**
boy	**halëk**
girl	**jinëy; njëlëy**
baby boy	**(dë ghezhi) mâshum**
baby girl	**(dë ghezhl) mâshuma**
child	**bachay; kamkay**
children	**kamkiyân**
teenager *boy*	**zalmay**
teenager *girl*	**peghla**
elder *old person*	**mëshër; spinzhiray**
person	*m* **sa̱ray;** *f* **sh̲ëdza**
people	**khalak**
orphan	**yatim**

—Religion

The Pashtoons are mostly Sunni Muslims with some Shi'is in Pakistan. (For more, see "Religious Heritage" on page 169).

What is your religion?	**Pë kum din ye?**
I am (a) . . .	**Zë . . . yam.**
Muslim	**Musulmân**
Buddhist	**Budâyi**
Orthodox	**Ortudoks**
Christian	**Isawi**
Catholic	**Kâtulik**
Hindu	**Hindu**
Jewish	**Yahud**
I am not religious.	**Zë maz-habi na yam.**

4. LANGUAGE

Aside from the many local languages spoken throughout the region, many Pashtoons know Dari in Afghanistan and Urdu in Pakistan. Some will also know a smattering at least of one or more European languages — such as English and Russian. Because Pashtoons are scattered over a wide region you will find quite a few speakers of national languages like Baluchi, Tajik and Uzbek, depending on the area they live in, and also Classical Arabic, particularly because of the obvious influence of Islam.

Do you know* Pashto?	**Pë Pashto pohezhe?****
Do you know Dari?	**Pë Dari pohezhe?**
Do you know English?	**Pë Inglisi pohezhe?**
Do you know Russian?	**Pë Rusi pohezhe?**
Do you know German?	**Pë Jarmani pohezhe?**
Do you know French?	**Pë Farânsawi pohezhe?**
Do you know Farsi?	**Pë Fârsi pohezhe?**
Do you know Tajik?	**Pë Tâjik pohezhe?**
Do you know Uzbek?	**Pë Ozbaki pohezhe?**
Do you know Chinese?	**Pë Chinâyi pohezhe?**
Do you know Urdu?	**Pë Urdu pohezhe?**
Do you know Hindi?	**Pë Hindi pohezhe?**
Do you know Arabic?	**Pë Arabi pohezhe?**
Does anyone know English?	**Tsuk pë Inglisi pohezhi?**
I know a little . . .	**Zë pë . . . lëzh pohezham.**
I don't know any . . .	**Zë pë ... në pohezham.**
I understand.	**Zë pohezham.**
I don't understand.	**Zë në pohezham.**
Please point to the word in the book.	**Lutfan pë kitâb ke kalima râwëshaya.**

* "Know" is used here as a broader alternative to "speak".
** **Pohezhe** is "you speak" informal; **pohezhëy** is "you speak" formal/plural.

Please wait while I look up the word.	**Lutfan tar hagho che dâ kalima pë kitâb ke guram, sabar wakra.**
Could you speak more slowly, please?	**Lutfan keday shi lëzh nor sawka khabëri wëkrëy.**
Could you repeat that?	**Keday shi tikrâr ye krëy?**
How do you say . . . in Pashto?	**. . . ta pë Pashto tsë wâyâst?**
What does . . . mean?	**. . . tsë mânâ lari?**
How do you pronounce this word?	**Dâ kalima tsënga talafuz kezhi?**
I know . . .	**Zë pë . . . pohezham.**
Arabic	**Arabi**
Armenian	**Armâni**
Chinese	**Chinâyi**
Danish	**Dinmârki**
Dutch	**Hâlayndi**
English	**Inglisi; Angrezi**
Farsi	**Fârsi**
French	**Farânsawi**
German	**Jarmani**
Greek	**Yunâni**
Hindi	**Hindi**
Italian	**Itâliyâyi**
Japanese	**Jâpâni**
Kirgiz	**Qirghizi**
Russian	**Rusi**
Spanish	**Haspânawi**
Tajik	**Tâjiki**
Tibetan	**Tibiti**
Turkish	**Turki**
Turkmen	**Turkmani**
Uzbek	**Ozbaki**

5. BUREAUCRACY

Note that many forms you encounter may also be written in Dari, Urdu or English.

name	**num**
surname	**takhalus**
middle name	**mandzway num;** **duham num**
address	**pata; âdras**
date of birth	**dë ze<u>zh</u>edo ne<u>t</u>a**
place of birth	**dë ze<u>zh</u>edo dzây**
nationality	**miliyat**
citizenship	**tâbe'iyat**
age	**umar**
sex: female	**<u>shë</u>dzina**
male	**nârina**
religion	**din**
reason for travel:	**dë safar waja**
business	**tijârat**
tourism	**torizam**
work	**kâr**
personal	**shakhsi**
profession	**maslak**
marital status	**dë tâhul wazi'ayat**
single *male*	**mujarad**
female	**mujarada**
married *male*	**mutâhil**
female	**peghla**
divorced *female*	**talâqashaway**
date	**ne<u>t</u>a**
date of arrival	**dë rârasedu ne<u>t</u>a**
date of departure	**dë rawânedu ne<u>t</u>a**
passport	**pâspor<u>t</u>**
passport number	**pâspor<u>t</u> shmera;** **pâspor<u>t</u> numra**

visa	**weza**
currency	**paysa**

—Enquiries

Is this the correct form?	**Âyâ dâ ye sama bana da?**
What does this mean?	**Dâ tsë mânâ lari?**
Where is . . . 's office?	**Dë . . . daftar cheri day?**
Which floor is it on?	**Pë kum por ke day?**
Does the lift work?	**Lift kâr kawi?**
Is Mr./Ms. . . . in?	**Shâghalay/Merman . . . shta?**
Please tell him/her that I am here.	**Lutfan hëghë/haghe ta wawâya che zë dalta yam.**
I can't wait, I have an appointment.	**Intizâr në sham kawalay, lë châ sara me wakht tâkalay.**
Tell him/her that I was here.	**Hëghë/Haghe ta wawâya che zë dalta râghalay wëm.**

—Ministries*

Ministry of Defense	**Dë Difâ Wizârat**
Ministry of Agriculture	**Dë Karhane Wizârat**
Ministry of Home Affairs	**Dë Kuranëyo Châro Wizârat**
Ministry of Foreign Affairs	**Dë Bahranëyo Châro Wizârat**
Ministry of Health	**Dë Rughtiya Wizârat**
Ministry of Education	**Dë Pohane Wizârat**
Ministry of Higher Education	**Dë Loru Zdakru Wizârat**
Ministry of Justice	**Dë Adle Wizârat**

* For reference only as the exact wording tends to change.

6. TRAVEL

PUBLIC TRANSPORT — When running, buses are generally too crammed for comfort. Far more practical are taxis or private cars hailed in the street or the minibuses called **minibas** (in Kabul you may hear them called **nisân-pikâp** "Nissan pick-up") which stop at pre-determined pickup points. You pay the driver or his assistant as you get out. When the railway lines are opened again, you will find rail travel slow, subject to long delays mid-journey and less safe than by road. Travel anywhere, even by air, is problematic due to the sustained and systematic destruction of Afghanistan's infrastructure. Bicycles and motorbikes are not difficult to find but are not much use outside of the town spaces.

What time does . . . leave/arrive?	**. . . kala rârasezhi/ rewânezhi?**
the airplane	**alwutëka; tayâra**
the boat	**berëy**
the bus	**bas; sarwes**
the train	**orgâday**
The plane is delayed.	**Alwutëka dzandedale da.**
The plane is cancelled.	**Alwutëka kinsil shawe da.**
The train is delayed.	**Orgâday dzandedalay day.**
The train is cancelled.	**Orgâday kinsil shaway day.**
How long will it be delayed?	**Tsumra ba wëdzandezhi?**
There is a delay of . . . minutes.	**. . . daqiqe dzandëdalay.**
There is a delay of . . . hours.	**. . . sâ'ata dzandëdale**

| Excuse me, where is the ticket office? | **Wëbakhsha, tikit-plorandzay cheri day?** |
| Where can I buy a ticket? | **Cheri tikit akhistay sham?** |

I want to go to . . .	**Zë ghwâram . . . ta lâr sham.**
I want a ticket to . . .	**Dë . . . tikit ghwâram.**
I would like . . .	**. . . ghwâram.**
a one-way ticket	**yaw tarafa tikit**
a return ticket	**dwa tarafa tikit**
first class	**lumray daraja**
second class	**duham daraja**
Do I pay in dollars or in afghanis/rupees?	**Dâlar darkram ka afghânëy/rupëy?**
You must pay in dollars.	**Dâlar râkra.** *or* **Bâyad dâlar râkre.**
You must pay in afghanis/rupees.	**Bâyad afghânëy/rupëy râkre.**
You can pay in either.	**Dwâra manu.**
Can I reserve a place?	**Dzây rizarf kawalay sham?**
How long does the trip take?	**Pë safar tsumra wakht lagezhi?**
Is it a direct route?	**Mustaqim parwâz day?**

—Air

Is there a flight to . . . ?	**Dë . . . lëpâra parwâz shta?**
When is the next flight to . . . ?	**. . . të bël parwâz kala day?**
How long is the flight?	**Mazël tsumra day?**
What is the flight number?	**Parwâz nambar tsë day?**
You must check in at . . .	**Bäyad pë . . . ke ye ogure.**

Is the flight delayed?	**Parwâz dzandedalay day?**
How many hours is the flight delayed?	**Parwâz tsu sâ'ata dzandedalay day?**
Is this the flight for . . . ?	**Âyâ dâ dë . . . parwâz day?**
Is that the flight from . . . ?	**Âyâ dâ parwâz lë . . . tsakha day?**
When is the Karachi flight arriving?	**Dë Karâchëy parwâz kala rârasezhi.**
Is it on time?	**Pë khpël wakht râdzi?**
Is it late?	**Dzandedalay day?**
Do I have to change planes?	**Âyâ bâyad alwutaka badala kram?**
Has the plane left Karachi yet?	**Âyâ alwutaka lë Karâchëy tlële da?**
What time does the plane take off?	**Kala alwutaka wâlwuta?**
What time do we arrive in Kabul?	**Kala Kâbël ta rasezhu?** *or* **Pë tsu bajo Kâbël ta rasezhu?**
excess baggage	**izâfa sâmân**
international flight	**narëywâl alwut/parwâz**
internal flight	**kuranay alwut; dâkhili alwut**

—Bus

bus stop	**tamdzay**
bus station	**ada**
Where is the bus stop?	**Tamdzay cheri day?**
Where is the bus station?	**Ada cheri da?**
Please take me to the bus station.	**Lutfan, mâ dë basunu ade të warwala.**
Which bus goes to . . . ?	**Kum bas ... ta dzi?**
Does this bus go to . . . ?	**Âyâ dâ bas ... ta dzi?**

How often do buses pass by?	**Basuna tsu dzali terizhi?**
What time is the . . . bus?	**... bas tsë wakht day?**
next	**bël**
first	**lumray**
last	**wrustay**

Will you let me know when we get to . . . ?	**Keday shi râta wëwâyâst kala . . . ta rasezhu?**
Stop, I want to get off!	**Wadarezha, ghwâram shkata sham!**
Where can I get a bus to . . . ?	**Dë . . . lëpâra cheri bas mondalay sham?**
When is the first bus to . . . ?	**Dë . . . lumray bas kala rawânezhi?**
When is the last bus to . . . ?	**Dë . . . wrustay bas kala dzi?**
When is the next bus to . . . ?	**Dë . . . bël bas kala day?**
Do I have to change buses?	**Âyâ bâyad basuna badal kram?**

I want to get off at . . .	**Zë ghwâram che pë . . . ke shkata sham.**
Please let me off at the next stop.	**Lutfan, mâ pë râtlu nki tamdzi ke shkata kra.**
Please let me off here.	**Lutfan, mâ dalta shkata kra.**

How long is the journey?	**Tsumra mazal day?**
What is the fare?	**Kirâya tsumra da?**
I need my luggage, please.	**Khpël sâmân ghwâram.**

That's my bag.	**Dâ zmâ baks day.**

—Rail

Passengers must . . .
    change trains.
	Swarlëy bâyad . . .
	    orgâday badal
	    kri.

change platforms.	paletfârëm badal kri.
Is this the right platform for . . . ?	Âyâ dâ dë . . . lëpâra sam paletfârëm day?
The train leaves from platform . . .	Orgâday lë . . . paletfârëma rawânezhi.
Is there a timetable?	Mahâlwesh shta?
Please take me to the railway station.	Lutfan, mâ dë orgâdi steshan ta bodza.
Which platform should I go to?	Kum paletfârëm ta bâyad lâr sham?
platform one	lumri paletfârëm ta
platform two	duham paletfârëm ta
You must change trains at . . .	Të bâyad pë . . . ke orgâday badal kre.
Where can I buy tickets?	Cheri tikit akhistay sham?
Will the train leave on time?	Orgâday bë pëkhpël wakht rawân shi?
There will be a delay of . . . minutes.	. . . daqiqe ba wdzandezhi.
There will be a delay of . . . hours.	. . . sâ'ata ba wdzandezhi.

—Taxi

Some taxis are marked, while others are not. You can also wave
down and negotiate a fare with any private car willing to go your

way, although this is not always as safe. To avoid unpleasant surprises, agree to fares in advance. It is useful to be able to tell the driver your destination in Dari or Urdu too (or have it written down on a piece of paper). Be warned, however, that some drivers will have as little idea as you as to the precise whereabouts of your destination. A reliable option is to call up one of the growing number of radio taxi (**tilifun ṭaksi**) companies.

Taxi!	**Ṭaksi!**
Where can I get a taxi?	**Cheri ṭaksi mondalay sham?**
Please could you get me a taxi.	**Lutfan, keday shi yaw ṭaksi râta wënisëy?**
Can you take me to . . . ?	**. . . ta me rasawalay shëy?**
Please take me to . . .	**Lutfan, mâ . . . ta warasawëy.**
How much will it cost to . . . ?	**Tar . . . puri tsu kezhi?**
How much?	**Tsu akhle?**
To this address, please.	**Lutfan, de âdras ta.**
Turn left.	**Kin lor ta tâw sha.**
Turn right.	**Shi lor ta taw sha.**
Go straight ahead.	**Negh dza.**
Stop!	**Wadarezha!**
Don't stop!	**Më darezha!**
I'm in a hurry.	**Bira me da.**
Please drive more slowly!	**Lutfan, lëzh sawka dza!**
Here is fine, thank you.	**Dâ dzây sam day, manana.**
The next corner, please.	**Râtlunkay pechumay.**
The next street to the left.	**Kin lor ta râtlunke kutsa.**
The next street to the right.	**Shi lor ta râtlunke kutsa.**

Stop here!	**Dalta wadarezha!**
Stop the car, I want to get out.	**Motar wadarawa, ghwâram shkata sham.**
Please wait here.	**Lutfan, dalta intizâr wakra.**
Please take me to the airport.	**Lutfan. mâ hawâyi dagar ta warasawa.**

—General phrases

I want to get off at . . .	**Zë ghwâram che pë . . . ke shkata sham.**
Excuse me!	**Bakhshana ghwâram!**
I want to get out (of the bus).	**Ghwâram shkata sham.**
These are my bags.	**Dâ zmâ baksuna di.**
Please put them there.	**Lutfan, halta ye kezhda.**
Is this seat free?	**Âyâ dâ sit khâli day?**
I think that's my seat.	**Fikar kawam dâ zmâ sit day.**

—Extra words

airport	**hawâyi-dagar**
airport tax	**dë hawâyi-dagar tiks**
ambulance	**ambolâns**
arrivals	**râtlunkay; rârasedunkay**
bag	**baks**
baggage	**baksuna; sâmân**
baggage counter	**dë sâmân dzây**
bicycle	**bayskil**
boarding pass	**alwut-kârt**
boat	**berëy; mâku**
border	**sarhad; pula; wesh**

bus stop	**tamdzay**
camel *dromedary*	**ush**
car	**motar**
cart *horse-drawn*	**karâchëy; bagëy; tânga** (*Pakistan*)
check-in	**talâshi**
check-in counter	**dë talâshëy dzây-barkha/mez**
closed	**band**
customs	**gumrëk**
delay	**dzand**
departures	**rawânedâ; harakat**
donkey	**khar**
emergency exit	**iztirâri wato lâr**
entrance	**dë nanawato lâr**
exit	**dë wato lâr**
express	**chatak; garanday**
ferry	**berëy**
foot: on foot	**pë psho**
frontier	**sarhad; pula**
4-wheel drive	**jip; pijâro**
helicopter	**churlaka; hilikâptara**
horse	**as; âs**
information	**ma'lumât; itlâ'ât**
ladies/gents	**âghële/shaghali**
local	**dzâyi; mahali**
lorry	**lârëy; trak** (*Pakistan*)
luggage	**baksuna; sâmân**
motorbike	**motërsaykël**
mule	**kachër**
no entry	**nanawatël man'a di**
no smoking	**sigret man'a di**
open	**khlâs; prânistay**
path	**raw; lâr**
platform number	**paletfârëm nambar**
railway	**relwe**

reserved	**sâtalay**
radio taxi	**tilifun taksi**
road	**sarëk; wât**
tarmac road	**qir sarëk**
sign	**nasha**
sleeping car	**silipar**
station	**ada**
bus station	**dë basunu ada**
train station	**steshan**
subway; underground	**metro**
telephone	**tilifun**
ticket office	**dë tikitunu daftar**
timetable	**mahâlwesh**
toilet(s)	**kenârâb; tashnâb**
town center	**dë shâr markaz**
truck	**lârëy; trak**
van	**wâgun; daba**

Some common expressions . . .

Here are a few expressions you'll hear in everyday conversation:

âyâ...?	well...?; I wonder...
sama da!	all right!; okay!
âfarin!; shâbas!	bravo!
hây hây!; ay!	alas!
wâ!	oh! *(in admiration or surprise)*
akh!	ow!
yâne	I mean...; that's to say...
afsus!; armân-armân!	what a pity!
bas!	enough!; well now!
na, bikhi!	not at all!
rishtiyâ?	really?
wëli nê?	why not?
sha!	well!
parwâ në lari!	no problem!

7. ACCOMMODATION

The hotel and guesthouse network in Afghanistan is slowly being built up again. Should adequate accommodation be found away from the major towns, you will find that room service is not available, and breakfast or other meals will have to be negotiated and paid for separately. In Pakistan things are similar away from the main hotels in the larger towns and cities that do provide service to European/U.S. standards. An excellent option in more rural areas is to have your accommodation arranged at a private house, where traditional hospitality will guarantee that you are well looked after and, as always in Pashtonkhwa, well fed. Note that **hotal** means "guesthouse" and "hostel" as well as "hotel".

Where is a hotel?	**Hotal cheri day?**
I am looking for a hotel.	**Zë pë hotal pase gardzam.**
Is there anywhere I can stay for the night?	**Dë shpe terawëlo lëpâra kum dzây shta?**
Where is . . .	**. . . cheri day?**
a cheap hotel	**arzân hotal**
a good hotel	**shë hotal**
a nearby hotel	**nëzhde hotal**
a clean hotel	**pâk hotal**
What is the address?	**Âdras ye tsë day?**
Could you write the address please?	**Lutfan âdras ye râta wëlikëy.**

—At the hotel

Do you have any rooms free?	**Khâli kuta larëy?**
I would like . . .	**Zë . . . ghwâram.**
a single room	**yaw kasiza kuta**
a double room	**dwa kasiza kuta**
We'd like a room.	**Munzh yawa kuta ghwâru.**

ACCOMMODATION

We'd like two rooms.	**Munzh dwe kute ghwâru.**
I want a room with . . .	**Zë yawa dâsi kuta ghwâram che . . . walari.**
a bathroom	**tashnâb**
a shower	**shâwar**
a television	**tilwezyun**
a window	**karkëy**
a double bed	**dwa kasiz takht**
a balcony	**tarâs**
a view	**manzara**
I want a room that's quiet.	**Yawa ârâma kuta ghwâram.**
How long will you be staying?	**Tsumra pâte kezhe?**
How many nights?	**Tsu shpe?**
I'm going to stay for . . .	**Zë ghwâram . . . pâti sham.**
one day	**yawa wradz**
two days	**dwe wradzi**
one week	**yawa onëy**
Do you have any I.D.?	**Âyâ kum pezhankârt larëy?**
Sorry, we're full.	**Wabakhsha, dzây na laru.**
I have a reservation.	**Mâ kota niwale.** *or* **Mâ kota rizarf kare da.**
My name is . . .	**Zmâ num . . . day.**
May I speak to the manager please?	**Lutfan kedây shi la manejar sara khabëri wakram?**
I have to meet someone here.	**Bâyad dalta la châ sara wëwinam.**

How much is it per night?	**Dë yawe shpe kirâya tsumra da?**
How much is it per week?	**Dë yawe onëy kirâya tsumra da?**
How much is it per person?	**Dë yawë tan kirâya tsumra da?**
It's . . . per day.	**Dë yawe shpe kirâya . . . da.**
It's . . . per week.	**Dë yawe onëy kirâya . . . da.**
It's . . . per person.	**Dë yawë tan kirâya . . . da.**
Can I see the room?	**Âyâ kuta lidalay sham?**
Are there any others?	**Nur tsuk shta?**
Is there . . . ?	**. . . shta?**
airconditioning	**irkandeshan**
a telephone	**telifun**
hot water	**tawde obë**
laundry service	**dobi**
room service	**dë kuto khidmat**
No, I don't like it.	**Na, dâ me në khwashezhi.**
It's too . . .	**Dâ dera . . . da.**
cold	**sara**
hot	**tawda**
big	**loya**
dark	**tiyâra**
small	**wara**
noisy	**lë shura daka; nâ-rama**
dirty	**chatala**
It's fine, I'll take it.	**Dâ shë da, wëbë ye nisam.**
Where is the bathroom?	**Tashnâb cheri day?**
Is there hot water all day?	**Tula wradz tawde obë lari?**

ACCOMMODATION

Do you have a safe?	**Sayf larëy?**
Is there anywhere to wash clothes?	**Dë jâmu mindzalo dzây lari?**
Can I use the telephone?	**Âyâ telifun isti'mâ lawalay sham?**

—Needs

I need candles.	**Zmâ shame pëkâr di.**
I need toilet paper.	**Zmâ tashnâb kâghaz pëkâr day.**
I need soap.	**Zmâ sâbun pëkâr day.**
I need clean sheets.	**Zmâ pâka rujâyi pëkâr da.**
I need an extra blanket.	**Zmâ izâfi kambala pëkâr da.**
I need drinking water.	**Zmâ dë tsëshâk obë pëkâr di.**
I need a light bulb.	**Zmâ kamzoray grup pëkâr day.**
Please change the sheets.	**Lutfan, rojâyi badala krëy.**
I can't open the window.	**Kërkëy na sham khlâsawalay.**
I can't close the window.	**Kërkëy na sham bandawalay**
I have lost my key.	**Kili me wraka shwe.**
Can I have the key to my room?	**Dë kute kili râkrëy.**
The toilet won't flush.	**Dë kamod tânkëy kâr na kawi.**
The water has been cut off.	**Obë bande shawi di.**
The electricity has been cut off.	**Breshnâ qata da.** *or* **Barq qata day.**

ACCOMMODATION

The gas has been cut off.	Gâz qata day.
The heating has been cut off.	Markaz garmi banda da.
The heater doesn't work.	Bukhârëy kâr na kawi.
The airconditioning doesn't work.	Irkandeshan kâr na kawi.
The phone doesn't work.	Telifun kâr na kawi.
I can't flush the toilet.	Kamod ta obë na sham achawalay.
The toilet is blocked.	Kamod band day.
I can't switch off the tap.	Tsushkay na sham khlâsawalay.
Where is the plug socket?	Sâket cheri day?
wake-up call	dë râwishawëlo zang
Could you please wake me up at . . . o'clock.	Lutfan, keday shi mâ pë . . . bajo wish kërey.
I am leaving now.	Os dzam.
We are leaving now.	Os dzu.
May I pay the bill now?	Payse os darkawalay sham?

—Extra words

bathroom	tashnâb
bed	kat
blanket	kambala
candle	shama
candles	shame
chair	chawkëy
cold water	sare obë
cupboard	almârëy
door	war; darwâza
doorlock	kolp; qolf

ACCOMMODATION

electricity	**breshnâ; barq**
excluded	**istël**
floor *story*	**manzël; pur**
fridge	**yakhchâl;**
	frij *(Pakistan)*
hot water	**tawde obë**
included	**shâmilawël**
key	**kili; kunji**
lamp	**tsirâgh**
laundry service	**dobi**
light *electric*	**lâsi tsirâgh**
mattress	**toshak**
meals	**khwârë**
mirror	**hindâra**
name	**num**
noisy	**lë shura dak**
padlock	**kolp**
pillow	**bâlësht**
plug (bath)	**sarposh; sar**
plug (electric)	**palak**
quiet	**ghalay; chup**
quilt	**brastën**
roof	**bâm**
room	**kuta**
room number	**dë kute nambar**
sheet	**rojâyi**
shelf	**almârëy**
shower	**shâwar**
stairs	**pwrëy**
suitcase	**baks**
surname	**takhalus**
table	**mez**
towel	**toliya; qadifa**
veranda	**baranda**
wall	**dewâl**
water	**obë**
window	**karkëy; orsëy**

8. FOOD & DRINK

Food plays an important part of Pashtoon life, and important events in all aspects of life and the year are marked with a feast of one form or another. Food is a very important part of hospitality — it is both the host's duty to make sure his guests are eating and the guest's duty to partake of what is offered. **Palaw** is king in Pashtoon cuisine, and new guests are traditionally fed this dish above all others. In normal times, you will be offered a dazzling variety of dishes, delicacies and drinks, which vary from area to area and from season to season. Any menu you may encounter may be written in Pashto, Dari, Urdu or English.

breakfast	**nâray; sabnâray**
lunch	**dë gharme dodëy**
dinner, supper	**dë mâshâm dodëy**
dessert	**khwâzha**

MEALS — In practise, Pashtoons do not use separate names for meals as in English. The terms given above are rather literal terms. Lunch and dinner are usually just called **dodëy** "food" or "meal".

I'm hungry.	**Wazhay yam.**
I'm thirsty.	**Tazhay yam.**
Have you eaten yet?	**Dodëy dë khorale da?**
Do you know a good restaurant?	**Yaw shë resaturân dar ma'lum day?**
Do you have a table, please?	**Lutfan yaw mez larëy?**
I would like a table for . . . people, please.	**Yaw . . . kasiz mez ghwâram.**
Can I see the menu please?	**Keday shi mino wagoram?**
I'm still looking at the menu.	**Zë lâ tar osa mino goram.**
I would like to order now.	**Os ghwâram farmâyash darkram.**

FOOD & DRINK

What's this?	**Dâ tsë shay day?**
Is it spicy?	**Masâla dâra da/day?**
Does it have meat in it?	**Ghwâsha pake shta?**
Do you have . . . ?	**Tâso . . . khorëy?**
We don't have . . .	**Munzh . . . në khoro.**
What would you recommend?	**Tâso dë tsë farmâyash warkaray?**
Do you want . . . ?	**Âyâ . . . ghwârëy?**
Can I order some more . . . ?	**Keday shi yaw tsë nor . . . waghwâram?**
That's all, thank you.	**Bas hamdumra, manana.**
That's enough, thanks.	**Bas di, manana.**
I haven't finished yet.	**Lâ me khatma karay na da.**
I have finished eating.	**Dodëy me bas karay.**
I am full up!	**Zë mor yam.**
Where are the toilets?	**Tashnâb cheri day?**
I am a vegetarian.	**Zë sabzi khora yam.**
I don't eat meat.*	**Zë ghwâsha në khoram.**
I don't eat chicken or fish.	**Dë chërg yâ kab ghwâsha në khoram.**

CULTURAL NOTE — While in the West it is perfectly OK to state dietary preferences, in Pashtoon society this is interpreted as an insult to the host: you are in effect telling them that the food isn't good enough for you. In traditional Pashtoon society (and many other Asian societies) people will be baffled that someone would voluntarily choose not to eat meat. Better to say that you have medical reasons for doing so.

I don't drink alcohol.	**Alkol/Sharâb në tsëshëm.**

* Since Pashtoons are an Islamic people, you will not be offered pork. For reference purposes or use abroad, "I don't eat pork" is **Dë khuk ghwâsha na khoram**.

I don't smoke.	**Sigre<u>t</u> në tsikawam.**
I would like . . .	**Lutfan . . . râw<u>r</u>ëy.**
an ashtray	**ironay; khâkistardânëy**
the bill	**bel**
a glass of water	**yaw gilâs obë**
a bottle of water	**yaw botal obë**
another bottle	**bël botal**
a bottle-opener	**sarprânistunay**
a corkscrew	**sarprânistunay**
dessert	**khwâ<u>zh</u>ë**
a drink	**tsë<u>sh</u>âk**
a chair	**chawkëy**
a plate	**qâb; pale<u>t</u>** *(Pakistan)*
a bowl	**kâsa**
a glass	**gilâs; istikân**
a cup	**piyâla**
a napkin	**kâghazi dusmâl**
a glass	**gilâs; istikân**
a fork	**panja**
a knife	**châ<u>r</u>ë**
the menu	**menyu**
a jug	**jag**
a spoon	**kâchogha**
a table	**mez**
a teaspoon	**châykhori-kâchugha**
a toothpick	**ghâ<u>sh</u>khalay;**
	ghâ<u>sh</u>tumbunay
the sugar bowl	**qandânëy**
a washbowl	**chelëmchi**

▬Tastes & textures

fresh	**tâza**
raw; uncooked	**um; khâm**
cooked	**powkh**

FOOD & DRINK

ripe	**pokh; rasedalay**
tender	**naram**
tough *meat*	**sakhta**
spicy (hot)	**trikh**
stale	**bâsi**
sour	**triw**
sweet	**kho<u>zh</u>**
bitter	**trikh**
hot	**garm; tawda**
cold	**yakh; so<u>r</u>**
salty	**mâlgin**
taste	**maza; khwand**
tasteless	**bekhwënda**
tasty	**khwëndawar;**
	mazadâr *(Pakistan)*
bad/spoiled	**bad/kharâb**
too much	**<u>d</u>er ziyât**
too little	**<u>d</u>er lë<u>zh</u>**
not enough	**nâ kâfi**
empty	**tësh**
full	**<u>d</u>ak**
good	**<u>sh</u>ë**

—General food words

burger	**bargar**
butter	**kwëch**
bread *flat*	**<u>d</u>o<u>d</u>ëy**
loaf	**ma<u>r</u>ëy**
cake	**kek; kolcha**
candy	**sherini**
cheese	**paner**
cottage cheese	**chaka**
chewing gum	**zhawli**
coriander	**da<u>n</u>yâ; gashniz**
egg	**hagëy**
fat *animal*	**wâzga**
flour	**wr<u>ë</u>**

french fries	**chips**
garlic	**ozha**
ghee	**ghwari**
ginger	**sond**
gravy	**qurma**
honey	**shât**
ice-cream	**âys-krim**
jam; jelly	**morabâ**
ketchup	**kichap; sâs**
mint	**welanay; nânâ**
mustard	**awrëy**
nut	**maghz; zaray**
almond	**bâdâm**
pistachio	**pista**
salty apricot pits	**shorkhasta**
walnut	**ghoz**
oil	**mâye ghwari**
pasta	**makaruni**
pepper *black*	**tormrëch**
pepper *hot*	**srë mrëch**
pizza	**pitsa**
provisions	**sawdâ**
rice	**wriji**
salad	**salâta**
salt	**mâlga**
sandwich	**sândiwich**
sauce	**qurma**
shopping	**sawdâ**
soup	**shorwâ**
spice	**mësâla**
sugar	**bura**
syrup	**sharbat**
tablecloth	**distarkhân**
tray	**patnus**
teapot	**châynak(a)**
vinegar	**sëirka**
yogurt	**maste**

> **RICE** — **Wriji** is uncooked rice. All cooked rice in Pashtoon cuisine becomes pilau (**palaw**) or some other term depending on the dish. It's not eaten as plain white rice.
>
> **BREAD** — The general word for bread is **do<u>d</u>ëy**, but there are lots of special varieties, including: **marëy** and **<u>t</u>ikala**; flat barley **ro<u>t</u>a** or **dë jwar do<u>d</u>ëy**; flat maize **sokrëk**; flat wheat **ghalmina; ghanamina**.

—Vegetables

aubergine	**tor bânjân**
beans	**bag<u>ri</u>; gung<u>ri</u>**
green beans	**fâsuliya**
beetroot	**jaghwandër**
cabbage	**karam**
carrot	**gâzëra**
cauliflower	**gobay**
chickpeas	**nakhwëd**
cucumber	**bâdrang**
eggplant	**tor bânjân**
fennel	**bâdyân**
lentils	**dâl; mëshëng; nësk**
lettuce	**kâhu**
okra	**ben<u>d</u>ëy**
onion	**pyâz**
peas	**më<u>t</u>ër**
pepper	**mrëch**
potatoes	**âlu; kachâlu**
pumpkin	**kadu**
radish	**mulëy**
salad	**salâta**
spinach	**sâg; pâlëk**
tomato	**srë bânjan; rumi bânjân**
turnip	**<u>t</u>epër; shalghama**
vegetables *ready to eat*	**tërkâri; sabzi**

—Fruit

almond	**bâdâm**
apple	**ma<u>n</u>a**
apricot	**zardâlu;**
	khormânëy
banana	**kela**
cherry	**gilâs; âlubâlu**
fruit	**mewa**
grapefruit	**chëkotara**
grapes	**angur; kwar**
lemon	**lemu**
lime	**lemu; nimbu**
melon	**kha<u>t</u>ëkay**
mulberry	**tut**
orange	**nârinj; mâlta;**
	santara
peach	**shaftâlu**
pear	**nâk;**
	nashpâtay *(Pakistan)*
plum	**âlu; âlucha**
pomegranate	**anâr**
raisins	**mamiz; oske**
watermelon	**hind wâ<u>n</u>a**

—Meat

beef	**dë ghwayi ghwa<u>sh</u>a**
chicken	**dë chërg ghwa<u>sh</u>a**
egg	**hagëy**
boiled egg	**yëshedële**
	hagëy
fat *noun*	**wâzga; ghwâ<u>r</u>**
fish	**kab**
goat *meat*	**dë oze ghwa<u>sh</u>a;**
	dë chelëy ghwa<u>sh</u>a
kebab	**kabâb; tike** *(Pakistan)*
lamb *meat*	**dë wri ghwa<u>sh</u>a**

meat	**ghwasha**
mutton	**dë psë ghwasha;**
	dë gëd ghwasha
veal	**dë skhundar**
	ghwasha

—Drinks

Remember to ask for modern soft drinks by brand name.

alcohol(ic drinks)	**alkoli tsëshâk**
beer	**bir**
bottle	**botal**
can	**dabay**
coffee	**kâfi; qahwa**
coffee with milk	**lë shido sara kâfi**
fruit juice	**dë mewe obë;**
	jus *(Pakistan)*
ice	**yakh; yakhay**
milk	**pëy; shide**
mineral water	**ma'dani obë**
tea	**chây**
black tea	**tor chây**
green tea	**shin chây**
tea with milk	**shodu chây;**
	shir chây
no sugar, please!	**lutfan trikh!** *or*
	lutfan bebure!
water	**obë**
wine	**sharâb**

More on food & drink . . .

The diet of most Afghan villagers consists mainly of unleavened flat bread called **dodëy**, soups, a kind of yogurt called **qwërët** or **kwërët**, vegetables, fruit, and occasionally rice and meat. Tea is the favorite drink. Traditionally, twice a year groups of nomads may pass through villages on their routes from summer highland grazing grounds to the lowlands where they camp during the winter. The villagers traditionally permit the nomads to graze their animals over the harvested fields, which the flocks fertilize by depositing manure. The nomads buy supplies such as tea, wheat, and kerosene from the villagers; the villagers buy wool and milk products from the nomads. For food and clothing, the nomads depend on the milk products, meat, wool, and skins of their flocks; for transportation they depend on their camels. Each part of Afghanistan has its unique cuisine with its own special flavor. There is a wide variety of rice and noodle based dishes, and several varities of soups. Some common specialities include:

palaw — rice with lamb or chicken or vegetables

qabuli palaw — rice with carrots and sultanas plus meat

rosh — lamb with onion

karayi — lamb with tomatoes and peppers

sabzai chalaw — spinach and white rice

qurma chalaw — meat and white rice

perakay or **bolani** —vegetable or meat patties covered in flour and fried in oil

shami kabâb — a mixture of ground meat with onion, eggs and vegetables

chapli kabâb — mince meat fried with onion, tomatoes and peppers, sometimes with eggs in oil, sometimes fat

mantu — steamed dumplings stuffed with sauteed onions and mince beef served with yogurt sauce and topped with yellow peas

borani banjân – sliced sauteed aubergine served with garlic yogurt sauce

chaynaki — soup served in a teapot

kofta — ground beef, onion green paper garlic and salt

âsh — noodles with meat and yogurt

shorwâ — soup, made of beef or lamb meat, served with sliced bread

chopâni kabâb — lamb kebab

lândi palaw — rice with dried, salted lamb normally served in winter or early spring

lândi shorwâ — soup made of dried salt meat

kichri qurat — well-done rice with yogurt and mince meat

tika kabâb — chunks of lamb kebab

Accompanying the above will be seasonal greens and other finger food. Finish off your meal with **ferni** (a light pudding made with milk and sugar), **suji halwâ** (a sugary sweet cooked in oil),.or fruit — all washed down with the ubiquitous Afghan **chây** (tea).

9. DIRECTIONS

Where is . . . ?	**. . . cheri da?**
the academy	**akâdimi**
the airport	**hawâyi-dagar**
the art gallery	**hunari gâlari**
a bank	**bânk**
the church	**kalisâ**
the city center	**dë shâr zr̄ë;**
	markaz
the consulate	**qunsulgari**
the . . . embassy	**. . . sifârat**
the . . . faculty	**dë . . . pohandzay**
the hotel	**hotal**
the information office	**dë ma'lumâto**
	dafter
the main square	**asli chawk**
the market	**mârket; bâzâr**
the Ministry of . . .	**dë . . . Wizârat**
the mosque	**jumât; masjid**
the museum	**muzyam**
parliament	**pârlimân**
lower house	**wëlisi jirga**
upper house	**mashrâno jirga**
traditional parliament of	**loya jirga**
Pashtoons & Afghans	
the police station	**mâmuryat;**
	tâna *(Pakistan)*
the post office	**posta;**
	posti-daftar
the railway station	**dë orgâdi steshan**
the telephone center	**dë telifun markaz**
the toilet(s)	**kenârâb; tashnâb**
the university	**pohantun**
What . . . is this?	**Dâ kum . . . day?**

bridge	**pul**
building	**wadânëy; ta'mir**
city	**<u>sh</u>âr**
district	**wulaswalëy**
river	**sin**
road	**wâ<u>t</u>**
street	**kutsa**
town	**shârgay;**
	shârgo<u>t</u>ay
village	**kalay**

What is this building? **Dâ dë tsë shi wadânëy da?**

What is that building? **Hagha dë tsë shi wadânëy da?**

What time does it open? **Kala khlâse<u>zh</u>i?**

What time does it close? **Kala bande<u>zh</u>i?**

Can I park here? **Dalta mo<u>t</u>ar darawalay/ pârkawalay sham?**

Are we on the right road for . . . ? **Dë . . . khwâ ta pë sama rawân yu?**

How many kilometers is it to . . . ? **Tar . . . puri tsu kilomtira lara da?**

It is . . . kilometers away. **. . . kilomitra da.**

How far is the next village? **Bël kalëy tsumra leri day?**

Where can I find this address? **Dâ dzây cheri mundalay sham?**

Can you show me on the map? **Pë naqsha ke ye râ<u>sh</u>odalay she?**

How do I get to . . . ? **. . . ta tsanga raseday sham?**

I want to go to . . . **Zë ghwâ<u>r</u>am che . . . ta la<u>r</u> sham.**

Can I walk there? **Pë p<u>sh</u>o wartlây sham?**

Is it far? **Leri day?**

DIRECTIONS

Is it near?	**Nazhde day?**
Is it far from here?	**Lë dë dzâya leri day?**
Is it near here?	**Dë dzây ta nazhde day?**
It is not far.	**Leri na day.**
Go straight ahead.	**Negh lâ<u>r</u> sha.**
Turn left.	**Ki<u>n</u> lor ta wâw<u>r</u>a.**
Turn right.	**<u>Sh</u>i lor ta wâw<u>r</u>a.**
to the left	**ki<u>n</u> lor ta; chap lâs ta**
to the right	**<u>sh</u>i lor ta; <u>sh</u>e lâs ta**
to one side	**tsang ta**
at the next corner	**pë râtlunki pechumi**
at the traffic lights	**ke dë tarâfik lë ishâre sara**
behind	**shâta; wrusta**
far	**leri**
in front	**mëkh ta**
left	**ki<u>n</u>; chap**
near	**nazhde**
on	**pë**
opposite	**mëkhâmëkh**
outside	**dëbândi**
right	**<u>sh</u>ay**
straight on	**negh**
under	**lânde**
bridge	**pul**
corner	**kwanj; pechumay**
crossroads	**taqâtu'**
one-way street	**yaw tarafa sa<u>r</u>ëk**
north	**shamâl**
south	**jënub**
west	**lwedidz; gharb**
east	**khatidz; sharq**

10. SHOPPING

Where can I find a . . . ?	**. . . cheri mundalay sham?**
Where can I buy . . . ?	**. . . cheri akhistalay sham?**
Where's the market?	**Bâzâr cheri day?**
Where's the nearest . . . ?	**Tar tolo nazhde . . . cheri day?**
Can you help me?	**Lë mâ sara mrasta kawalay she?**
Can I help you?	**Tsë mrasta kawalay sham?**
I'm just looking.	**Zë ye yawâzi goram.**
I'd like to buy . . .	**Ghwâram che . . . wâkhlam.**
Could you show me some . . . ?	**Yaw tsë . . . râshodalay she?**
Can I look at it?	**Katalay ye sham?**
Do you have any . . . ?	**. . . larëy?**
This.	**Dâ.** *or* **Dagha.**
That.	**Hagha.**
I don't like it.	**Dâ me në khwashezhi.**
I like it.	**Dâ me khwash day.**
Do you have anything cheaper?	**Tar de kum arzâna shay lare?**
cheaper/better	**arzân/shë**
larger/smaller	**ghât/wur**
Do you have anything else?	**Bël tsë shay lare?**
Sorry, this is the only one.	**Wëbakhsha, yawâzl hamdâ day?**

I'll take it.	**Dâ ba wâkhlam.**
How much/many do you want?	**Tsu ghwâre?**
How much is it?	**Dâ pë tsu di?**
Can you write down the price?	**Keday shi baya wëlikëy?**
Could you lower the price?	**Keday shi baya lëzh kama krëy?**
I don't have much money.	**Zë deri payse në lâram.**
Do you take credit cards?	**Tâso kredit kârt akhlëy?**
Would you like it wrapped?	**Wenghâram, wepecham?**
Will that be all?	**Bas hmadâ, nor khu tsë na ghwârëy?**
Thank you, goodbye.	**Manana, khudây pë amân.**
I want to return this.	**Ghwâram che dâ berta râwram.**

—Outlets

auto spares shop	**dë purzo dukân**
baker's	**nânwâyi**
bank	**bânk**
barber's	**salmâni; nâyi** (Pakistan)
I'd like a haircut please.	**Lutfan, weshtan me kam krëy.**
bookshop	**kitâb plorandzay**
butcher's	**qasâbi**
pharmacy	**darmaltun**
clothes shop	**dë poshâk plorandzay**
dairy goods store	**dë labanyâto dukân**
dentist	**dë ghâsh dâktar**

department store	**zandziri plorandzay; sopar mârket**
dressmaker	**khayâti**
electrical goods store	**dë aliktruniki wasâyalo dukân**
florist	**gwël plorandzay**
greengrocer	**sabzi plorandzay**
hairdresser	**salmâni; nâyi** *(Pakistan)*
hospital	**rughtun**
kiosk	**ghurfa**
laundry *place*	**dobi dukân**
market	**bâzâr**
newsstand	**dë wradzpâno ghurfa**
shoeshop	**bot plorandzay; dë botuna dukân**
shop	**dukân; plorandzay**
souvenir shop	**dë sawghâti shiyânu dukân**
stationer's	**qirtâsiya**
supermarket	**soparmârket**
travel agent	**tikit-plorandzay; trewal-ijint**
vegetable shop	**dë sabzo dukân**
watchmaker's	**sâ'atsâzi**

—Gifts

boots		**moze**
box		**baks**
bracelet		**washay; lâswand; disband**
candlestick		**shamadân**
carpet	*felt*	**lemtsay**
	knotted	**ghâlëy; qâlin**
	woven	**gëlam**
chain		**zandzlr**
chest *box*		**sandoq**

clock	**dewâli sâ'at**
copper	**mis**
crystal	**bilawr; kristal**
curtain	**parda**
cushion	**bâlësht**
earrings	**wâlëy**
emerald	**zamarud**
gold	**srë zar**
handicraft	**lâsi san'at**
headscarf	**tikray; parunay**
iron	**waspana**
jewelry	**zargari**
kilim	**gëlam**
leather	**tsarmën**
metal	**filiz**
modern	**naway; asri**
necklace	**nikil**
pottery	**kulâli**
ring	**gota; chila**
rosary	**tasbe**
silver	**spin zar; nuqra**
steel	**polâd**
stone	**dabara; tizha**
traditional	**dodiz; ana'nawi**
turban	**langota; patkay**
vase	**guldânëy**
watch	**sâ'at**
wood	**largay**

—Clothes

bag	**baks**
belt	**kamarband**
boot	**moza**
boots	**moze**
rubber boots	**kalawshe**
bra; brassiere	**sinaband**

bracelet	**wa_shay; disband; kara**
button	**tanëy**
buttonhole	**kâj**
cloth	**tukar; tota**
clothes	**jâme; kâli; po_shâk**
coat	**kurtëy**
collar	**ghâra**
cotton	**katân; pumba**
dress	**kâli**
fabric	**tukar**
gloves	**diskâshe; lâsputuni**
handbag	**lâsbaks**
handkerchief	**dësmâl**
heel	**punda**
jacket	**jampar**
jumper	**jâkat; banyân**
leather	**tsarmën**
material	**tukar; tota**
necktie	**nektâ'i**
overcoat	**ozhd jampar; kot**
pin	**stën; sinjâq**
pocket	**jëb**
sandals	**tsaplëy**
scarf	**dë ghâre shâl**
scissors	**biyâti; qaychi**
shawl	**shâl**
shirt	**kamis**
shoes	**bot**
silk	**wrë_shëm**
silken	**wreshmin**
socks	**jurâbe; kërâma**
sole *of shoe*	**tali**
stick: walking stick	**amsâ**
suit *of European clothes*	**dirishi**
sweater	**banyân**
thimble	**gotma**
thread	**târ**

tie *necktie*	**nektâ'i**
tights	**chasp patlun**
trousers	**partug; patlun**
umbrella	**chatrëy**
underwear	**siltirâg**
waistcoat *jacket*	**be lastunu banyân**
vest	**wâskat**
walking stick	**amsâ**
wool	**warëy**
zipper	**zip; zandzir**

Traditional clothing . . .

Traditional Pashtoon costume takes on a variety of guises depending from region to region. Headgear is important in Afghan and Pakistani society and can be a good indication of where the wearer comes from. Apart from the more conventional hats (**khwalëy**), there's quite an assortment on offer, including the turban (**lungëy**), the big bell-shaped Astrakhan hat, made from soft karakul lambswool (**karakuli**), and the "roll-top" Nuristani cap (**pakol**). Traditional clothing and fabrics are still very much in evidence in towns as well as the countryside. Women in many areas wear a variety of headscarves and veils – the garment that covers the head and body ("chadour") is called **burqa** in Kandahar and Peshwar, and **châdari** in Kabul and other areas.

—Toiletries

aspirin	**aspirin**
brush	**bors; bursh**
comb	**zhmandz**
condom	**pukanëy**
cotton wool	**mâluch**
deodorant	**buy zid**
hairbrush	**dë weshto bors**
lipstick	**labsirin**
mascara	**rânjë**
mouthwash	**khulëmindzunke**
nail-clippers	**nâkhungir**
nail-polish	**nukrang; ranginâkhun**

perfume	**atar**
powder	**po_d_ar**
razor *electric*	**dë _zh_ire mâshin**
razorblade	**pâki; châ_r_a**
safety pin	**ping; qwalfi stan**
shampoo	**shâmpu**
shaving cream	**dë _zh_ire krim**
sleeping pills	**dë khob gulëy**
soap	**sâbun**
sponge	**spanj**
sunblock cream	**dë lmar zid krim**
thermometer	**tarmâmitar; mizânulharâra**
tissues	**kâghazi dusmâl**
toilet paper	**tashnâb kâghaz**
toothbrush	**dë ghâ_sh_o bors**
toothpaste	**dë ghâ_sh_o krim**
toothpick	**ghâ_sh_khalay**

—Stationery

ballpoint	**qalam; khudkâr**
book	**kitâb**
dictionary	**qâmus; sin**
envelope	**pâka_t_**
guidebook	**lâr_sh_od kitâb**
ink	**rang; siyâhi**
magazine	**majala**
map	**naqsha**
road map	**dë sa_r_akuno naqsha**
a map of Peshawar	**dë Pe_sh_awër naqsha**
newspaper	**wradzpâ_n_a**
newspaper in English	**Angrezi wradzpâ_n_a**
notebook	**kitâbcha**

novel	**nâwêl**
novels in English	**Angrezi nâwël; dë Angrezi zhabe nâwël**
paper	**kâghaz**
a piece of paper	**yawa tota kâghaz**
pen	**qalam**
pencil	**pinsil**
postcard	**postkârt**
scissors	**biyâti; qaychi**
writing paper	**dë lik likalo kâghaz**
Do you have any foreign publications?	**Kuma bahranëy nashriya larëy?**

—Photography

How much is it to process (and print) this film?	**Dâ film pë tsu mindzëy aw châpawëy?**
When will it be ready?	**Kala ba tayâr shi?**
I'd like film for this camera.	**Dë de kâmre lëpâra film ghwâram.**
black and white film	**tor aw spin film**
camera	**kâmra**
color film	**ranga film**
film	**film; filam**
flash	**flash**
lens	**linz**
light meter	**ranâ-mech**

—Electrical equipment

adapter	**idâptar**
battery	**betrëy**
cassette	**kasit; pata; fita**
CD	**sidi; tikalëy**

CD player	**sidi tip**
fan	**pakay**
hairdrier	**drâyi**
heating coil	**skârë**
iron (for clothing)	**otu; istri** *(Pakistan)*
kettle	**châyjosha**
plug *electric*	**plâg**
portable T.V.	**wrël kedunay**
	tiliwizun
radio	**râdiyo**
record	**rikât**
tape (cassette)	**kasit; pata; fita**
tape recorder	**tip; tayp**
television	**tiliwizun**
transformer	**tarânsfârmar**
video (player)	**wediyo**
videotape	**wediyo kasit**

> **LANGUAGE TIP** — For hi-tech stuff like cassettes, videos/ video-players or transformers you are more likely to be understood if you use the English terms.

—Sizes

small	**wor**
big	**ghat; stër**
heavy	**drund**
light	**spëk**
more	**nor**
less	**lëzh**
many	**dër; ziyat**
too much/many	**khwrâ der; zësht der**
enough	**kâfi**
That's enough.	**Kâfi di/day/da.**
also	**ham; hamdâ râz**
a little bit	**yaw tsë**

Do you have a carrier bag? **Khalta lare?**

11. WHAT'S TO SEE

Do you have a guidebook?	**Tâso lârshod kitâb larëy?**
Do you have a local map?	**Tâso dë sime naqsha larëy?**
Is there a guide who speaks English?	**Kum lârshod che pë Angrezi ghazheday shi, shta?**
What are the main attractions?	**Tsë shay pë zrë pori di?**
What is that?	**Hagha tsë shay day?**
How old is it?	**Tsu kalan day?**
May I take a photograph?	**Keday shi yaw aks ye wakhlam?**
What time does it open?	**Pë tsu baje prânistal kezhi?**
What time does it close?	**Pë tsu baje bandezhi?**
Is there an entrance fee?	**Dë nanawato fis lari?**
How much?	**Tsu?**
What is this monument/ statue?	**Dâ yâdgâr/mujasima dë tsë shi da?**
Who is that statue of?	**Dâ mujasima dë châ da?**
Are there any night clubs/ discos?	**Âyâ kum dë shpe-klâb/disko shta?**
How much does it cost to get in?	**Dë nanawato tikit tsu day?**
What's there to do in the evening?	**Mâzigar tsë wëkru?**

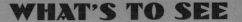

Is there a concert?	**Kansart shta?**
When is the wedding?	**Wâdë kala day?**
What time does it begin?	**Pë tsu bajo payl kezhi?**
Can we swim here?	**Dalta lâmbalay shu?**

classical music	**klâsika musiqi**
concert	**kansart**
dancing	**natsâ-raqs**
disco	**disko**
disk-jockey	**ghazh kantrolawunkay**
elevator	**lift**
escalator	**barqi-zine**
exhibition	**nandârtun**
folk dancing	**wolësi natsâ**
folk music	**wolësi musiqi**
jazz	**jâz**
lift	**lift**
nightclub	**dëshpe klab; nâytklab**
opera	**opira**
party	**pârtëy; bandâr**
pop music	**pâp-musik**
pub	**pab; sharâbkhâna; bâr**

—Buildings

academy of sciences	**dë ulumo akâdimi**
apartment	**apârtmân**
apartment building	**apârtmâni wadânëy; blâk**
archaeological	**larghunay**
art gallery	**hunari gâlari**
bakery	**nânwâyi**
bar	**bâr**
(apartment) block	**blâk**

WHAT'S TO SEE

building	**wadânëy**
casino	**qimârkhâna**
castle	**kalâ**
cemetery	**hadera**
church	**kalisa**
cinema	**sinamâ**
city map	**dë shâr naqsha**
college	**kâlij**
concert hall	**dë kansart hâl**
embassy	**safârat**
hospital	**rughtun**
house	**kor**
housing estate/project	**dë koruno purozha**
library	**kitâbtun**
main square	**asli chawk**
market	**bâzâr**
monument	**yâdgâr**
mosque	**jumât; masjid**
museum	**muzyam**
old city	**zor shâr**
opera house	**dë oparâ dzây**
park	**pârk**
parliament (building)	**dë pârlimân wadânëy**
restaurant	**rasturân**
ruins	**kandwâle**
saint's tomb	**ziyârat**
school	**showandzay; maktab**
shop	**dokân**
shrine	**ziyârat**
stadium	**lobghâlay**
statue	**mujasima**
store	**dokân**
street	**kutsa; sarëk**
tea house	**samâwâr**
temple	**daramsâl**
theater	**tiyâtar; nëndâre**

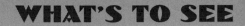

tomb	**qabër**
tower	**brëj**
university	**pohantun**
zoo	**zhoba<u>n</u>**

━Occasions

birth	**zok<u>r</u>a; ze<u>zh</u>edana**
death	**m<u>r</u>ina**
funeral	**dë jinâze marâsim**
wedding	**wâdë**
circumcision	**sunati; khatna**

Religious heritage . . .

Pashtoons are Muslims — mostly Sunni with some Shi'i communities. Scattered throughout Afghanistan are the flag-covered graves of saintlike people who are revered and petitioned for help in childbearing, settlement of disputes, moral leadership, or in other capacities. Mosques and madrasas (religious schools) have always played an important part in the development of the Pashtoons in Afghanistan and Pakistan, and Islam makes its presence felt through the often stunning religious buildings still standing throughout the two nations.

HOLIDAYS & FESTIVALS — There are a wide variety of traditional festivals celebrated in every village and area. Important dates in the national calendar are **Rozha** (Ramadan, the month of fasting), **Kuchinây Akhtar** (Id al-Fitr) when the end of Ramadan and fasting is celebrated, and **Luy Akhtar** (Id al-Adhâ) which is the eve before pilgrims traditionally celebrate going on hajj to Mecca. Both are normally three or four days holiday. **Mawlud**, the Prophet Muhammad's Birthday, is also celebrated. **Nawruz** is the Afghan New Year or Spring Festival (March 21st).

12. FINANCE

CURRENCIES — The official currency in Afghanistan is the **afghâni** (Af), divided into 100 **pul**. In Pakistan it is the **rupee** (Rp), divided into 100 **paisa** — 50 paisa is called **atë aniz** or **atânëy**, 25 paisa is **tsalor âniz**. Unofficially in use, but still accepted everywhere outside of government establishments and retail outlets, are U.S. dollars. These may be refused however if notes are creased, torn, old or simply a low denomination. Be prepared to accept change in afghanis or rupees.

CHANGING MONEY — Aside from the banks, money can also be changed in any bureau de change, where you will find reliable, up-to-date exchange rates prominently displayed on a board. The cashiers will often know a European language or two, and almost all will show the workings of the exchange on a calculator for you and give you a receipt. Many shops and kiosks will also be happy to change money for you.

I want to change some dollars.	**Ghwâram yaw tsë dâlar badal kram.**
I want to change some euros.	**Ghwâram yaw tsë iru badal kram.**
I want to change some pounds.	**Ghwâram yaw tsë pawnd badal kram.**
Where can I change some money?	**Cheri payse badlawalëy sham?**
What is the exchange rate?	**Dë badledo baya tsumra da?**
What is the commission?	**Kameshan tsumra day?**
Could you please check that again?	**Lutfan, biyâ ye wëgorëy?**
Could you write that down for me?	**Keday shi zmâ lëpâra ye wëlikëy?**

dollar	**dâlar**
euro	**iru**
ruble	**robal**
pound (sterling)	**pawnd**

bank notes	**bânk not; lot**
calculator	**dë hisâb mâshin**
cashier	**mahâsib**
coins	**sike**
credit card	**kridit kârt**
commission	**kameshan**
exchange	**dë payso badlun**
foreign echange	**as'âr**
loose change	**mâte; mayda payse**
receipt	**rasid**
signature	**lâslik**

Courtesy ...

Pashtoons pride themselves on being a courteous people and this is reflected in the expressions they use towards guests and superiors. Some related expressions you'll commonly hear are:

pë khayr râghle!	welcome! *to one person*
pë khayr râghlëy!	welcome! *to more than one person*
	To which the response is :
	khayr ose! *to one person, or*
	khayr osëy! *to more than one person*
kor di wadân!	may your home be forever!
salâmat ose!	health and peace to you *singular*!
salâmat osëy!	health and peace to you *plural*!
mehrabani wëkrëy!	come to the table!; please eat/drink!; help yourself!
stâso khpël kurdëy!	our door is always open for you!
harkala râshëy!	come again and again!

13. COMMUNICATIONS

TELECOMMUNICATIONS — It is likely that when Afghnistan's new telephone system is fully connected up, cell phones will be the preferred way to talk to one another. Satellite telephone links are costly but represent a reliable and secure method of communication in and out of the region.

POSTAL SERVICES — When operational, the postal service in Afghanistan is not always reliable. For important messages it would be best to stick to fax, telex, the telephone, couriers or e-mail. If you expect to receive mail, have it sent to the nearest headquarters of a host organization.

Where is the post office?	**Posti daftar cheri day?**
When does the post office open?	**Posti daftar kala khlâsezhi?**
When does the post office close?	**Posti daftar kala bandezhi?**
Where is the mail box?	**Postbaks cheri day?**
Is there any mail for me?	**Zmâ lëpâra kum lik shta?**
How long will it take for this to get there?	**Dâ ba pë tsumra wakht ke halta warasezhi?**
How much does it cost to send this to . . . ?	**. . . ta dë de pë lezhalo tsu lagezhi?**
I need some stamps.	**Tsu posti tikituna me pëkâr di.**
I would like to send . . .	**Ghwâram che . . . walezham.**
a letter	**lik**
a postcard	**postkârt**
a parcel	**pârsal**
a telegram	**tiligrâm**

air mail	**hawâyi post**
envelope	**pâkat**
mailbox	**postbaks**
to parcel up	**lezhël; pârsalawël**
registered mail	**râjistar**
stamp	**posti tikit**

—Tele-etiquette

I would like to make a phone call.	**Ghwâram yaw tilifun wakram.**
I would like to send a fax.	**Ghwâram che yaw fâks walezham.**
I would like to fax this letter.	**Ghwâram che dâ like fâks kram.**
I would like to send a telex.	**Ghwâram che yaw tiliks walezham.**
Where is the telephone?	**Tilifun cheri day?**
May I use your phone?	**Stâ tilifun kârawalay sham?**
Can I telephone from here?	**Lë de dzâya tilifun kawalay sham?**
Can you help me get this number?	**Dâ nambar râta rukh kawalay shëy?**
Can I dial direct?	**Mustaqim ye rukh kawalay sham?**
May I speak to . . . .?	**Keday shi lë . . . sara khabëri wakram?**
Can I leave a message?	**Payghâm warta preshodalay sham?**
Who is calling?	**Tsuk khabëri kawi?**
Who are you calling?	**Châ ta tilifun kawëy?** *or* **Tsuk ghwârëy?**
Can I take your name?	**Stâso num?**
Which number are you dialing?	**Kum nambar di rukh karây?**

COMMUNICATIONS

He/She is not here at the moment — would you like to leave a message?	**Hagha os dalta në shta — ghwâray che payghâm warta prezhdëy?**
This is not . . . You are mistaken. This is the . . . office.	**Dâ . . . na day. Ghalat karëy mu day. Dâ dë . . . daftar day.**
Hello, I need to speak to . . .	**Salâm, ghwâram che lë . . . sara khabëri wakram.**
I am calling this number . . . Please phone me.	**Mâ dâ . . . nambar rukh karay day. Lutfan, tilifun râta wakra.**
The telephone is switched off. I want to ring . . .	**Tilifun istal shaway day. Ghwâram che . . . ta tilifun wakram.**
What is the code for . . . ? What is the international code? The number is . . . The extension is . . .	**Dë . . . kod tsë day? Narëywal kod tsë day? . . . day. Warpase nambar ye . . . day.**
It's busy. I've been cut off. The lines have been cut.	**Masruf day. Tilifun qata shu. Layn qata day.**
Where is the nearest public phone?	**Tar tolo nazhde tilifunkhâna cheri da?**
digital e-mail fax fax machine	**dijital breshnâlik; imel faks dë fâks mâshin**

international operator	**narëywâl âpretar**
internet	**internit**
internet cafe	**internit-klâb**
line	**layn; karsha**
mobile phone; cell phone	**mubâyl**
modem	**naway; modim**
operator *male*	**âpritar**
female	**âpritara**
satellite phone	**satilâyt tilifun**
telephone center	**dë tilifun markaz; tilifunkhâna**
telex	**tiliks**
to transfer/put through	**hawâla kawël; intiqâlawël**

—Faxing & e-mailing

Where can I send a fax from?	**Lë kum dzâya faks lezhalay sham?**
Can I fax from here?	**Lë de dzâya ye faks kawalay sham?**
How much is it to fax?	**Pë tsu faks kezhi?**
Where can I find a place to e-mail from?	**Lë kum dzâya imel kawalay sham?**
Is there an internet cafe near here?	**Pë de shâwkhwâ ke internit-klab shta?**
Can I e-mail from here?	**Lë de dzâya imel kawalay sham?**
How much is it to use a computer?	**Dë kampyutar dë isti'mâl masraf tsu kezhi?**
How do you turn on this computer?	**Dâ kampyutar tsanga gul kezhi?**
The computer has crashed.	**Kampyutar kharâb shu.**

I need help with this computer.

Dë de kampyu_tar pë isti'mâl ke mraste ta zarurat laram.

I don't know how to use this program.

Dë de progrâm pë kârawëlo na pohe_zham.

I know how to use this program.
I want to print.

Dë de progrâm pë kârawëlo pohe_zham.
Ghwâ_ram châp ye k_ram.

LANGUAGE TIP — When answering the phone, you say **halo!** If the caller knows you, they will generally respond with **salâm alaykum!**, prompting your response **wa-alaykum wasalâm!** Now you are ready to start the conversation.

14. THE OFFICE

chair	**chawkëy**
computer	**kampyotar**
desk	**mez**
drawer	**rawaq**
fax	**faks**
file *paper*	**dusiya**
computer	**fâyl**
meeting	**ghwanda**
paper	**kâghaz**
pen	**qalam**
pencil	**pinsil**
photocopier	**dë futukâpi mâshin**
photocopy	**futukâpi;**
	futustet *(Pakistan)*
printer *computer*	**printar**
program *computer*	**progrâm**
report	**râpor**
ruler	**khatkash**
telephone	**tilifun**
telex	**tiliks**
typewriter	**tayp; tayprâytar**

15. THE CONFERENCE

article	**maqâla**
a break for refreshments	**waqfa; dama**
conference room	**dë kanfrâns khuna**
	dë kanfrâns sâlun
copy	**kâpi; naqal**
discussion	**bahs**
forum	**ghwanda**
guest speaker	**mëshër melma**
a paper	**tseraniza maqâla**
podium	**dë waynawâl mez**
projector	**projiktur**
session	**nâsta**
a session chaired by . . .	**dë ... pë mëshrëy**
	ghwanda
speaker	**wayând**
subject	**mawzo**

16. EDUCATION

to add	**jama' kawël**
addition	**jama'**
bench	**chawkëy**
biro	**khodkâr**
blackboard	**toratakhta**
book	**ketâb**
calculation	**hesâb; shmer**
to calculate	**shmerël**
chalk	**tëbâshir**
class	**t̲olgay; senf**
to copy	**kâpi kawël**
to count	**shmerël**
crayon	**ranga qalam**
difficult	**grân; mushkil**
to divide	**taqsimawël**
division	**taqsim**
easy	**âsân**
eraser	**takhtapâk**
exam	**âzmoyana; emtihân**
exercise book	**(dë tamrin) kitâbcha**
to explain	**tashrih kawël**
felt-tip pen	**tush**
geography	**joghrâfiya**
glue	**sri̲sh**
grammar	**girâmar**
history	**târikh**
holidays	**rokhsati**
homework	**koranay kâr**
illiterate	**besawâda**
language	**zhëba**
laziness	**t̲ambali**
to learn by heart	**pë yâdo yâdawël; hifzawël**

lesson	**lwëst**
library	**ketâbkhâna; kitâbtun**
literature	**adabyât**
madrasa	**madrasa**
maths	**riyâzi**
memory	**hâfiza; yâd**
multiplication	**zarb**
to multiply	**zarbawël**
notebook	**(dë yâdâsht) ketâbcha**
page	**mëkh; safa**
paper	**kâghaz**
to pass *an exam*	**kâmyâbedël**
pen	**qalam**
pencil	**pinsël**
progress	**parmakhtag**
to punish	**jazâ war-kawël**
pupil	**shâgird**
to read	**lwastël**
to repeat	**tikrârawël**
rubber *eraser*	**pinsëlpâk**
ruler *instrument*	**khatkash**
satchel	**baks**
school	**<u>sh</u>owundzay; maktab**
sheet *of paper*	**kâghaz**
slate	**sële<u>t</u>**
student *university*	**mohasel**
to subtract	**manfi kawël**
subtraction	**manfi; tafriq**
sum	**payse**
table	**mez**
teacher	**ostâz; <u>sh</u>owunkay**
to test *academic*	**imtihân akhistël**
time	**wakht**

17. AGRICULTURE

agriculture	**zërâ'at; karana**
barley	**wërbëshe**
barn	**dë ghale godâm**
cattle	**mâl**
combine harvester	**kombâyn**
corn	**jwâr**
cotton	**pumba**
crops	**fasal; hâsil**
to cultivate	**karël**
earth *land*	**mdzaka; dzmaka**
soil	**khâwra**
fallowland	**yawe shawe mdzaka**
farm	**karwanda**
farmer	**karwandgar; dehqân**
farming	**karwandgari; dehqâni**
to feed an animal	**shuma warkawël/ achawël**
fertilizer	**sara**
field	**paṯay**
fruit	**mewa**
furrow	**kil**
garden	**ba<u>n</u>; bâgh**
grass	**wâ<u>sh</u>ë**
to grind	**o<u>r</u>ë kawël**
to grow *crops*	**karël**
harvest	**law**
hay	**beda**
haystack	**pro<u>r</u>a**
irrigation	**oba-lagawana**
leaf	**pâ<u>n</u>a**
livestock	**mâl**

maize	**jwâr**
manure	**sara**
marsh	**jaba**
meadow	**warsho**
to milk *an animal*	**lwashël**
mill	**zhranda**
miller	**zhrandagëray**
millstone	**pal**
orchard	**ban; bâgh**
to plant	**niyâlawël**
plow	**qolba; yawe**
to plow	**qolba kawël;**
	yawe kawël
potato	**âlu; kachâlu**
poultry	**chërgân**
rape seed	**sharsham**
to reap	**rebal**
rice	**wriji**
root	**risha**
rye	**jawdër**
season	**mosam; fasal**
seeds	**dâna; tukhum**
to shoe *a horse*	**nâlawël**
sickle	**lor**
silkworms	**dë wreshamo**
	chinjay
to sow	**karël**
straw	**bus; pror(a)**
tractor	**tëraktor**
tree	**wëna**
trunk *of tree*	**sëta**
vine	**angur; kwar**
wheat	**ghanëm**
well *of water*	**kohay; tsâ**

18. ANIMALS

bat	**shâperak**
bear	**yazh**
boar	**khanzir**
bull	**ghwayay**
calf	**khosay**
camel	**ush**
cat	**pisho**
cow	**ghwâ**
deer	**hosëy**
dog	**spay**
donkey	**khar**
ewe	**gëda; mezha**
fish	**kab**
flock *of sheep*	**rama**
fox	**gidër**
gazelle	**ghërtsë; husëy**
goat	**wuza**
hare	**swëy**
herd	**goram**
hound: Agfhan hound	**tâzi**
horse	**âs; as**
hyena	**kozh**
jackal	**surlanday**
lamb	**wray**
leopard	**prâng**
lion	**zmaray**
mare	**aspa**
mole	**mëzha**
monkey	**bizo; shâdo**
mouse	**muzhak**
mule	**kachar**
ox	**ghwayay**
pig	**khuk**

pony	**ta̱tu**
rabbit	**suy**
ram	**më̱zh; psë**
rat	**ma̱zha**
sheep	**psë**
sheepdog	**dë rame spay**
squirrel	**mu̱zhakprâng**
stag	**ghartsë**
stallion	**as**
wolf	**lewë**

—Birds

bird	**mërghëy**
chicken	**chërgu̱ray**
crow	**kârghë**
dove	**gogoshtu; qumri**
duck	**helëy**
eagle	**'oqâb**
falcon	**bâz; shâhin**
goose	**qâz**
wild goose	**zâ̱na**
hawk	**bâz**
hen	**chërga**
nightingale	**bâjo; bulbëla**
owl	**kwëng; gungay**
parrot	**tuti**
partridge	**zërka**
peacock	**tâus**
pheasant	**dashti chërg**
pigeon	**kawtara**
quail	**ma̱rëz**
rooster	**bângi; chërg**
sparrow	**chinchë̱na; mërghëy**
sparrowhawk	**shâhin**
turkey	**filmorgh; khë̱rtumi-chërg**
vulture	**ta̱pus**

—Insects & amphibians

ant	**me<u>zh</u>ay**
bee	**muchëy**
butterfly	**patang**
caterpillar	**dë wane chinjay**
cicada	**chërchirak**
cobra	**kapcha**
cockroach	**gë<u>r</u>ëndëy**
crab	**chungâ<u>sh</u>**
cricket	**kirë<u>r</u>ay**
dragonfly	**bambirak**
fish	**mâhi; kab**
flea(s)	**wrë<u>zh</u>a**
fly	**mëch**
frog	**chungë<u>sh</u>a**
grasshopper	**malëkh**
hedgehog	**jushkuray**
hornet	**ghumbësa**
insect	**hashara**
lizard	**karbo<u>r</u>ay**
louse	**spë<u>zh</u>a**
mosquito	**mâsha**
scorpion	**la<u>r</u>ëm**
snail	**halzun**
snake	**mâr**
grass snake	**dë obo mâr**
spider	**ghë<u>na</u>**
termite	**wayna**
tick	**richa**
viper	**mëngaray**
wasp	**ghumbësa**
worms	**chinjay**

19. COUNTRYSIDE

avalanche	**barf koch; râshay**
canal	**kânâl; oblâr**
cave	**smëtsa**
dam	**band**
earth	**dzmëka**
earthquake	**zëlzëla**
fire	**or**
flood	**sel; selâw**
foothills	**dë ghrë lamën**
footpath	**tsënglâr; pyâdaraw**
forest	**dzangal**
hill	**ghund̲ëy**
lake	**jahil**
landslide	**dë dzmëke shwayedâ**
marsh	**jaba**
mountain	**ghar**
mountain pass	**gharanëy-lâr**
mountain range	**dë ghrono lar̲ëy**
peak	**dë ghrë tsuka**
plain	**awâra**
plant	**but̲ay**
pond	**d̲and̲; nâwër**
ravine	**nâw; tanga dara**
river	**sin**
river bank	**dë sin ghâr̲a**
rock	**kamar**
sand	**shëga**
soil	**dzmëka; khâwra**
slope	**dzwër̲**
spring *of water*	**china**
stone	**kân̲ay; tiz̲ha; d̲abara**

stream	**wyâla**
mountain stream	**khwër**
summit	**tsuka; dë ghrë tsuka**
swamp	**jaba**
torrent	**khwër**
tree	**wëna**
valley	**dara**
waterfall	**âbshâr**
a wood	**dzangal**

Social organization . . .

FAMILY — Pashtoons place great value on social bonds and their society teaches respect for tradition and one's elders. This has been carried over into the active mechanism of authority. Pashtoons have always traditionally turned to their elders for all major decisions, embodying as they do one of the three pillars of family, tradition and religion on which the nation has been built and which has helped it survive against all odds. The village elders are the **spinzhiri** ("grey-beards"), and include the **olemâ** ("wisemen" or ulema, Muslim scholars), the **qâzi** ("qadi" or Muslim judge), and the **molla** ("mullah" or Muslim clergyman). The **khân**, or "large landowner", is also expected to have influence on local matters. There are various titles for the secular heads of the communities: the head or mayor of a village is the **arbâb** or **malëk** ("headman"), in a town he is the **walaswâl** ("district head") and in a city he is the **wâli** ("governor"). The smaller meetings over which they preside are called **jirga**, while the great congress that is called from year to year to consult and make joint decisions on matters of national importance is called the **loya-jirga**.

LAW – The concept of law reflects this mixture. Normal law in the sense of law and order is **qânun**, while an individual law is called a **moqarara**. Many Pashtoons also appeal to **shari'a**, Islamic law, or even the customary law of their forefathers, known as **Pështunwali**.

20. WEATHER

What's the weather like?	**Hawâ tsënga da?**
The weather is . . . today.	**Hawâ nën ... da.**
cold	**sara**
cool; fresh	**mu'tadila; tâza**
cloudy	**wredz**
foggy	**larjëna**
hot	**tawda**
misty	**larjëna; khupjana**
very hot	**dera tawda**
very cold	**dera sara**
windy	**bâd**

It's going to rain.	**Hawâ bârâni da.**
It is raining.	**Bârân ori.**
It is snowing.	**Wâwra ori.**
It's becoming very cold.	**Hawâ dera sara shwa.**
It is sunny.	**Lmar day.** *or* **Âsmân shin day.**

—Climate words

air	**hawâ**
climate	**âb aw hawâ**
cloud	**wredz**
dew	**shabnam**
drought	**wëchkâli**
famine	**kâkhti**
fog	**lara**
to freeze	**kangal kedël**
frost	**parkha**
hail	**zhalëy**

heatwave	**tawda tsapa;**
	dë garmëy tsapa
ice	**kangal**
lightning bolt	**breshnâ**
lightning	**tandër**
mist	**lara**
moon	**spozhmëy**
new moon	**myasht**
full moon	**spozhmëy**
rain	**bârân**
rainbow	**dë budëy tâl;**
	shna zar ghuna
shower *of rain*	**jarëy**
sky	**âsmân**
sleet	**gëre gëray**
snow	**wâwra**
snow flakes	**dë wâwre potsënay**
star	**storay**
stars	**sotri**
storm	**tufân**
rain storm	**sheba**
thunderstorm	**jâkër**
sun	**lmar**
to thaw	**wiledël**
thawed	**wili**
thunder	**tâlanda**
weather	**hawâ**
wind	**bâd**

—Seasons

summer	**oray; dobay**
autumn	**mënay**
winter	**zhëmay**
spring	**psarlay**

21. CAMPING

Where can we camp?	**Cheri kamp* darawalay shu?**
Can we camp here?	**Dalta kamp darawalay shu?**
Is it safe to camp here?	**Dâ dzây dë kamp darawëlo lëpâra khwandi day?**
Is there drinking water?	**Halta dë tsë<u>sh</u>âk obë shta?**
May we light a fire?	**Or lagawalay shu?**

—Equipment

ax	**tabër**
backpack	**baks**
bucket	**satil; bâl<u>t</u>ëy**
campsite	**kamp dzây**
can opener	**sar prânistuni**
compass	**qotbnomâ**
firewood	**bu<u>t</u>i; dë swang largi**
flashlight	**lâsi tsirâgh**
gas canister	**dë gâz <u>d</u>aba**
hammer	**tso<u>t</u>ak**
ice-ax	**dë yakh mâtawëlo tso<u>t</u>ak**
ice-box	**âys baks**
lamp	**lampa; tsirâgh**
mattress	**tushak; nâlëy**
penknife	**qalamtarâsh**
rope	**pa<u>r</u>ay; rasëy**
sleeping bag	**safari-bistira**
stove	**ish<u>t</u>op**
tent	**tâmbo; khayma**
tent pegs	**dë ki<u>zh</u>dëy maw<u>zh</u>ay**
water bottle	**dë obo botal**

* **Khayma** is also commonly used instead of **kamp**.

22. EMERGENCY

COMPLAINING — If you really feel you have been cheated or misled, raise the matter first with your host or the proprietor of the establishment in question preferably with a smile. Pashtos are proud but courteous, with a deeply felt tradition of hospitality, and consider it their duty to help any guest. Angry glares and shouting will get you nowhere.

CRIME — Pashtoons are law-abiding people, but petty theft does occur. Without undue paranoia, take usual precautions: watch your wallet or purse, securely lock your equipment and baggage before handing it over to railway or airline porters, and don't leave valuables on display in your hotel room. On buses, look out for pickpockets – keep valuables in front pockets and your bag close to your side. If you are robbed, contact the police. Of course in the more remote areas, sensible precautions should be taken, and always ensure that you go with a guide. In general, follow the same rules as you would in your own country and you will run little risk of encountering crime.

LOST PROPERTY — If you lose something, save time and energy by appealing only to senior members of staff or officials. If you have lost items in the street or left anything in public transport, the police may be able to help.

DISABLED FACILITIES — The terrain and conditions throughout most of Pashtonkhwa do not make it easy for any visitor to get around in a wheelchair even at the best of times. Access to most buildings in the cities is difficult, particularly since the majority of lifts function irregularly. Facilities are rarely available in hotels, airports or other public areas.

TOILETS — You will find public utilities located in any important or official building. You may use those in hotels or restaurants. You may sometimes encounter failed plumbing and absence of toilet paper. Similar to Turkey and countries in the Middle East, people in Afghanistan and Pakistan tend to use any available paper as toilet paper, and occasionally a jug of water (rural areas).

wheelchair	**tsarkh-chawkëy**
disabled	**ma'yub**
Do you have seats for the disabled?	**Dë ma'yub lëpâra chawkëy larëy?**
Do you have access for the disabled?	**Dë ma'yubâno lëpâra lâr larëy?**

Do you have facilities for the disabled?	**Dë ma'yubâno lëpâra asântiyâ lârëy?**
Help!	**Mrasta!**
Could you help me, please?	**Râsara mrasta kawalay shëy?**
Do you have a telephone?	**Tilifun larëy?**
Where is the nearest telephone?	**Tar tolo nazhde tilifun chiri day?**
Does the phone work?	**Tilifun kâr kawi?**
Get help quickly!	**Zhër mrasta tarlâsa kra!**
Call the police.	**Polis khabër kra.**
I'll call the police.	**Zë ba polis khabër kram.**
Is there a doctor near here?	**Dalta nazhde dâktar shta?**
Call a doctor.	**Dâktar râwëghwâra.**
Call an ambulance.	**Ambulâns râwëghwâra.**
I'll get medical help!	**Zë ba tibi mrasta tarlâsa kram!**
Where is the doctor?	**Dâktar chiri day?**
Is there a doctor?	**Kum dâktar shta?**
Where is the hospital?	**Rughtun chiri day?**
Where is the pharmacy?	**Darmaltun chiri day?**
Where is the dentist?	**Dë ghâsh dâktar chiri day?**
Where is the police station?	**Dë poliso mâmuriyat chiri day?**
Take me to a doctor.	**Mâ dâktar ta budza.**
There's been an accident.	**Halta takar shaway day.**
Is anyone hurt?	**Tsuk zhobël shawi day?**

This person is hurt.	**Dâ yaw zhobël shaway day.**
There are people injured.	**Halta khalak zhobël shawil di.**
Don't move!	**Më khwadza!** *or* **Më shura!**
Go away!	**Dza!** *or* **Lâr sha!**
Stand back!	**Shâ ta wadarezha!**
I am lost.	**Mâ lâra wraka kare da.**
I am ill.	**Nârogh yam.**
I've been robbed.	**Lë mâ ghlâ shawe da.**
Stop, thief!	**Wadarawa, ghal day!**
My . . . has been stolen.	**Lë mâ . . . ghlâ shawe da.**
I have lost . . .	**Zmâ tsakha . . . wrak shaway.**
my bags	**zmâ baksuna; zmâ bekuna**
my camera equipment	**zmâ dë kâmre wasâyêl**
my handbag	**zmâ baks**
my laptop computer	**zmâ dë ghezh kampyutar**
my money	**zmâ payse**
my passport	**zmâ pâsport**
my sound equipment	**zmâ dë ghazh wasâyël**
my travelers' checks	**zmâ safari chikuna**
my wallet	**zmâ batwa**
My possessions are insured.	**Zmâ sâmânuna bema di.**

I have a problem.	**Yawa stunza laram.**
I didn't do it.	**Mâ dâ në di kër̲i.**
I'm sorry.	**Bakh̲shana ghwâr̲ëm.**
I apologize.	**Mazrarat ghwâr̲ëm.**
I didn't realise anything was wrong.	**Poh në shwëm che kum shay nâsam di.**
I want to contact my embassy.	**Ghwâr̲ëm lë khpël sifârat sara tamâs wënisam.**
I speak English.	**Zë pë Angrezi khabëri kawëm.**
I need an interpreter.	**Tarjumân ta ar̲tiyâ laram.**
Where are the toilets?	**Tashnâbuna chiri di?**

LANGUAGE TIP — Pashto has a special 'vocative' ending – **-a/-e** – that you can use when addressing people, e.g. **wror-a!** 'brother!' (from **wror**), **mor-e!** 'mother!' (from **mor**), **mëlgëre!** '(my) friend!' (from **mëlgëray**).

23. HEALTHCARE

INSURANCE — Make sure any insurance policy you take out covers Afghanistan, although this will only help in flying you out in case of a serious accident or illness. Consult your doctor for any shots required or recommended when making any trip outside of North America and Western Europe.

PHARMACIES — Chemists are not always easy to find and tend to be chronically understocked or simply empty even in peacetime. Particularly if planning to travel off the beaten track, it is probably best to bring a sufficient supply of any medication you require — even basics such as aspirin, cotton wool or sunscreen. But most of the familiar range of medicines can be found in the larger towns. Don't forget to check the "best before" date.

What's the trouble?	**Tsë taklif lare?**
I am sick.	**Nârogh yam.**
My companion is sick.	**Zamâ malgaray nârogh day.**
May I see a female doctor?	**Keday shi lë <u>d</u>âktari sara wegoram?**
I have medical insurance.	**Tibi bema laram.**
Please take off your shirt.	**Lutfan kamis obâsa.**
Please take off your clothes.	**Lutfan kâli obâsa.**
How long have you had this problem?	**Tsumra wakht ke<u>zh</u>i chi dâ taklif larëy?**
How long have you been feeling sick?	**Lë kala râhisi taklif ihsâsawëy?**
Where does it hurt?	**Kum dzây di khu<u>zh</u>i<u>zh</u>i?**
It hurts here.	**Dâ dzây me khu<u>zh</u>i<u>zh</u>i.**
I have been vomiting.	**Khwâ me gërdzi.**
I feel dizzy.	**Sar râbânde churli.**
I can't eat.	**Tsë në shëm khwarëlay.**
I can't sleep.	**Khob në sham kawalay.**

HEALTHCARE

I feel worse.		**Lâ badtara shaway yam.**
I feel better.		**Yaw tsë <u>sh</u>ë shaway yam.**
Do you have diabetes?		**Shakar lare?**
Do you have epilepsy?		**Mergi lare?**
Do you have asthma?		**Sâlan<u>d</u>i lare?**
I'm pregnant.		**Omedwâra yam.**
I have . . .		**Zë . . . laram.**
You have . . .	*formal*	**Tâso . . . larëy.**
	informal	**Të . . . lare.**
a pain.		**dard; khwë<u>zh</u>**
a sore throat.		**da stuni dard**
a temperature.		**tabë**
an allergy.		**hasâsyat**
an infection.		**ufunat**
an itch.		**khârë<u>sh</u>t**
a rash.		**dâna; dzwânaka**
backache.		**mlâ dard**
constipation.		**qabzyat**
diarrhea.		**is-hâl**
fever.		**tabë**
hepatitis.		**hipâti<u>t</u>**
indigestion.		**bad hazmi; dë hâzime kharâbi**
influenza.		**influyënzâ**
a heart condition.		**dë zr<u>ë</u> taklif**
pins and needles		**dard aw sway**
stomachache		**nas dard**
a fracture		**mât; darz**
toothache		**ghâ<u>sh</u> dard**
I have a cold.		**Zë zukâm yam.**
You have a cold.	*formal*	**Tâso zukâm yâst.**
	informal	**Të zukâm ye.**

I have a cough.	**Zë tokhezham.**
You have a cough. *formal*	**Tâso tokhezhëy.**
informal	**Të tokhezhe.**
I have a headache.	**Zë sardard yam.**
You have a headache. *formal*	**Sardardi lare.**
informal	**Tâso sardardi larëy.**

I take this medication.	**Dâ dawâ khwram.**
I need medication for. . .	**Dâ . . . lë pâra mi dawâ pëkâr da.**
What type of medication is this?	**Dâ tsanga dawâ da?**
What pill is this?	**Dâ tsanga golëy da?**
How many times a day must I take it?	**Dâ wradzi ye tso wâri okhram?**
When should I stop?	**Kala ye bas kram?**

I'm on antibiotics.	**Zë antibyutik khuram.**
I'm allergic to antibiotics.	**Zë lë antibyutik sara hasâsiyat laram.**
I'm allergic to penicillin.	**Zë lë pinsilin sara hasâsiyat laram.**
I have been vaccinated.	**Zë wâksin shaway yam.**
I have my own syringe.	**Khpëla pichkâri laram.**

Is it possible for me to travel?	**Âyâ safar kawalay sham?**

—Health words

AIDS	**eydz**
alcoholism	**dë sharâb tsëshëlo âdat**
to amputate	**pre kawël; qata kawël**

anemia	**kamkhuni**
anesthetic	**behushi**
anesthetist	**anistizist**
antibiotic	**antibyutik**
antiseptic	**ufuni zid**
appetite	**eshtihâ**
artery	**shiryân**
artificial arm	**masnuyi lâs**
artificial eye	**masnuyi stërga**
artificial leg	**masnuyi p<u>sh</u>a**
aspirin	**aspirin**
bandage *medical*	**patëy**
bandaid	**palastar**
bladder	**spoghz; masâna**
blood	**wina**
blood group	**dë wine grup**
blood pressure	**dë wine fishâr**
high blood pressure	**lwë<u>r</u> fishâr**
low blood pressure	**<u>t</u>it fishâr**
blood transfusion	**dë wine badlun**
bone	**ha<u>d</u>ukay**
brain	**mâghzë**
bug *insect*	**khasak; ka<u>t</u>mël**
burn *medical*	**swan**
cancer	**saratân**
catheter	**nal; majrâ**
cholera	**kulâra**
clinic	**klinik; katandzay**
cold *medical*	**rezish**
constipated: Are you constipated?	**Qabzyat ye?** *or* **Qabzyat yâst?**
cotton wool	**pomba**
cough	**<u>t</u>okhay**
cream *ointment*	**malham; mâlish**
dentist	**dë ghâ<u>sh</u> <u>d</u>âktar**
diarrhea	**es-hâl**

diet	**parez**
dressing *medical*	**pa<u>t</u>ëy**
drug *medical*	**dawâ**
drug *narcotic*	**nashayiz mawâd**
dysentery	**pech**
ear	**ghwa<u>zh</u>**
ears	**ghwa<u>zh</u>una**
ear drum	**dë ghwa<u>zh</u> parda**
edema	**pë<u>r</u>sob**
epidemic	**sâri nâroghi**
eye	**stërga**
eyes	**stërge**
femur	**dë wrânë hadukay**
fever	**tëba**
flea	**wrë<u>zh</u>**
flu	**zukâm; infloyënzâ**
frostbite	**yakh wahalay**
gall bladder	**trikhay;**
	dë safrâ kisa
gently!	**wro wro!**
germs	**mikrob**
gut	**kulma**
guts	**kulme**
hand: left hand	**chap lâs**
right hand	**<u>sh</u>ay lâs**
hard! *vigorously*	**qawi!**
health	**sihat; roghtiyâ**
heart attack	**dë zrë hamla**
heel	**punda**
hip	**kunâ<u>t</u>ay**
hips	**kunâ<u>t</u>i**
hygiene	**hefz-ol siha**
infant	**mâshum; kuchinay**
infected: It is infected.	**Zawab ye kë<u>r</u>ay.** *or*
	Ufunat ye kë<u>r</u>ay.
infection	**ufunat; gazak**
intestine(s)	**kulma**

HEALTHCARE

joint	**band**
kidney	**poshtawërgay**
kidneys	**poshtawërgi**
lice	**spëzha**
limbs	**wri**
maternity hospital	**zezhantun**
milk: *mother's*	**dë mor shode**
cow's	**dë ghwâ shode**
goat's	**dë wze shode**
powdered	**wëche shode**
mouth	**khwlë**
muscle	**azala**
navel	**num**
needle	**dë pichkâri stën**
nerve	**asab**
newborn child	**mâshum; warukay**
nose	**poza**
nurse	**narsa; nars**
ointment *cream*	**malham; mâlish**
operating theater	**dë amaliyât khuna**
(surgical) operation	**amaliyât**
organ *of body*	**ghëray**
oxygen	**aksijan**
painkiller	**musakin; musakin dâro**
palm *of hand*	**talay**
pancreas	**toray**
physiotherapy	**fizyotrâpi**
placenta	**prewân; zëlândz**
plaster *medical*	**patëy; palastar**
pupil *of eye*	**kësay**
rabies	**dë lewani spi dârl**
rib(s)	**poshtëy**
rib cage	**gogal**
saliva	**lâre; nâre**
shoulder blade	**ozha; wëlay**

shrapnel	**chara**
side *of body*	**arkh**
skin	**postëkay**
skull	**koprëy; kaparëy**
sleeping pill	**dë khob golëy**
snake bite	**mâr chichël**
sole *of foot*	**talay**
spinal column; spine	**dë mlâ tir**
stethoscope	**stâtiskop**
stump *of limb*	**dë ghëri awushtël**
surgeon	**jarâ; jarâh**
(act of) surgery	**jarâhi**
syringe	**pichkâri**
syrup *medical*	**sharbat**
thermometer	**tarmâmitar**
thigh	**patun; wrun**
thorax	**tatar**
throat	**stunay**
tibia	**pandëy**
to vomit	**qay kawël; khwa gërdzwël**
tooth	**ghâsh**
teeth	**ghâshuna**
torture	**karâw**
trachea	**stunay**
tranquilizer	**musakin**
tuberculosis	**sil; naray randz**
umbilical cord	**num**
urine	**mityâze; idrâr**
vein	**rag**
vertebra	**dë mlâ mërëy; dë mlâ hadukay**
vitamins	**witâmin**
waist	**mlâ**
windpipe	**stunay; marëy**

—Eyecare

I have broken my glasses.	**Aynake me mâte kare di.**
Can you repair them?	**Tarmimawalay ye she?**
I need new lenses.	**Nawi linz me pakâr di.**
When will they be ready?	**Kala ba tayêr(e) shi?**
How much do I owe you?	**Tsumra de porawaray yam?**
contact lenses	**linz**
contact lens solution	**dë linz mindzunkay (mahlul)**

ELECTRIC CURRENT — Afghanistan is 220-volt electric current; Pakistan is 220-240 volts. However, it may not be constantly at full voltage strength and lengthy power failures may be common, particularly away from the larger towns, where the local transformers of villages that have a supply can overload. Although many buildings and villages may now have their own back-up generators in case of power failure, be sure to keep a flashlight or supply of candles.

24. RELIEF AID

Can you help me?	**Zamâ sara mrasta kawëlay shëy?**
Can you speak English?	**Pë Angrezi khabëri kawëlay she?**
Who is in charge?	**Tsok masul day?**
Fetch the main person in charge.	**Asli masul/mudir paydâ kra.**
What's the name of this town?	**Da de shâr num tsë day?**
How many people live there?	**Pë de shâr ke tsumra khalak osi?** *or* **Dâ shâr tsumra nufus lari?**
What's the name of that river?	**Dâ sin tsë numezhi?**
How deep is it?	**Tsumra zhawër day?**
Is the bridge down?	**Pul mât day?**
Is the bridge still standing?	**Pul os ham jor day?**
Where can we ford the river?	**Cheri lë sina tereday shu?**
What is the name of that mountain?	**Dâ ghar tsë numezhi?**
How high is it?	**Tsumra lwër day?**
Where is the border?	**Wesh/Sarhad cheri day?**
Is it safe?	**Be-khatara day?**
Show me.	**Râ weshaya.**
Is there anyone trapped?	**Tsuk halta band di?**

—Checkpoints

checkpoint	**dë talâshëy posta**
roadblock	**band sërëk**
Stop!	**Dresh!**
on roads	**Stâp!**

Do not move!	**Më khudza!** or **Dresh!**
Go!	**Dza!** or **Lâr sha!**
Who are you?	**Tsuk ye?**
Don't shoot!	**Daz më kawa!** or
	Më me wala!
Help!	**Mrasta!**
Help me!	**Râsara mrasta wakra!**
no entry	**nanawëtël man'a di**
emergency exit	**iztirâri khoroj;**
	wato-lâr
straight on	**negh**
turn left	**kin lâs ta wâwra**
turn right	**shi lâs ta wâwra**
this way	**pë de lâr**
that way	**hagha lâr**
Keep quiet!	**Ghalay sha!**
You are right.	**Stâ khabara sama da.**
You are wrong.	**Stâ khabara sama në da.** or **Dâsi në da.**
I am ready.	**Zë tayâr yam.**
I am in a hurry.	**Bira laram.**
What's that?	**Dâ tsë day?**
Come in!	**Dananë râsha!**
That's all!	**Hëmdâ wu!**

—Food distribution

feeding station	**pakhlandzay**
How many people are in your family?	**Stâ dë koranëy tsu ghari di?**
How many children?	**Kuchinyân tsumra di?**
You must come back . . .	**Bâyad ... berta râshe.**
this afternoon	**nën mâspa shin**
tonight	**nën shpa**
tomorrow	**sabâ**
the day after tomorrow	**bël sabâ**
next week	**râtlunke unëy**

There is water for you.	**Obë darta shta.**
There is grain for you.	**Ghala darta shta.**
There is food for you.	**Khwârë darta shta.**
There is fuel for you.	**Swang darta shta.**
Please form a queue (here/there)!	**Lutfan (dalta/halta) qatâr wëdarezhëy!**

—Road repair

Is the road passable?	**Sarëk da teredu war day?** *or* **Sarëk khlâs day?**
Is the road blocked?	**Sarëk band day?**
We are repairing the road.	**Muzh sarëk tarmim kawu.**
We are repairing the bridge.	**Muzh pul tarmim kawu.**
We need . . .	**Muzh . . . ta zarurat laru.**
wood	**largi**
a rock	**dabara**
rocks	**dabaro**
gravel	**jaghal**
sand	**shaga**
fuel	**swang; swang mawâd**
Lift!	**Porta kra!**
Drop it!	**Wâ ye chawa!**
Now!	**Os!**
All together!	**Yaw dzây!**

—Mines

mine *noun*	**mâyn**
mines	**mâynuna**
minefield	**mâyn larunke sima**
to lay mines	**mâyn ishodël**
to hit a mine	**mâyn shandawël**
to clear a mine	**mâyn pâkawël**

mine detector	**mâyn kashfawnkay**
mine disposal	**mâyn shanda wunkay**
Are there any mines near here?	**Dalta nazhde kum mâyn shta?**
What type are they?	**Kum dawl di?**
anti-vehicle	**arâda-zid**
anti-personnel	**parsunal-zid**
plastic	**palâstiki**
magnetic	**miqnâtisi**
What size are they?	**Luywâlay ye tsumra day?**
What color are they?	**Tsë dawl rang lari?**
Are they marked?	**Pë nasha shawi di?**
How?	**Tsanga?**
How many mines are there?	**Halta tsumra mâynuna shta?**
When were they laid?	**Kala ishodël shawi wu?**
Can you take me to the minefields?	**Mâ mâyn larunke sime ta bewalay she?**
Are there any booby traps near there?	**Âyâ dzân ta dë khatar luma shta?**
Are they made from grenades, high explosives or something else?	**Âyâ lë lâsi-bam, qawi châwdonku mawâdu yâ bël shi jor shawi di?**
Are they in a building?	**Pë koruno ke di?**
on paths?	**pë lâro ke?**
on roads?	**pë sarakuno ke?**
on bridges?	**pë pluno ke?**
or elsewhere?	**aw ka bël dzây?**
Can you show me?	**Râ shodalay ye she?**
Don't go near that!	**Më warnazhde kezha!**
Don't touch that!	**Lâs më warwra!**

—Other words

airforce	**hawâyi dzwâk**
ambulance	**ambulâns**
armored car	**pawdzi gâday**
army	**pawdz; urdu**
artillery	**top; topkhâna**
barbed wire	**azghën sim**
bomb	**bam**
bomber	**bambâr**
bomblet	**bamgay**
bullet	**golëy; kârtus**
cannon	**top**
cluster bomb	**klastar bam;**
	ghunchayi bam
disaster	**ghamiza**
drought	**wëchkâli**
earthquake	**zilzila**
famine	**kâkhti**
fighter	**jangyâlay**
gun *pistol*	**tamâncha; topancha**
rifle	**topak**
cannon	**top**
machine-gun	**mashingan;**
	mâshindâr
missile	**tughanday**
missiles	**tughandi**
mortar *weapon*	**hâwân**
natural disaster	**tabi'i ghamiza**
navy	**samandari dzwâk;**
	bahriya
nuclear power	**atomi qudrat**
nuclear power station	**atomi batëy**
officer	**afsar**
parachute	**parâshut**
peace	**sola**
people	**khalak**

pistol	**topancha**
refugee camp	**dë kadwâlu kamp**
refugee	**kadwâl; mahâjir**
refugees	**kadwâl; mahâjir(in)**
relief aid	**mrasta**
sack	**bojëy**
shell	**dë top golëy**
shelter	**panâ**
submachine gun	**kuchinay mâshingan**
tank	**tânk**
troops	**askar; dzwakuna**
unexploded ammunition	**nâchâwdale golëy**
unexploded bomb	**nâchâwdalay bam**
unexploded ordnance	**nâchâwdale wasle**
war	**jang; jagra**
weapon	**wasla**

Weights & measures . . .

Afghanistan and Pakistan use the metric system. Here is a list of international units — for reference translations are included for the most common imperial units:

kilometer	**kilomitir**
meter	**mitir**
mile	**mil**
foot	**fot**
yard	**gaz**
acre	**ikar**
gallon	**gelon**
liter	**litir**
kilogram	**kilogrâm**
ton; tonne	**tan**
gram	**grâm**

Special words used for units of weight are:

pâw	pound/half kilo
chârak	4 pounds/2 kilos
ser	16 pounds/7 kilos
	(note this can also mean a single kilo in Pakistan)
man *Afghanistan*	16 pounds/7 kilos
pokh man *Pakistan*	50 kilos
darëy *Pakistan*	4 kilos

25. TOOLS

binoculars	**durbin**
brick	**khë<u>sh</u>ta**
brush	**burs; bursh**
cable	**kebal**
cooker	**bukhâr deg**
crane	**jarsaqil**
crowbar	**jabal**
drill	**barma**
gas bottle/canister	**<u>d</u>ablay**
hammer	**tso<u>t</u>ak**
handle	**lâstay**
hose	**u<u>zh</u>de jurâbe**
insecticide	**hashara zid**
ladder	**zina**
machine	**mâshin**
microscope	**mâykruskop**
nail	**nuk**
padlock	**kwëlp**
paint	**rang**
pickaxe	**kulang**
plank	**da<u>r</u>a**
plastic	**palastik**
rope	**rasëy**
rubber	**rabë<u>r</u>**
rust	**zang**
saw	**ara**
scissors	**byâti; qaychi**
screw	**pech**
screwdriver	**pechtâw; pechkash**
sieve	**ghalbel**
spade	**bel**
spanner *wrench*	**wrinch**
string	**târ; spa<u>n</u>say**
telescope	**<u>t</u>iliskop**
varnish	**wârnis**
wire	**sim**

26. THE CAR

> **DRIVING** — Unless you already know the country well, it is inadvisable to bring your own vehicle to Afghanistan or Pakistan. If you do, you will need an international driving license, car registration papers and insurance. It is unlikely you will find spare parts for any vehicle other than those made in India or the ex-USSR. Driving conditions used to be good, although the recent conflicts have taken their predictable toll on the road system. Roads used to be well marked. Street lighting is sporadic, and traffic lights, if they exist, rarely work. Certain areas have parking restrictions, although it is not always obvious where they are nor what the restrictions are. It is important to note that vehicles drive on the right-hand side of the road in Afghanistan (like the U.S.), while in Pakistan they drive on the left-hand side of the road (like the U.K.).

Where can I rent a car?	**Cheri moṯar kirâya kawalay sham?**
Where can I rent a car with a driver?	**Cheri lë ḏrewar sara moṯar kirâya kawalay sham?**
How much is it per day?	**Dë wradze pë tsu day?**
How much is it per week?	**Dë hafte pë tsu day?**
Can I park here?	**Dëlta ye darawalay sham?**
Are we on the right road for. . . ?	**. . . ta pë sama lâr rawân yu?**
Where is the nearest filling station?	**Dë telo ṯër ṯelo nëzhde ṯânk cheri day?**
Fill the tank please.	**Lutfan ṯânkëy ḏaka krëy.**
normal/diesel	**mâmuli/ḏizal**
Check the oil/tires/ battery, please.	**Lutfan tel/ṯayruna/ beṯrëy chik krëy.**

THE CAR

—Emergencies

I've broken down.	**Motar me kharâb shaway.**
I have a puncture.	**Tayr me panchar shaway.**
I have run out of gas.	**Dë motar tel me khlâs shawi.**
Our car is stuck.	**Motar mu nëshatay.**
There's something wrong with this car.	**Dë de motar kum shay kharâb di.**
We need a mechanic.	**Mistari me pëkâr day.**
Where is the nearest garage?	**Nëzhde warakshâp cheri day?**
Can you tow us?	**Motar me kashawalay she?**
Can you jumpstart the car? (by pushing)	**Tela kawalay ye she?**
There's been an accident.	**Takar shaway day.**
My car has been stolen.	**Motar me ghlâ shaway day.**
Call the police.	**Pulis khabër kra.**
The tire is flat.	**Tayr hawâ në lëri.**

—Car words

driving license	**laysans; lesans**
insurance policy	**bema**
car papers	**dë motar asnâd**
car registration/numberplate	**dë motar nambar-palet**
accelerator	**aksiletar**
air	**hawâ**
anti-freeze	**yakh-zid**
battery	**betrëy**
bonnet/hood	**bânat**
boot/trunk	**tolbaks**

brake	**brik**
bumper/fender	**bampar**
car park	**pârking**
clutch	**kalach**
driver	**motarwân;**
	chalawunkay;
	drâywar
engine	**injin; mâshin**
exhaust	**igzâs(t)**
fan belt	**panjbolt; fanbolt**
gear	**ger**
indicator light	**ishâra**
inner-tube	**tiyub**
jack	**jak; jag**
mechanic	**mistari**
neutral drive	**notal**
oil	**tel**
oilcan	**gelan(a)**
passenger	**swarli; musâfër**
petrol	**pitrol**
radiator	**râdiyâtor**
reverse	**rewars; (pë) shâ**
seat	**sit; chawkëy**
spare tyre/tire	**ishtapni (tâyr)**
speed	**spid; surat**
steering wheel	**shtring**
tank	**tânkëy**
tyre/tire	**tâyr**
tow rope	**kebal**
windscreen wipers	**shishapâk;**
	wâypar *(Pakistan)*
windscreen/windshield	**(dë motar) dë mëkh**
	shisha

27. SPORTS

Wrestling, polo, and horse-racing are particularly favorite traditional sports in Pashtoon society. If you're lucky, in northern Afghanistan, you may even witness a game of **buzkashi**, a game played on horseback in rural areas in which teams of horsemen compete to deposit the carcass of a large headless calf in a goal circle. More recent sports adopted include judo and other martial arts, basketball, cricket, and, of course, soccer.

athletics	**dzghâsta**
ball	**top**
basketball	**bâskitbâl**
chess	**shatranj**
cricket	**kriket**
goal	**gol**
horse racing	**âs-dzghâsta**
horse-riding	**âs-sparli**
match	**musâbiqa; maych**
soccer match	**dë futbâl maych**
pitch	**maydân**
referee	**rifri; hakam**
rugby	**rakbi**
skiing	**ski**
soccer	**futbâl**
stadium	**lobghâlay; stodiyum**
swimming	**lâmbo**
team	**tim; lobdala**
wrestling	**ghezh; pâlawâni**

Who won?	**Châ wëgatala?**
What's the score?	**Tsumra goluna shwi di?**
Who scored?	**Châ gol wëwâhë?**

28. THE BODY

ankle	**bârkay; dë pshe tiqay**
arm	**mët**
back	**mlâ; shâ**
beard	**zhira**
blood	**wina**
body	**tan; badan**
bone	**hadukay**
bottom	**kwana**
breast	**tay; sina**
chest	**tatar; sina**
calf *leg*	**pandëy**
cheek(s)	**bârkho; anangai**
chin	**zëna**
ear	**ghwazh**
elbow	**tsangël**
eye	**stërga**
eyebrow	**wrudza**
eyelashes	**bânë**
face	**mëkh**
finger	**gwëta**
fingers	**gwëte**
fist	**mutay**
foot	**psha**
feet	**pshe**
genitals	**tanâsuli âle**
hair *singular/collective*	**weshtë**
hairs	**weshtân**
hand	**lâs**
head	**sar**
heart	**zrë**
index finger	**dë shahâdat gwëta**
jaw	**zhâma**
kidney	**pështawërgay**

knee	**gunda; zangun**
leg	**lengay**
lip	**shunda**
liver	**dzigar; ina**
lung	**sëzhay**
mustache	**bret**
mouth	**khwlë**
nail *of finger/toe*	**nuk**
navel	**num**
neck	**ghâra; wërmezh**
nose	**poza**
rib(s)	**pushtëy**
shoulder	**ozha**
skin	**post**
stomach	**nas; me'da; kheta**
throat	**stunay**
thumb	**ghata gwëta**
toe	**dë pshe gwëta**
tongue	**zhëba**
tooth	**ghâsh**
teeth	**ghâshuna**
womb	**rahem; zilândz**
wrist	**marwënd**

29. Politics

aid worker	**mrastanduy; dë khayriya mwasise kârkawunkay**
ambassador	**safir**
to arrest	**niwël; bandi kawël**
assassination	**qatal**
assembly *meeting*	**ghwanda**
parliament	**jirga**
autonomy	**korwâki**
cabinet	**kâbina**
a charity	**mrasta**
citizen	**shâri**
civil rights	**madani huquq**
civil war	**koranëy jagra**
coalition	**itilâf; talwâla**
condemn	**ghandël; mahkumawël**
constitution	**asâsi qânun**
convoy	**kârwân**
corruption	**fasâd; darghali**
coup d'etat	**kodatâ**
crime	**jurm; jinâyat**
criminal	**jinâyatkâr; mujrim**
crisis	**karkech; buhrân**
dictator	**diktâtur; zorwâk**
debt	**por**
democracy	**dimukrâsi; wolëswâki**
dictatorship	**diktâturi; zorwâki**
diplomatic ties	**diplumâtike arike**
displaced person	**bedzâya shaway kas**
displaced persons/people	**bedzâya shawi khalak**
election	**intikhâbât**
embassy	**safârat**
ethnic cleansing	**qawmi tasfiya**
exile	**jalawatan(a)**

free	**âzâd**
freedom	**âzâdi**
government	**hukumat**
guerrilla	**chirik; tsaryâlay**
hostage	**yarghamal; baramta**
humanitarian aid	**bashari mrasta**
human rights	**bashari huquq**
imam	**imâm**
independence	**khpëlwâki**
independent	**khpëlwâk**
independent state	**khpëlwâk hewâd**
judge	**qâzi**
killer	**qâtil; wëzhunkay**
king	**pâchâ**
law court	**mahkama**
law	**qânun**
lawyer	**wakil; huquqpoh**
leader	**ledar; (siyâsi) mëshër**
left-wing	**kin-arkh**
liberation	**zhghorana; nijât**
majority	**aksaryat**
mercenary	**malesha; ojrati dzwâk; ajir**
minister	**wazir**
ministry	**wizârat**
minority	**aqalyat**
ethnic minority	**qawmi aqalyat**
minority vote	**dë aqalyat râya**
murder	**qatl; wazhla**
opposition	**mukhâlif arkh; apozisun; apozeshan** (*Pakistan*)
parliament	**pârlimân**
upper house	**mëshrâno jirga**
lower house	**wolisi jirga**
(political) party	**gwand**
politics	**siyâsat**

POLITICS

peace	**sola**
peace-keeping troops	**sola sâtay dzwâk;**
	sola sâti
politician	**siyâsatwâl; siyâsatpoh**
president	**wolësmëshër;**
	jamhur rayis
prime minister	**lumray wazir;**
	sadri azam
prison	**zindân; band**
prisoner-of-war	**jangi asir**
POW camp	**dë jangi asirâno kamp**
protest	**a'tirâz; ihtijâj** *(Pakistan)*
reactionary *adjective*	**murtaje**
Red Crescent	**Sra Miyâsht**
Afghan Red Crescent	**Dë Afghâni Sra**
Society	**Miyâsht Tolana**
Red Cross	**Sur Salib**
refugee	**mahâjër; kadwâl**
refugees	**mahâjër(in); kadwâl**
revolution	**inqilâb**
right-wing	**shay arkh**
robbery	**ghlâ**
seat (in assembly)	**chawkëy; kursëy** *(Pak.)*
secret police	**khufiya polis**
socialism	**susiyâlizëm; sushalizëm**
socialist	**susiyâlist; sushalist**
spy	**jâsus; mukhbir**
struggle	**mubâriza**
to testify	**shâhidi warkawël**
theft	**ghlâ**
trade union	**sawdâgri itihâdiya**
treasury	**khazâna**
United Nations	**Malgëri Milatuna**
veto	**weto**
vote	**râya; wut** *(Pakistan)*
vote-rigging	**taqalub**
voting	**râyachawëna; râygiri**

30. WAR

airplane	**tayâra; jâz; alwutaka**
air-raid	**hawâ'i hamla**
ambush	**hamla**
ammunition	**marmëy; gülëy**
anti-aircraft gun	**dâfe hawâ top;**
	zid-e hawâ'i top
armored car	**zire posh;**
	zghar gâday
arms	**wasla**
army	**urdu**
artillery	**top qowa; topchi**
assault; attack	**hamla**
aviation	**hawâ'i qowa**
bayonet	**barcha**
to beat *overcome*	**niwël**
belt	**kamarband**
cartridge belt	**gërdanëy**
bomb	**bam**
bombardment	**bambâri**
butt *of rifle*	**qondâgh**
to camouflage	**pëṯawël**
captain	**turan**
cartridge	**kârtus**
ceasefire	**orband**
chief of staff	**loydrastiz**
to command	**qumanda wërkawël**
to conquer	**fatah kawël; gatël**
dagger	**chorkëy; këtara;**
	peshqawza
defeat	**mâta; shikast**
to defeat	**gatël; fatah kawël;**
	mâta warkawël
to destroy	**wrânawël;**
	kharâbawël

detonation	**châwdël**
enemy	**do<u>sh</u>man**
to evacuate	**tashawël; pre-<u>sh</u>odël**
to explode	**chawël**
to free	**âzâdawël; khushi kawël**
freedom	**khpëlwâki; âzâdi**
general	**<u>d</u>agër janrâl**
grenade	**lâsi bam**
gun	**<u>t</u>opak**
gun barrel	**mil**
helicopter	**elikoptar**
hostage	**bëramta**
to invade	**tajâwoz kawël; hamla kawël**
jihad	**jihâd**
to kill	**wazhël**
to liberate	**âzâdawël**
liberty	**khpëlwâki; âzâdi**
lieutenant	**bridman**
lieutenant-colonel	**<u>d</u>agër-man**
lieutenant-general	**turan-janrâl**
to loot	**tâlânawël**
to lose	**baylël; mâta khwë<u>r</u>ël; shikast kawël**
machine gun	**mâshindâr**
major-general	**brid-janrâl**
martyr	**shahid**
military university	**harbi pohantun**
military school	**harbi <u>sh</u>owandzay**
mine: anti-personnel	**personal zid mâyn**
anti-tank	**<u>t</u>ânk zid mâyn**
munitions	**gulëy; marmëy**
objective	**hadaf**
opponent	**mokhâlif**
patrol	**gazma; payra**
peace	**sola**
to make peace	**sola kawël**

personnel *military*	**pezhantun**
pilot	**pilot**
pistol	**tëmâncha**
plane	**alutaka**
prisoner	**bandi**
to take prisoner	**bandi kawël**
to pursue	**taqibawël**
raid	**hamla; yarghal**
air-raid	**hawâ'i hamla**
regiment	**gwënd**
reinforcements	**komaki qowa**
to resist	**moqâwimat kawël**
to retreat	**shâtag kawël**
rifle	**topak**
rocket	**râket**
rocket-launcher	**râket lënchar**
shell *military*	**dë top marmëy/golëy**
shelter	**panâdzây**
to shoot down	**wishtël**
shrapnel	**dë bam pârcha; chara**
siege	**mohâsera; kalâband**
soldier	**askar**
spy	**jâsus; mokhbir**
staff *army*	**pezhand**
submachine gun	**mâshindâr**
to surrender	**taslimedël**
to surround	**mohâsera kawël**
to take shelter	**kada kawël; panâ wrël**
tank	**tânk**
tracer bullet	**rasâm marmëy**
truce	**orband**
victory	**baray; fatah**
war	**jang**
weapon	**wasla**
to win	**gatël**
to wound	**zakhmi kawël; zhobledël**

31. TIME

century	**perëy**
decade	**lasiza**
year	**kal**
month	**myâsht**
week	**wunëy; hafta**
day	**wradz**
hour	**sâ'at**
minute	**daqiqa**
second	**sânya**
dawn	**speda châwd;**
	sabâwun
sunrise	**lmar khâtë**
morning	**sahâr; gahidz**
daytime	**wradz**
noon	**gharma**
afternoon	**mâspashin**
evening	**mâshâm**
sunset	**lmar lwedë;**
	mazigar
night	**shpa**
midnight	**nima shpa**
three days before	**lâ âbël parum**
the day before yesterday	**âbël parun;**
	warma wradz
yesterday	**parum**
today	**nën**
tomorrow	**sabâ**
the day after tomorrow	**bël sabâ**
three days from now	**lâ bël sabâ**

the year before last	**wëram kâl**
last year	**parosazhkâl**
this year	**sazhkâl**
next year	**bël kâl; râtlunkay kâl**
the year after next	**kâl na bël kâl**
last week	**tera hafta**
this week	**dâ hafta**
next week	**bëlâ hafta**
last night	**tera shpa; begâ**
this morning	**nën sahâr**
just now	**os os; hamdâ os**
now	**os**
this afternoon	**nën mâspashin**
this evening	**nën mâshâm**
tonight	**nën shpa**
yesterday morning	**parun sahâr**
yesterday afternoon	**parun mâspashin**
yesterday night	**tera shpa; begâ**
tomorrow morning	**sabâ sahâr**
tomorrow afternoon	**sabâ mâspashin**
tomorrow night	**sabâ shpa**
in the morning	**dë sahâr pë wakht**
in the afternoon	**dë mâspashin pë wakht**
in the evening	**dë mâshâm pë wakht**
past	**ter**
present	**os**
future	**râtlunkay**
What day is it?	**Nën dë tsë shi wradz da?**
What date is it today?	**Tsoma neta da?**
What time is it?	**tso baje di?**
It is . . . o'clock.	**. . . baje di.**

TIME

—Seasons

summer	**oray; dobay**
autumn	**mënay**
winter	**zhëmay**
spring	**psarlay**

—Days of the week

> The second line of names is used mainly in Pakistan.

Monday	**Doshamba; Gwël**
Tuesday	**Seshamba; Nahi**
Wednesday	**Chârshamba; Shuro**
Thursday	**Panjshamba; Ziyârat**
Friday	**Jom'a**
Saturday	**Shamba; Khâli**
Sunday	**Yakshamba; Itbâr**

—Months

January	**Jinwari**
February	**Fibriwari**
March	**Mârch**
April	**Epril**
May	**Mey**
June	**Jûn**
July	**Julây**
August	**Agist**
September	**Siptambar**
October	**Âktobar**
November	**Nawembar**
December	**Disambar**

Afghanistan months

The names of the (solar) months used in Afghanistan correspond to the signs of the zodiac. The second line of names are direct Pashto translations of the original months commonly used in the media. The Afghan year starts on March 21.

Hamal; Wray	Aries
Sawr; Ghwayay	Taurus
Jawzâ; Ghbargolay	Gemini
Saratân; Chingâsh	Cancer
Asad; Zmaray	Leo
Sonbola; Wazhay	Virgo
Mizân; Tala	Libra
Aqrab; Laram	Scorpio
Qaws; Lindëy	Sagittarius
Jadi; Marghomay	Capricorn
Dalwa; Salwâgha	Aquarius
Hot; Kab	Pisces

Islamic months

You will also hear dates given according to the Islamic calendar, which comprises 12 lunar months. **Ramazân** ("Ramadan") is the month when Muslims fast, **Zulhajj** is the month when Muslims traditionally go on the hajj — the pilgrimage to Mecca. The second line of names are the Pashto versions.

Muharram; Imâmâno Miyâsht *(the first month)*
Safar; Safara
Rabi'ul-Awwal; Lumrëy Khor
Rabi'ul-Âkhir; Dohama Khor
Jimâdâl-Awwal; Dreyama Khor
Jimâdâl-Âkhir; Wrustëy Khor
Rajab; Dë Khudây Miyâsht *or* **Bzërga**
Sha'abân; Barât
Ramazân; Rozha
Shawwâl; Kamkay Akhtër
Zulqida; Myâna
Zulhajj; Luy Akhtër *(the last month)*

32. NUMBERS

0	sifar		
1	yaw; yëw	31	yaw-dersh
2	dwa	32	dwa-dersh
3	dre	33	dri-dersh
4	tsalor	34	tsalor-dersh
5	pindzë	35	pindzë-dersh
6	shpa<u>zh</u>	36	shpa<u>zh</u>-dersh
7	owë	37	owë-dersh
8	atë	38	atë-dersh
9	nahë	39	nahë-dersh
10	las	40	tsalwe<u>sh</u>t
11	yiwo-lës	41	yaw-tsalwe<u>sh</u>t
12	do-lës	42	dwa-tsalwe<u>sh</u>t
13	dyâr-lës	43	dri-tsalwe<u>sh</u>t
14	tswâr-lës	44	tsalor-tsalwe<u>sh</u>t
15	pindzë-lës	45	pindzë-tsalwe<u>sh</u>t
16	shparës	46	shpa<u>zh</u>-tsalwe<u>sh</u>t
17	owë-lës	47	owë-tsalwe<u>sh</u>t
18	atë-lës	48	atë-tsalwe<u>sh</u>t
19	nu-lës	49	nahë-tsalwe<u>sh</u>t
20	shël	50	pandzos
21	yaw-wisht	51	yaw-pandzos
22	dwa-wisht	52	dwa-pandzos
23	dër-wisht	53	dri-pandzos
24	tsalor-wisht	54	tsalor-pandzos
25	pindzë-wisht	55	pindzë-pandzos
26	shpa<u>zh</u>-wisht	56	shpa<u>zh</u>-pandzos
27	owë-wisht	57	owë-pandzos
28	atë-wisht	58	atë-pandzos
29	nahë-wisht	59	nahë-pandzos
30	dersh	60	shpetë

61	yaw-shpetë	81	yaw-atyâ
62	dwa-shpetë	82	dwa-atyâ
63	dri-shpetë	83	dri-atyâ
64	tsalor-shpetë	84	tsalor-atyâ
65	pindzë-shpetë	85	pindzë-atyâ
66	shpazh-shpetë	86	shpazh-atyâ
67	owë-shpetë	87	owë-atyâ
68	atë-shpetë	88	atë-atyâ
69	nahë-shpetë	89	nahë-atyâ
70	awyâ	90	nawi

71	yaw-awyâ	91	yaw-nawi
72	dwa-awyâ	92	dwa-nawi
73	dri-awyâ	93	dri-nawi
74	tsalor-awyâ	94	tsalor-nawi
75	pindzë-awyâ	95	pindzë-nawi
76	shpazh-awyâ	96	shpazh-nawi
77	owë-awyâ	97	owë-nawi
78	atë-awyâ	98	atë-nawi
79	nahë-awyâ	99	nahë-nawi
80	atyâ	100	sël

105	yaw sël o pindzë	3,000	dre zëra
		4,000	tsalor zëra
200	dwa sawa	5,000	pindzë zëra
300	dre sawa	6,000	shpazh zëra
400	tsalor sawa	7,000	owë zëra
500	pindzë sawa	8,000	atë zëra
600	shpazh sawa	9,000	nahë zëra
700	owë sawa	10,000	las zëra
800	atë sawa		
900	nahë sawa	50,000	pandzos zëra
		100,000	sël zëra;
1,000	zër		yaw lak
2,000	dwa zëra	1,000,000	miliyun

first	**lomray**	eighth	**atam**
second	**doham**	ninth	**naham**
third	**dreyam**	tenth	**lasam**
fourth	**tsaloram**		
fifth	**pindzam**	fifteenth	**pindz(a)-**
sixth	**shpëzham**		**lasam**
seventh	**owëm**	twentieth	**shalëm**

once	**yaw wâr; yaw dzal**
twice	**dwa wâri; dwa dzali**
three times	**dre wâri; dre dzali**

one-half	**nim; nimâyi**
one-quarter	**tsalorama barkha**
three-quarters	**dre barkhe**
one-third	**pë dro ke yawa barkha;**
	dreyama barkha
two-thirds	**pë dro ke dwe barkhe**

33. OPPOSITES

beginning—end	**payl—pây**
clean—dirty	**pâk—chatal/nâwalay**
comfortable—uncomfortable	**hosa/ârâm—nâ-ârâm/nâkarâr**
fertile—barren *land*	**sherâz/hâsilkhez—shâr**
happy—unhappy	**khwash—nâkhwash**
life—death	**zhwand—marg**
friend—enemy	**dost—doshman**
modern—traditional	**asri—dodiz**
modern—ancient	**osanay—pakhwânay**
open—shut	**prânistay—puri**
wide—narrow	**prâkh—naray**
high—low	**lwër—tit**
peace—violence/war	**sola—shkhara/jagra**
polite—rude	**mu'adab—be-adaba/stëgh**
silence—noise	**chuptiyâ—shur**
cheap—expensive	**arzân—grân**
hot/warm—cold/cool	**tod—sor**
health—disease	**roghtyâ—nâroghi**
well—sick	**rogh—nârogh**
night—day	**wradz—shpa**
top—bottom	**sar; bekh**
backwards—forwards	**wrusta—mëkhta**
back—front	**mëkh—shâ**
dead—alive	**mër—zhwënday**
near—far	**nazhde—leri**
left—right	**kin—shay**
inside—outside	**danana—dëbândi**
up—down	**porta—shkata**
yes—no	**ho—na/ya**
here—there	**dalta—halta**

soft—hard	**post—klak**
easy—difficult	**âsân—grân/sakht**
quick—slow	**chatak—sawka**
big—small	**ghat—wor**
old—young	**budâ—dzwân**
tall—short *people*	**dang/lwar—tit/landi**
tall—short *things*	**awzhd—land**
strong—weak	**ghështalay— kamzoray**
success—failure	**baray/kâmyâbi— nâkâmi**
new—old	**naway—zor**
question—answer	**pushtana—dzawâb**
safety—danger	**amniyat—khatar**
good—bad	**shë—bad**
true—false	**sam—nâsam**
light—heavy	**spëk—drund**
light—darkness	**ranâ—tiyâra**
well—badly	**shë—bad**
truth—lie	**rishtiyâ—durogh**